10 SCOTLAND STREET

10 SCOTLAND STREET

Leslie Hills

Published in 2023 by
SCOTLAND STREET PRESS
EDINBURGH

All rights reserved
Copyright © Leslie Hills
Foreword Copyright © Val McDermid

The author's right to be identified as the author of this book under the
Copyright, Designs and Patents Act 1988 has been asserted.

A CIP record for this book is available from the British Library.

ISBN: 978-1-910895-979

Printed on responsibly sourced paper

Cover image by Alex Strouts
Cover design by Mirrin Hutchison
Typset by Hewer Text UK Ltd, Edinburgh

for Uta Ganschow
1947 – 2021

CONTENTS

Foreword by Val McDermid ... ix
Acknowledgements ... xiii
List of Illustrations ... xv

Introduction ... 1
1 WHYTTS OF FIFE ... 7
2 THE LEITH STATION AT WAR ... 16
3 WEDDINGS ... 31
4 TO SCOTLAND STREET ... 49
5 PROBLEMS AND THE PADONS ... 64
6 DEATHS AND A SECRET ... 68
7 ALEXANDER HENDERSON WHYTT ... 90
8 THE FINAL YEARS ... 105
9 'OBSCURE MUSIC SELLER' ... 114
10 WHYTE AND COMPANY, GEORGE STREET ... 131
11 GRACE AND HER MISSIONARY ... 158
12 10 SCOTLAND STREET AFTER DAVID ... 179
13 TEN IN FORTY-ONE ... 205
14 DECLINE AND RESURRECTION ... 218
15 EPILOGUE: WALKING WITH GHOSTS ... 231

Select Bibliography ... 245
Resources ... 251

FOREWORD

Buying a house, we hope will become a home, is one of the exceptional rites of passage we undergo along the road to feeling like a grown-up. And who among us hasn't studied those title deeds and wondered who were those people who lived here before us? What were their names? What kind of lives did they lead? What was the history absorbed by these four walls before we overlaid it with our possessions?

With most of us, that's where it stops. We might spend an evening poring over our new abode's history, exclaiming over the spidery copperplate of a Victorian clerk; trying to make sense of some obscure Georgian legalese; or just confused by what exactly a covenant means for us. But we tuck the paperwork away in a file, shove it in a drawer and forget about it till we sell up or pass it on to the next generation. If you're anything like me, you'll even forget which drawer it's in and spend a frantic morning trying to unearth the vital documents.

Leslie Hills chose a different road. She decided she really did want to know whose ghosts inhabited her home at 10 Scotland Street, Edinburgh. She lives in the ground floor flat of a fine-looking sandstone tenement in the New Town of Edinburgh, an early example of formal town planning that transformed the city at the turn of the nineteenth century. The New Town is a grid of imposing buildings dotted with formal private gardens, constructed in response to the cramped, insanitary and inconvenient buildings on the far side of what had been the Nor' Loch, a broad ditch that the denizens of Edinburgh had used as a dumping ground for their waste products.

Now, the noisome ditch was filled in, and the Old Town was linked to the New Town by bridges across the newly created valley. It must have been with a huge sense of relief that the gentry and the emerging middle classes moved across town to the new accommodations, but still within easy reach of the University, the Law Courts, the City Council chambers, the castle and the cathedral.

The flat that the Hills family moved into on a freezing January day in 1974 was not exactly the same as the one that David Kedie Whytt moved into in 1824. He bought it direct from the builders, though without the new housing guarantee given to modern buyers! The intervening two centuries have seen some structural changes to 10 Scotland Street, a not uncommon feature of New Town properties. But those changes are only a tiny fraction of the fascinating story that lies behind that imposing black door.

The story that Leslie unfolds for us spreads its threads across the globe. And it moves through different strata of society, painting a kaleidoscopic portrait of social, political, fiscal and financial life in Scotland and beyond, all through the lens of a single flat in a single city. Leslie takes us from the slave plantations of the Caribbean to the trading tentacles of the East India Company, from a blacksmith in New Zealand to a Victorian surgeon in Bonar Bridge in the Scottish Highlands. (The surgeon's practice, by one of the many odd coincidences in this exploration, was in the very parish where the Hills family rented a remote cottage for two decades . . .)

We learn how property and wealth were passed through families, not always in the straight lines we imagine inheritance to travel in. It's not hard to read between the lines of wills and gifts to picture some of the loves and dislikes, the disapprovals and the determination to make good past wrongs. As a writer of fiction, I found myself itching to lift some of these characters from the page into the fertile fields of my own imagination.

Leslie's research has brought this crowd of ghosts back to life. We learn what they did for a living; we learn how families lived together and dispersed. We see births, marriages and deaths – the heart-breaking loss of infants and young children, the debilitating injuries and illnesses that limited lives, the uprooting of young people from their known world thanks to marriage and the necessity to make their way in the world. And because families pass names down from generation to generation, Leslie guides us through those levels by interposing simplified family trees at crucial points.

The prospect of taking on a research project like this is daunting. Where do you start? How do you find what you need to know? I imagine many people start digging into their home's history only to give up when they hit the first brick wall.

But in Scotland, we are particularly fortunate in our available records. The Scotland Land Registry runs the Register of Sasines, a historical account of ownership with all the transactions there have been since 1905. Details of older deeds are kept in the National Archives of Scotland, so it's possible to track who owned property, when it changed hands, and how much was paid.

Scotland's People is an invaluable website that incorporates official records of births, marriages and deaths; church and parish registers; census returns; valuation rolls that itemise owners, tenants and occupiers of properties; wills; and they're starting to digitise migration records from the Highlands and Islands. It's a rabbit hole I've nearly fallen down myself . . .

Other gaps can be filled via the National Library of Scotland and the National Records of Scotland. Although Leslie's research started here, it took her a long way from home. But this is no dry recitation of records. Leslie's own family's experiences weave in and out of the extraordinary lives that have passed through 10 Scotland Street. As a film maker, she's accustomed to teasing out the narrative threads that bring stories to life. And thanks to the bee in her bonnet that has driven her over the years to unravel the past of her own home, she has given us a fascinating account of the role of one house in the history of her city, her country, her world.

Val McDermid
2023

THANKS

Several decades ago, when I first became enmeshed in this story, I sent a very short draft to my friend, the indefatigable researcher and writer, George Rosie. In response he told me I had the makings of a first-class bore. Thus encouraged, I proceeded. Thank you to Val McDermid, who, when we sat together looking over the North Sea, on a long-ago morning after the party-night before, listened to my stories and told me I should be writing a book. And thank you, Val, for all the years of friendship. Thank you to the serendipity which brought Jean Findlay to live for a while with a view into my office window, and to found Scotland Street Press. My thanks to this brilliant, inventive press and all who sail in her. Thank you, Lee Randall, scrupulous first reader, and to my second readers, Sara Sheridan, always intuitive and supportive, and Andy Arthur, pointillist local historian, who made the fine family trees. Thank you to Alan McCreadie, Robin Gillanders, May Matthews, Ruairidh Campbell and Laic Khalique, to Ben Tindall, John Stamp and Jacqueline Cahif and James Hamilton, Alan McIntosh and the Spurtle, and all the curators, librarians and archivists I've bothered and relied on. Thank you to Moira Forsyth for encouragement, to Anna Girling, to Diana Paton and Esther Breitenbach, to the late Ian Duffield for access to his restless, well-stocked mind. I've missed people out and as soon as I've signed this off, their names will come to haunt me. So, a general but no less heartfelt thank you to all the unsung who have helped. Finally, thank you to Ward, Stephanie and Frances (and Ben) for encouragement, comment and love.

ILLUSTRATIONS

Cover
Front: watercolour of 10 Scotland Street, Alex Strouts, 2023
Back: Charles Wilkins; after John Hoppner. Lady Charlotte Campbell 1775–1861. Writer and Famous Beauty. National Galleries of Scotland
To the honourable the magistrates of Leith, this plan of the City Harbour Wet Dock and other improvements. Edinburgh: Abernethy and Walker, ca 1808 to 1809. Reproduced with the permission of the National Library of Scotland.

Builders Sketch and Petition for 10 Scotland Street. Edinburgh City Archives, Dean of Guild Plan Collection
Grassmarket and Bow. James Skene 1823. City of Edinburgh Council – Libraries www.capitalcollections.org.uk
Rev Robert Dickson of South Leith Church. Author's own
Water's Close by Jessie M King. The Grey City of the North TN Foulis 1910
Ann Henderson's Mirror. Author's own
The Vaults Leith. Courtesy of Ben Tindall
JG Thomson Ink Stamp. Author's own
Bell and Bradfute Doorstep. With kind permission of Makar's Gourmet Mash Bar Edinburgh
David Kedie Whytt's Letter to the Admiralty. The National Archives, ref. ADM6/195/302
Number 10's locks. Author's own
The Whytt Grave 2021. Author's own

Mr Lister's Case Notes 1, 2 and 3. Courtesy of the Royal College of Surgeons Edinburgh

Lady Charlotte Campbell, Charles Wilkin, after John Hoppner, Lady Charlotte Campbell 1775–1861. Writer and Famous Beauty. National Galleries of Scotland

William Whyte's proposed alterations frontage. Edinburgh City Archives, Dean of Guild Plan Collection

William Whyte's proposed alterations layout. Edinburgh City Archives, Dean of Guild Plan Collection

Mrs Leckie's Receipt. Author's own

Cowgatehead Church 2021. Author's own

Thomas Smith in Calcutta, Colesworthey Grant. Sketches of the Public Characters of Calcutta 1835–1853

Thomas Smith by John Henry Lorimer. Courtesy of Laic Khalique. Image Dr Ruairidh Campbell

Thomas Carson's Discharge Paper. Author's own

Thomas Carson, Paterfamilias. Author's own

Edwin Eyre Gulland. Reproduced with the permission of the National Library of Scotland

Robert Lawson. ©Imperial War Museum (Documents.8192)

Freda White as a Young Woman. Author's own

Willie Taylor. © Rob Smith

Frances Gordon as a Young Woman. Author's own

MAPS

MAP ONE   Plan of the City of Edinburgh including all the latest and intended improvements 1823. Wood, John, ca. 1780–1847; Brown, Thomas, fl. 1785- 1820. Reproduced with the permission of the National Library of Scotland.

MAP TWO   To the honourable the magistrates of Leith, this plan of the City Harbour Wet Dock and other improvements. Edinburgh: Abernethy and Walker, ca 1808 to 1809. Reproduced with the permission of the National Library of Scotland.

MAP THREE   Sketch map of the City of Edinburgh and Leith with the Estate of Prestonfield and lands adjacent. David Crawford, Surveyor, 1824. Reproduced with the permission of the National Library of Scotland.

INTRODUCTION

We moved to 10 Scotland Street on a snowy day in January 1974 – and moved out again two days later because the buyers of our former house had not handed over the cash. Between our agreement on the deal and the payment date, the worst of a stock market collapse had hit the purchasers, who decided to renege. I shut the door behind me with one bag slung over my shoulder, and my babe-in-arms wrapped in my grandmother's shawl against the falling snow. I felt bemused relish at the drama of the shawl, the babe, the snow. The problem was quickly sorted out. At that time an agreement was an agreement, and our young but tough Edinburgh solicitor was not having any nonsense from the buyer's lawyer. After two nights in the spare room of a good friend, we, my then-husband and our first daughter, were settled into the home which would be my refuge and base for half a century.

Number 10 was in a sorry state. It was bought by David Kedie Whytt from the builders in 1824 and was the family home until his death over thirty years later. The house then sheltered tenants and transients for almost seventy years. A succession of owners for the next fifty showed it little love. By 1973, it was dingy and neglected, as was much of the street. Demolition had been mentioned.

Two centuries earlier, the leading citizens of Edinburgh were considering, with some dismay, their cramped and noisome city. According to Webster's census of 1755, more than thirty-one thousand people lived in barely one elongated square mile of towering, close-packed buildings, on either side of the medieval road that runs down from Edinburgh Castle to Holyrood Palace. Advocates, aristocrats, paupers and many children lived huggermugger in rickety, insanitary tenements which on occasion fell down without notice, frequently caught fire and bred crime and disease. Something had to be done to establish, in stone, the city whose leading citizens were generating the ideas of the Scottish Enlightenment and the dynamic trade in goods, ideas and scholarship between Scotland, Europe and beyond. George Drummond, politician and accountant, who was six times Lord Provost between 1725 and 1764, set to.

Under the northern skirts of Edinburgh was the Nor' Loch, into which the city's effluent disgorged, and beyond were fields and open country. The City Fathers drained the Loch, bought up land, and held a blind competition to design a New Town. When anonymity was lifted, they found that the design they had chosen was that of a young architect, James Craig. The Council minutes show that the City Fathers had their doubts. They commissioned one of their number, William Mylne, to produce a rectified plan. Mylne, with Craig consulting, delivered a simplified grid of wide streets and squares and private gardens which was approved in July 1767.

Between then and the late 1780s, fine sandstone terraces of spacious, well-appointed houses and shops gradually covered the slopes up from Princes Street to George Street and down again to Queen Street where they looked over Lady Blair's gardens and to the River Forth and the hills of Fife. Spoil created by the digging of foundations was carted up to the Nor' Loch where it formed the basis of the modern Mound. The houses were quickly filled with the new professional classes, the gentry, and the multitude of tradespeople they required to keep them comfortable. The Council decreed the development of a second New Town, below Lady Blair's gardens – now Queen Street Gardens. For the next twenty years, terraces were laid out on the sloping ground, moving eastward and northwards towards the old village of Broughton and the Bellevue Estate.

Introduction

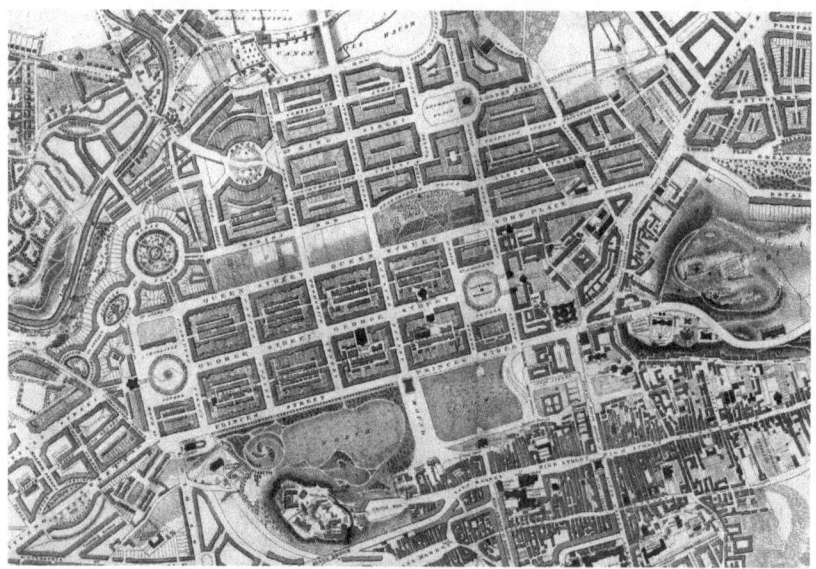

MAP ONE   Plan of the City of Edinburgh including all the latest and intended improvements 1823. Wood, John, ca. 1780–1847; Brown, Thomas, fl. 1785- 1820. Reproduced with the permission of the National Library of Scotland.

The Council bought the Estate and Bellevue House round which Drummond Place was built. The City Fathers called for interest in building on Scotland Street in 1813 but it was not until 23 June 1823, that they invited prospective buyers to view plans at the City Chambers for a block of 140 feet, comprising numbers 4,6,8 and 10 Scotland Street. The corner pavilion on Drummond Place, which houses number 2 Scotland Street, had recently been finished and inhabited. There, on 9 October 1823, Mary Yates, wife to Captain William Cargill of the 74th Regiment, stationed at Edinburgh Castle, gave birth to Edward, the first child to be born on Scotland Street. Edward and his father later sailed off to New Zealand's South Island where Edward became Mayor of Dunedin.

In March 1824, the builders William and Alexander Lewis Wallace, a father and son partnership, submitted a proposal following the mandatory over-arching plan and ensuring that the external features – the stonework, stairways, basement areas and windows, complied. However, behind the doors of the New Town, builders might, and mostly did, vary the internal composition to suit their tastes. Soon after I moved into my first New Town flat, I discovered that it was accepted that a visitor might ask to inspect the layout, its nooks and crannies and unexpected corridors and plumbing arrangements.

The Wallaces built quickly. Large blocks of sandstone were carted from Craigleith Quarry, which furnished the stone for the New Town. Some years ago, I took a core from one of these stones. Streaked black on the ends, the core is as it was when the masons put it in place two hundred years ago – the colour of a fine butter. The picture in my head of the masons, many plagued by lung disease from the dust, pausing on wooden scaffolding to breathe and to look down over open ground to Canonmills with its distillers, tanners and dyers, suddenly switched from black and white to colour. The street is fine, but in the early 1820s, for a few years before the smoke soaked in, it must have been beautiful.

Maps from the 1840s show Scotland Street completed and the land to the north still used for pasture. Mid-century, the *Ordnance Survey Name Books* note that Scotland Street was a 'well-laid out street . . . it is well paved, drained and lighted up with gas. The houses are . . . in good repair and are all occupied by respectable families.'

Respectable and well-kept the street remained for many years. Not until the 1950s, when little maintenance had been done since before the First World War, and the perjink bungalows of the new westward-seeking suburbs became popular, did the street's downward trajectory reach for rock bottom. In 1973, there were deserted basement voids, at least one property deemed unfit for human habitation, and the odd crack in the masonry. This, we found to our dismay, had made the street un-mortgageable. We spoke to my mother who had been trained meticulously by a Miss Prentice in the Glasgow Meat Market of the 1920s, and now kept the books in copperplate ink for one of Glasgow's biggest estate agencies. She had a word with her boss, and he with the Bank . . . and all was well. The sum we contracted for was five very small figures.

We were not alone. A number of friends bought, in Scotland Street and its environs, relatively cheap properties in need of re-wiring, re-plumbing, window conservation – everything to make them habitable. We did most of the work ourselves and furnished the flat with other people's unwanted goods bought at auction, in junk shops and jumble sales, from a tea-strainer offered by a venerable doorstep hawker, to a battered but serviceable bath found on a tip. We were resourceful, of a generation who did their own repairs, and we lived well. But our street was regarded as being at the scruffy end of the New Town. It was busy and noisy with children, and gloriously heterogeneous, housing carpenters and teachers, architects and van drivers . . . The average age was low. There was an extensive babysitting circle whose currency was cardboard tokens, red for two hours, yellow for one. I babysat the children of several future professors, politicians and a future Nobel prize recipient. The cars on the street were few in number, generally decrepit and kept running with scrapyard finds. A man called Boris sourced second-hand tyres for us. Now the world has revolved, the street is once again respectable, and its properties are much sought-after. I believe only two of my contemporary neighbours, who made a lovely modernist home high on the corner pavilion, have been here longer than I.

When finally I paid off the mortgage on number 10, our solicitor handed me a substantial bundle of vellum deeds, dating back to that original sale to David Kedie Whytt. I laid them out on the floor of his drawing room and read until I reached 1974. It took a long time. The cursive penmanship was sometimes cramped and difficult, but with a bit of perseverance, the script yielded. A story unfolded. Vaguely, I decided I would have a look, someday, at the man who had bought my house when it was brand new. The bundle was set aside, and aside it stayed for quite some time, until one morning in the 1990s, researching a film – I had by then turned myself from teacher into producer – I visited the National Archives in Kew.

The building was recent and striking. Low sunlight lay over the fine, wide, wooden entrance pathway across the lake. There were a lot of geese. Having found what I needed for the film, I decided to look in the catalogue for David Kedie Whytt.

In among the toils of living, making and doing, there is sometimes a moment remembered viscerally. Someone you trust tells you a great big lie; you lock eyes with a very young baby and see it thinking; the right person takes your hand. That moment at the National Archives in Kew, when I opened the oilskin-wrapped letter, dated May 1836, and headed 10 Scotland Street, Edinburgh, is among my best.

In a flowing and elegant hand, David Kedie Whytt, retired paymaster and purser, of His Majesty's Royal Navy, is writing from 10 Scotland Street, Edinburgh, to claim the half-pay to which he is entitled, by virtue of his thirty-one years' service, during and after the Napoleonic Wars. The style and sentence structure match the quality of the handwriting. It is quite simply a beautiful letter. I left the archives and slid over the wooden walkway, made almost un-navigable by a day's worth of goose poo, knowing that after that crystalline moment in Kew's search room, I'd pursue Mr Whytt properly.

In the pre-internet days of microfiche and huge paper indexes, it took a lot longer than it would today. As I looked further into David's life, I discovered a complex, energetic character at the heart of an extended family, as it prevailed through conflict and change. Getting to know these people became a decades-long task, to be picked up and put down through times of trouble and of joy, sojourns in Berlin, deaths, births, illness and the odd moment of calm, when a whole day might be spent in a library. It won't ever be finished, of course. I won't ever know everything about this family and their wide-ranging business and friendship bonds. There will always be more to find, new documents to consult, fresh threads to pull loose. The pandemic of 2019 encouraged reflection. I decided it was time to sit down in the Whytt's dining room, and make some sense of it all.

What follows is the story of 10 Scotland Street; the world of the house, the street, and its connections far and wide; the lives, deaths, triumphs and failures of a gloriously varied bunch of characters, on an ever-changing panorama – their one common point, 10 Scotland Street. I'm not an historian but there is nothing here – except when I acknowledge speculation – which is not backed by original sources. I apologise for mistakes and inadvertent omissions.

ONE

WHYTTS OF FIFE

On Friday 8 April 1825, David Kedie Whytt and his wife Ann Henderson took possession of 10 Scotland Street. At forty-nine and forty-one years of age, David and Ann had at last settled down. As a young man, David was always on the move, trading with France and the Baltic Ports, and crossing the country in multiple roles for the Admiralty during the Napoleonic wars. In the eighteen years of her marriage, Ann had moved her growing family through five homes, each a mirror of increasing prosperity. Moored at last in Scotland Street, she and David sat at the centre of a far-flung family network which built its fortunes piece by patient piece.

Until the turn of the nineteenth century, the Whytt family's base was north of Edinburgh, across the River Forth, in and around the port of Kirkcaldy. The first Whytt to come to my attention was Robert Whytt, who, in October 1658, became Provost of Kirkcaldy, and bought the lands of Abbotshall and the estate of Bennochy, to which the Whytts would be connected for several centuries. The port of Kirkcaldy was busy and relatively prosperous with commercial and familial links across the North Sea and south to London and the coastal ports. Traces of these links are still to be found. The Somerset Heritage Centre holds the eighteenth-century bills and receipts of Robert Whytt of Kirkcaldy, who traded with Thomas Muffat of London. In 1774, the London magistrates awarded Robert Whytt a certificate to deal in flax from Fife into and out of London, and he or his successor pops up, over the years of this story, in partnership, litigation and bankruptcy in connection with the Whytts in London.

Through the centuries, the Whytts left a trail of official documents, employment records, newspaper articles and advertisements, wills, legal disputes, building warrants and letters. They were merchants, traders, mercantile shippers, physicians and surgeons, mariners in time of war, pastors, lawyers, clerks, booksellers and bookbinders with strong familial connections.

I found the unpicking of the Whytt web both fascinating and frustrating. Spelling wanders all over the place. Whyt, Whyte, Whytt, White and Quyt are used, in handwriting which ranges from exquisite to illegible scrawl. Keddie is sometimes Kedie and I have been faithful to the spelling of each original. In Scotland, until relatively recently, women kept their own surnames on marriage, and for the sake of clarity, and preference, I have followed this practice. Words are mis-transcribed and dates muddled. Most confusing was the multiple use of the same first names, particularly William. It took me a while to get my head round Whytt family relationships.

David's great-grandfather, Thomas Whytt, was born around 1679 and his great-grandmother, Margaret Philp, in 1683. Their son, William, David's grandfather, was born on 11 July 1714 in Linktown, a parish of Abbotshall, Kirkcaldy. In 1747, aged thirty-two, he married by declaration seventeen-year-old Nicholas Watt, and yes, she was called Nicholas, a relatively common female name at the time. Marriage by declaration was legal, though frowned upon by the church. My children's great-grandmother did it three times. It was sometimes made respectable by church blessing; especially if the bride was pregnant, as was Nicholas. On 11 February 1748, Nicholas and William's union was made official and recorded in the South Leith Church register. The couple were rebuked, exhorted and dismissed. Four months later, on 10 June, their son James, who would become David Kedie Whytt's father, was born in Linktown.

In 1766, a decade before David's birth, eighteen-year-old James Whytt was apprenticed for five years to the Edinburgh firm of Messrs Johnstone and Smith. James went to work in the Luckenbooths which were ancient buildings of four to six storeys, tottering down the ridge of the High Street against the north wall of St Giles High Kirk. They were still there well into the nineteenth century and housed many booksellers. James Whytt had been with Johnstone and Smith a short time when the firm moved across the High Street to the Exchange building, newly-built on a site freed up when a tenement collapsed. It is now Edinburgh City Chambers. From the Exchange, with its panoramic view across the fields to Leith and the River Forth, the firm carried out its diverse businesses, exchanging country notes not used in Edinburgh, for one penny per twenty-shilling note, and selling State Lottery tickets, competing against other licensed sellers with prizes such as yards of linen and silk stockings. In 1768, persons unknown broke into their counting house, using an illegal key. The leading newspaper, the *Caledonian Mercury*, published a notice asking the blacksmiths of Edinburgh, who made all the town's keys, to consult their records, and warned the thieves to return the stolen money, under threat of severe punishment.

One year after the end of James' apprenticeship, the firm of Johnstone and Smith was bankrupt. The trustees, winding up the business, concluded that it had been conducted with regularity, diligence and frugality and had failed because other businesses had not paid up on time. Friends raised enough to pay fifteen shillings in the pound to those least able to withstand loss. Amid all the gloom – including news of a cannon being shipped from Leith for use in the Mediterranean, the deaths of infants from cholera, and intelligence of yet another invasion of Poland – that little paragraph in the *Caledonian Mercury* is cheering.

Before catastrophe befell Johnstone and Smith, James Whytt had moved back across the river to Kirkcaldy to set up a bookbinding business. In January 1771, he married Janet Davidson. Their marriage would last for forty-one years, until her death. Janet was the sixth of eleven children of Grizell Keddie and Thomas Davidson. On the same page as the record of the marriage of James Whytt and Janet Davidson is that of Captain James Muffat of London and Elizabeth Whytt, daughter of Robert Whytt of Kirkcaldy. Perhaps that earlier commerce between Muffat and Whytt had resulted in romance – or perhaps their union was to strengthen a profitable business arrangement.

TREE ONE

```
Thomas Whytt ── m. 1704, Abbotshall, Fife ── Margaret Philp
                                │
        ┌───────────────────────┤
   William Whytt ── m. 1747, Linktown  ── Nicholas Watt      Thomas Davidson ── m. 1743, Dysart, Fife ── Grizel Kedie
   b. 1714, Linktown, Fife   & 1748, Leith
                                │                                                    │
                          James Whytt ──── m. 1771, Kirkcaldy, Fife ──── Janet Davidson
                          b. 1748, Linktown                              b. 1743, Dysart, Fife
                                │
     ┌──────────────────┬───────────────────┬──────────────────┐
  William Whytt    Grace (Grizel) Whytt   David Kedie Whytt   Janet Whytt
  b. 1772, Kirkcaldy  b. 1774, Kirkcaldy   b. 1776, England   b. 1783, At sea on *Belle Poule*
```

In Kirkcaldy, on 5 March 1772, James Whytt's wife, Janet Davidson, gave birth to her first child, William. A second, Grace, was born in 1774. Her given name was Grizel after Janet's mother, but it seems that, as soon as she had any say in the matter, it was Grace. Then came our David Kedie Whytt, born in England in 1776.

Two years later, Britain was again engaged in one of its interminable wars, as France, Britain and Spain competed for dominance in the Channel, the Mediterranean, the Indian Ocean and the West Indies. Kirkcaldy, a ship-building centre crucial to the northern and Baltic trade, prospered. The British Navy was mustered in time of war. In 1783, James Whytt and James Keddie were listed as Mariners on the sloop of war, *Belle Poule*. On board this unlikely maternity facility, Janet Davidson gave birth to her fourth child. Back on land in Kirkcaldy, Keddie's wife was also giving birth. When, a few days later, the two babies, were baptised together, Keddie stood witness for the Whytt baby while Janet's brother, Thomas Davidson, stood witness for the other. The Whytts, their family and friends were clearly a close-knit, extended network of some substance.

In 1790, Abbotshall and Kirkcaldy were described in the *Old Statistical Account of Scotland* as being, 'very pleasant with dry and healthy airs'. A minister of the Church of Scotland and a preacher of the Cameronian persuasion were in charge of 2136 souls, a parochial school and only six registered paupers – but the parish, they remarked, had some trouble looking after vagrants making their way to the Infirmary in Edinburgh. The people of Kirkcaldy were mainly in trade, though some now worked in the textile mills at the spinning jennies. The port did good business importing grain and other commodities directly from the Baltic, much of it for the meal markets of London. There were four brewers who kept decent houses – and several more who did not. William and David would have had their education at the excellent Burgh School of Kirkcaldy, the *alma mater* of Adam Smith.

After the union with England in 1707, parliamentarians and politicians and many of the nobility had moved south, but Scottish law, education and the established church remained completely separate and distinct. By the year of David's birth in 1776, a new middle class of lawyers, university men, scientists, architects, philosophers and the few women who were able to achieve an education, were thriving in Edinburgh and were central to the Scottish Enlightenment – and as a consequence of Scotland's close ties across the North Sea, to the Enlightenment in Europe. Much has been written of such luminaries as David Hume; not so much about the people of business and trade who kept the wheels turning and made Edinburgh a prosperous city. Firmly grounded in evangelical, sometimes positively marginal, religion, the Whytts were of the literate middle sort – energetic, innovative, pious, charitable and not averse to adventure or risk. They made their way to Edinburgh and considerable wealth.

At some point after 1785, the Whytts moved their bookbinding business and their young family across the river to Edinburgh and the West Bow which emerges from the depths of the Grassmarket and the Cowgate. David and his siblings spent their youth there, in the lee of the castle, at the epicentre of Edinburgh. The West Bow was the steep thoroughfare by which everyone, including royalty, diplomats, and the nobility entered Edinburgh, and the condemned made the reverse journey to execution in the Grassmarket. The street narrowed from the foot of the Bow until it was a precipitous passageway opening out into the Lawnmarket just under the Castle. It was a tortuous climb but wider than the wynds and closes between the Cowgate and the High Street and, with a bit of effort, a cart could be navigated up it. At the top of the West Bow were the courts, the booksellers and the coffee shops; down at the Grassmarket were the alehouses and taverns where much business was conducted.

Nearly thirty years ago, among uncatalogued papers in the Edinburgh City Archives, I found four very filthy ledgers. A vault, deep in the City Chambers, had recently been uncovered. When the trapdoor entrance was opened, the ledgers, and a wooden shop sign for Forsyth and Fowler, booksellers and stationers, were found. The ledgers had not been conserved and catalogued, but I was given gloves and allowed to look at them. A tattered index listed fourteen bookbinders to whom Forsyth and Fowler had sent books during 1788–1793, one of whom was James Whytt. On page 331, I found a long and diverse list of the books bound by the Whytts in the years 1791 to 1793. There were: one copy of *Modern Europe*, *25 Trav Memo Stitch* – which I assume is a stitched volume of Travel Memoirs; several treatises; medical textbooks – including six copies of a book on venereal disease; mathematics and chemistry textbooks; volumes of poetry; twelve copies of *Arabian Tales* and six copies of McLeod's *Casus Principis*, an *Essay towards the History of the Principality of Scotland*. This last is held in the great world libraries including the National Library of Scotland. Among petitions of the time to the Dean of Guild Court are complaints about windows, floors, ceilings and walls tottering and shaking due to the hideous crashing of heavy bookbinding presses. I can imagine the impact of a bookbinder's chopping house on the packed West Bow. I hope the Whytts' premises were not in Stinking Close. They were prosperous enough to engage a servant. In 1791, James Whytt of the West Bow paid a servant-tax of 2/6d for a Margaret Sinclair.

Edinburgh was in process of turning itself into a modern city. There were lots of innovations for David, Grace, William and Janet to absorb. Almost exactly their contemporary was George Sandy of Meal Market Close, Cowgate, a few steps from the Whytt home. George's lively, engaging diary is a fascinating snapshot of a young man's life at that time and in that place. The hunt for Deacon Brodie is on and its progress is avidly followed by George and his fellows as they walk by the Water of Leith, and by the route of a proposed

Eastern Road to swim in the sea, sustained by Crambambulie whisky and bread. One evening George attends a book auction and buys a collection of voyages and travels for fourteen pence. A bargain. He also buys a copy of *Don Quixote* in quires, that is, in sheets, which he takes to the bookbinders, but not to the Whytts. He laments that for want of a shilling, he does not have a copy of the Polygraphic Dictionary which would allow him to make his own paints and dyes. He was an avid draughtsman and is responsible for sole-surviving images of Edinburgh and Leith at that time. A friend suggests they might borrow the money from Walter Scott's brother, Tom, who has the needful. Thomas Scott, due to his financial incompetence, would go on to cause his brother, later Sir Walter, much grief over the years. From his friend Hugh Watson's windows, George Sandy watches a hanging on gallows erected by the Luckenbooths. He notes that Mrs Siddons is coming to town and the Greyfriars graveyard will be enlarged. This wonderful diary has been brought into the light by the Society of Writers to the Signet. Were George and the Whytt boys acquainted? Perhaps not. He would become a Writer to the Signet and deviser of the pioneering and internationally-lauded catalogue of the Signet Library, and they were in trade.

Peter Williamson, keeper of a coffee house in Parliament Close just off the High Street, was overhauling the penny post he had established in 1766. I am old enough to remember the second post, clattering through the letterbox, and my mother told me that in pre-war Glasgow a note sent at two of the afternoon would arrive in time to confirm a visit to the pictures at six. Williamson did even better. Dispatches were made to Leith and the suburbs eight times a day. Letters circulating within the city were delivered every hour – essential for the city's growing economy. The other invaluable innovation Williamson gifted the city was his street directory, covering both Edinburgh and Leith where much of the merchants' business was done.

In 1785, commissioners were appointed to oversee street lighting and cleaning, roads were named and houses numbered, so that rent might be collected and commissioners paid. In the Grassmarket, a Leerie – a lamplighter – looked after twelve oil lamps, and three on the dark West Bow where the Whytts lived. To my surprise, I realise that I may be one of the last to remember a lamplighter. My Leerie went about his work, his ladder on his shoulder in Kilchattan Bay, a little village lit by two oil lamps, at the far end of the Isle of Bute. I spent much of my youth there, washing in cold water at an iron sink, rattling down three flights of stairs with a milk can to have it filled from a churn by Hugh, the proprietor of a horse-drawn milkcart, crouching by the coal-fired kitchen range, in the evenings, reading by oil lamp. Bedroom heating in winter was by Dalek-like Valor paraffin stoves which emitted a horrible smell and no heat. I have a chiaroscuro memory of creeping in the small dark hours over cold linoleum to the heavy door, behind which lay the shared stairhead toilet.

By 1786, Edinburgh had a Chamber of Commerce. Steel-sprung coaches had reduced the journey from Edinburgh to London to ten days – though many went by sea. In 1789, Janet and James' last child, named for his father, was born in the West Bow. George Davidson, Janet's second brother, described as formerly a gunner on board the *Brune*, a Blonde-class frigate captured from the French, was a witness. Britain had been enjoying a short period of peace and George Davidson was again a civilian. But the year was 1789, and in France, a few months later, there was revolution. By early 1790, Britain and France were again on the brink of war.

James and Janet were still in the West Bow in 1796, but change was coming. In the mid-1790s, their elder son William crossed the divide between the Old and the New Town, served an apprenticeship as a music-seller and publisher, and set up for business on the corner of St Andrew Street and Princes Street. Much of the original Princes Street has been replaced, sometimes several times, but that corner building still stands four-square. William would rent several shops in the area, in the following thirty years or so, before moving to permanent premises.

Across the channel, Napoleon Bonaparte became the First Consul of France. The Napoleonic War, as it was known in Britain, involved the country in multiple fronts around the globe. Alliances came and went. The war ruined many, killed more, and affected all of Britain and many of its colonial possessions, not least the West Indies. The Whytts, however, prospered.

In Edinburgh, in 1793, at the start of Britain's war with revolutionary France, the conflict must have seemed distant, but, by 1797, when David Kedie Whytt was twenty-one, there were armed ships in the channel. Invasion seemed imminent. The merchants of Leith persuaded Admiral Duncan to protect their Baltic trade. He set up a convoy system, and topographical surveys were carried out along the coast – the ordnance survey would not appear in Scotland until 1847 – so that shutter telegraphs could replace the old flag system. The protection of the east coast ports turned into a battle among rival politicians. Finally, Lord Keith, in charge of the Admiralty in Scotland, but unwilling to leave Kent, agreed to have a ship posted to the Leith Station, on condition that its master be not Scottish. Admiral Richard Rodney Bligh – no relation to Captain Bligh of the mutiny on the *Bounty* – was appointed. Ships, their officers and crew, and all the trades which were needed to ready a ship for sail and keep it seaworthy, required provisioning. The Whytts moved down towards the sea and the centre of the action in the port of Leith.

TWO

THE LEITH STATION AT WAR

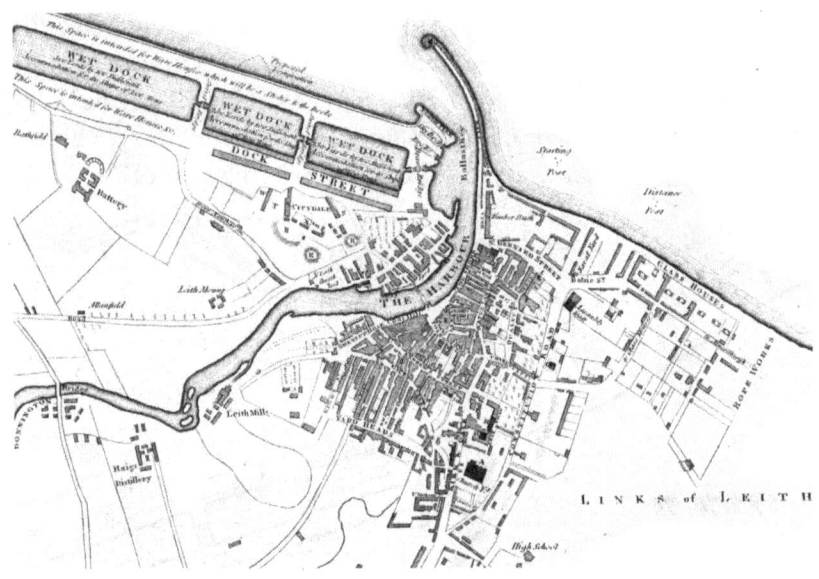

MAP TWO   To the honourable the magistrates of Leith, this plan of the City Harbour Wet Dock and other improvements. Edinburgh: Abernethy and Walker, ca 1808 to 1809. Reproduced with the permission of the National Library of Scotland.

Leith, before Glasgow overtook it, was Scotland's principal trading port, importing and exporting all sorts of goods, mostly with the Baltic ports but also with the Caribbean from as early as 1667 when the first ship returned to Leith packed with tobacco. Linen became a big export, much of it rough fabric for enslaved plantation workers. In 1764, the *Glasgow* sailed with Dundee linen from Leith to Gambia, where it picked up ninety-three enslaved people and transported them to Barbados. It returned with rum and sugar, which, by the first decade of the nineteenth century when the Whytts arrived in Leith, was feeding a substantial sugar-refining industry.

James Whytt and his son David set up in business as wine and spirit merchants on Sheriff Brae, close by the centre of the trade at the Vaults, in Giles Street. Little remains of the Sheriff Brae of the time, save for a low wall where one can sit looking over the Water of Leith, eating ice cream from the excellent parlour at the Brae's end. The Whytts made their home in Constitution Street, joined the ancient South Leith Parish Church where James' father had regularised his union with Nicholas and, together with William, bought ground in its graveyard for their future use. Their minister at South Leith was Robert Dickson DD, who was in post for thirty-eight years and officiated at the burials of their infants.

In the National Galleries of Scotland, there is a mezzotint of Reverend Dickson after a painting by Sir Henry Raeburn. Some years ago, I bought an old painting at an auction held close by South Leith Church. It is crazed oil on wood, and on the back, in what was once white paint, is written, 'Robt Dickson DD First Minister of South Leith, Nov 1783.' It's not the Raeburn, being much smaller and a copy, and actually pretty terrible as paintings go. I like it and it hangs above my desk.

During my digging, I came across the minister who preceded the respected Robert Dickson. He was John Logan, who arrived in South Leith in 1773. Logan was one of the founders of the Royal Society of Edinburgh, but he was also a depressive drunk who had already fathered a child by a servant girl when a second parishioner became pregnant. The Kirk Session gave him handsome annuity to go away.

When the Whytts joined Reverend Dickson's church, Leith was a thriving port where many Edinburgh merchants had their warehouses. There were numerous industries, among them shipyards, rope-works and bottle- and window-glass workshops, one of which was still operating in my memory. There were iron-works, soap-works, carpet and cloth manufacturers, woodyards and many small enterprises supplying the port's needs. Street lighting and a fresh water supply had been newly installed. Leith had its lanes and wynds, but there were also wide streets with classical buildings. In the latter years of the eighteenth century, Bernard Street, at Leith's heart, was regarded as one of the finest in Europe. It still stands, largely unchanged, except for the pick and mix shop signs and proliferation of bins. The burgh had its own administration, a Customs House, Assembly Rooms and a school.

In February 1799, in St Andrew's Church, George Street, Edinburgh, David's sister, Grace, married Captain John Gourley. The church, an elegant building with a fine curving oval interior, was just fifteen years old, and not yet greyed by the smoke of the multitude of chimneys roosting on New Town roofs. The steeple rises a precipitous fifty-one metres. In it hangs a unique peal of eight bells cast in 1788 by William and Thomas Mears at the Whitechapel Bell Foundry in London. The bells were refurbished relatively recently by the Foundry, which commenced business in 1570 in the reign of the first Elizabeth. For more than 200 years, it was housed in a glorious piece of early industrial architecture, now sitting bang in the path of the eastward crawl of the City of London and its current rocketing prices. Despite valiant efforts to save the Foundry, after 450 years of trading it was closed in 2017 and stands derelict. Grace and John were married to the peal of what is now the oldest complete ring in Scotland.

John Gourley was fifteen in 1781 when he entered the Royal Navy and boarded *Belle Poule*, on which his future wife's sister, Janet, would be born two years later. Was this where he first met the Whytts? Gourley joined the ship on 17 February, and, in April, just outside the mouth of the Forth, *Belle Poule*, along with *Berwick*, captured the fast, heavily-armed privateer, *Calonne*. Later that year, under Captain Philip Tatten with William Bligh as the ship's Master, *Belle Poule* took part in the battle of Dogger Bank, a particularly bloody battle in which many men on both sides were lost, to little effect on the conflict – the fourth Anglo-Dutch War – which was tied up in some impenetrable way with the American Revolutionary War. *Belle Poule* lost twenty-five men and fifty officers and men, were wounded. And yes, her Master was that William Bligh of the mutiny on the *Bounty*.

Belle Poule was broken up in 1801. Another fate awaited *Berwick*. It was captured by the French, put into their navy as a man of war and, in 1805, at the Battle of Trafalgar, was re-captured by *Colossus*, which proceeded to Portsmouth. From there, the French prisoners were taken to Norman Cross, a prisoner of war camp built for French and Dutch soldiers and sailors. Between 1796 and 1816, roughly 10,000 prisoners were held there. Many died and were buried in the camp's cemetery.

Only two of the crew captured on *Berwick* were not taken to Norman Cross. These were Martyn Campess, who was released to His Majesty's Service, 'being a German' – i.e., he was not from an enemy country – and Phillip Francis Hills, who was not released until 31 March 1806. The nature of his release may not have been a relief. He was to serve in the '60th Rgt', i.e., as a soldier in the British Army's 60th Regiment of Foot. Depending into which battalion of the regiment he was drafted, he would have been sent to the Caribbean, where very large numbers of British troops died of tropical diseases, or the newly-acquired Cape of Good Hope. At least one, perhaps more, of the 60th regiment's battalions was a penal battalion, with service under harsh discipline for men found guilty of serious military offences – like fighting for the enemy.

Phillip Francis Hills, a merchant seaman from Brightlingsea, Essex, was my children's great-great-great-great-great-grandfather on their father's side. It's likely that he was on a British merchant ship, taken by a French warship or privateer. He may then have been conscripted into or volunteered to fight in the French navy, in order to escape the miseries of internment, thus ending up on the *Berwick*. Whatever the truth of it, he survived the navy and the army, lived another twenty-five years, and had at least two sons, one of whom sent forward his genes and the name Phillip to the present generation, in the person of my grandson.

In fact, the manning of French, British and United States warships during this protracted period of warfare became extremely complicated. Because of crew losses through action, accident or infection, plus a high rate of desertion, these navies were not in the least bothered about placing enemy nationals as crewmen on their warships, especially if they were experienced seamen. A look at Nelson's *Victory* muster book at the time of Trafalgar shows that of his crew of 837 men, 319 were pressed from every country in the British Isles. Another forty-eight were described as 'foreigners', of whom one was a sailor from France, one was Swiss, a fair number came from Holland, Sweden, Denmark and Russia, twenty-three gave their birthplace as America, two of whom stated they were 'negroes'.

This was the navy John Gourley entered. He became a Midshipman, then Master's Mate, serving in several stations in the West Indies where he may have spent time with plantation owners, with consequences for two of his children. In Canada, he sailed under Admiral Vashon, later of Leith. In Puget Sound in Washington State lies Vashon Island, named by Commander George Vancouver in honour of his former Captain. Gourley also sailed with Vancouver as he steered *HMS Discovery* past the island larger than Wales which would become Vancouver Island. Here he would have found a beautiful and abundant land of abandoned villages, populated only by the dead. A pandemic of smallpox, an horrific disease which Europeans had learned to hinder by quarantine and, even before Jenner offered vaccination, by inoculation, had left the land empty. Some years earlier, before smallpox had been imported, *Discovery* would have been met by fleets of war-canoes, fortified towns and warriors in suits of armour, fashioned of metals sourced from Russian Alaska. Now the land, formerly heavily populated, seemed empty and for the taking.

Gourley transferred to *Victory*, at the time Lord Hood's flagship, which was in the Mediterranean when the French war started in 1793. He was promoted to Lieutenant and sent to command a floating battery, stationed by Toulon harbour. The French bombarded him unceasingly, until his vessel went down with her colours nailed to the top of her tattered mast, but with remarkably few casualties. I picture Gourley, hammer in hand, clinging to the top of that mast as it sank. He was then sent on a number of cruising and bombarding missions before being put in charge of *Vanneau*, recently captured from the French.

In June 1796, when Bonaparte took possession of Leghorn, Gourley helped rescue the stranded British, and a month later was at the surrender of Porto Ferrajo, in Elba, to Commodore Nelson, under whom Gourley had been a Lieutenant on *Agamemnon*. *Vanneau* was then wrecked and Gourley court-martialled, but Nelson intervened and the hearing was abandoned. Gourley then had a frantic couple of years until he was invalided home for six months. Perhaps that was when his engagement to Grace Whytt took place. In June 1798, he was appointed to *Fortitude*, in Portsmouth, which appears to have been a prison-boat.

Around this time, the Whytts moved their home from Constitution Street to a newly-built flat in Morton Street, now Academy Street, just along from the foot of Leith Walk. James Whytt would live there for over three decades. In 1804, by his side, he had his wife, Janet Davidson, two adult offspring – David and Janet – and a granddaughter. This reference to a granddaughter gave me pause. I looked for a birth record but could find nothing. James' eldest son, William, was selling books and stationery, music and pianos at 1 St Andrew Street and annoying the more-established merchants. His last-born, James, has disappeared off the record. At the time, children who lived to adulthood were regularly listed, but deceased infants often were not. We must conclude that James died young.

The Whytts' first floor home was on the south-west corner of Morton Street, with open land on two sides. It had four rooms and kitchen closets, landings and cellars, the stairway and a pump-well, with a cistern at the back from which the Whytt maid would carry water up the stairs. There was no mention of a water closet i.e., a toilet. Policing was done by the Leith High Constables and the Whytts were levied a proportion of the Police Duty which paid for them. The Admiralty Court records, which hold details of crimes at sea and in harbours, tell stories of robbery and battery, lewd behaviour and drunkenness, but I do not get the impression that the streets of Leith, walked by the Whytts, were particularly dangerous.

In 1803, when Britain's war with France re-commenced following a short break, John Gourley was called back to Leith and re-joined Grace and their first-born, Janet. Gourley's health had been badly affected by his extremely energetic, some might say foolish, feats of bravery, both in the Mediterranean and West Indies. He took charge of *Mary*, the Leith tender which David Kedie Whytt later hired to retrieve *Utrecht*. When Gourley left this post, the owners of Greenland ships based at Leith presented him with a gold watch, in gratitude for services rendered. The Dutch, then allies, were most complimentary about his seamanship and perseverance under difficulty and danger.

For a short time, David and his father were trading out of Water's Close, nearby the Shore and Leith Roads. I'm reminded, by the question of a puzzled friend, to point out that Leith Roads are not highways but the stretch of water just outside the entrance to the port of Leith, where anchorage was generally safe, and protected from gales by the conveniently-placed island of Inchkeith. The anchorage also provided early warning of possible invasion, so feared in Edinburgh. Jessy Allan, daughter of the proprietor of the *Caledonian Mercury*, wrote to her sister, Agnes, in Allahabad, British India, from her home at 28 Queen Street, that everyone was so weary of the war and annoyed that it had started up again – but that it was necessary as no-one could put up with Bonaparte's insolence. Her husband and brother had joined the Cavalry, and apparently had a fine time drilling in Musselburgh.

In 1805, with French warships in the channel, the wine trade was in the doldrums. Wartime meant disruption and swingeing government duty on liquor. James Whytt and Son added salvage and auctioneering to their portfolio. The country needed corn and wood, not wine and spirits. Leith, however, was packed and busy. Admiralty HQ was in Baltic Street, less than five minutes from his home in Morton Street for a fit young man. The Navy Victualling Board, at the heart of the war effort, was in Constitution Street, running parallel to Morton Street, past South Leith Parish Church. David was bang in the centre of the action.

The Victualling Board used contractors and pursers to provision the ships, so that they might sail and fight. Between the Board and its officers, the chain of bureaucracy generated reams of standard contracts and forms and rigid reporting protocols. A full-rigged frigate is the common signifier for the Napoleonic Navy. I now know that acres of boxes and miles of shelving would be more apposite. David Kedie Whytt, literate, numerate and with his finger in the wind, joined the Navy and became a purser.

As a purser, later promoted to paymaster, he had to have the capital and credit of a successful merchant behind him. His task was to ensure the supply and issue of victuals, clothes, coals for the galley and the officers' quarters, wood, candles, lanterns, turned wooden bowls and more. David had twelve pence a day – fourteen at sea – for each man. Pursers also acted as the officers' bankers. Before I explored the role, I had no idea of the crucial part played by the huge, unsung, administrative departments, quietly hidden in the apparatus of war. The pursers of my acquaintance sold tickets from a cubby-hole on Clyde steamers.

In 1804, Rear Admiral James Vashon replaced Admiral Bligh as Commander of the Northern Station, to be faced with the huge task of defending a long coastline, and operating the convoy system to protect Leith shipping against enemy ships and privateers. Alongside his role as purser, David became Vashon's Secretary Clerk and was soon joined by his brother-in-law, Gourley, who left *Mary* to become Vashon's Signal-Lieutenant.

In the Edinburgh City Archives, I found letters written by Vashon from his ship, *Texel*, at Leith. One, to the Lord Provost and Magistrates of Edinburgh, thanked them for granting him the freedom of the city. Vashon was promoted to Vice Admiral and offered the Channel Fleet but turned it down. He liked Leith. All his letters were written by David in his characteristic fine hand and signed rather shakily by Vashon. In the Archives, there are sketches of a system of signals for Leith Harbour, set up by Vashon to alert ships to the depth of water under their hulls. They are charmingly drawn and coloured, and no doubt were extremely useful. I do wonder if they are also by David's hand.

From 1805 to 1810, there were regular convoys to the Baltic, the Nore, Gothenburg, Archangel, Heligoland and the island of Walcheren. Defences were only breached once, when, in November 1808, a privateer captured a sloop on the east coast, between Stonehaven and Aberdeen. Vashon sent *Spitfire* after them, stationed three of His Majesty's cruisers in the area, and wrote to the Provost of Edinburgh that he shouldn't worry. The National Maritime Museum holds a long correspondence between Vashon and Admiral John Markham of the Admiralty in London, in which Vashon details his efforts in Leith. The prose on both sides is abundant, embellished and long-winded. I fear some of this may have rubbed off on mine.

Part of Vashon's work was recruiting for the Royal Navy and impressment: taking men off the street to serve as seamen. He appointed John Gourley as his impressment agent. Gourley was not happy. He left much of the local work to a Captain Nash who had fewer scruples and who was assured by the Lord Provost by letter that the Magistrates would always support him in manning the Navy. Gourley wrote to Vashon about the smugglers and the fishermen on the Northumberland coast against which the revenue cutters were no match. He is of the opinion that Mr Nash's press gangs would be better employed stopping the smuggling and a positive side-effect would be that the fishermen, for fear of them, would work harder at their trade. In 1810–12, he raised for the Navy 200 men and boys from the Scottish fishing industry, it would appear by persuasion rather than kidnap. Meanwhile, Nash's gangs roamed the streets, picking off likely men, and men who had been informed on. Prints of the time show men being brutally removed from taverns, their homes, and their beds. And, as always, there were informers: the Edinburgh City Archive holds nasty little letters to the Admiralty reporting on seamen who are evading the press. One letter dated 1805 to the Regulating Captain of the port of Leith, serves up 'a person of the name of William Bell a seafaring man at present working in the office of Messrs Lawrie and Co Printers, Libbertons Wynd. He is a middling siz'd man dark complexion and thin.' The letter is unsigned. The Edinburgh City Archives also hold many petitions for release from men with ruptures, or from those who were apprentices and thus exempt. Long after the war. Gourley published *On the great Evils of Impressment*, a masterful piece of vituperative invective. His argument, in essence, was that a volunteer Navy, properly trained, paid and looked after would attract a more sober and industrious kind of man.

In 1804 Donovan 's *Leith Directory* lists James Whytt and Son, Wine and Spirit dealers in Giles Street and Lang Gate Side, a triangular bit of land south of Giles Street, next to an area which went by the name Back of the Vaults. The building known as the Vaults stood and stands on a corner of Giles Street. It is the oldest building associated with wines and spirits in Leith and had been a focal point of the trade since the mid-16th century. James and David Whytt must surely have been in and out of the Vaults, day and daily. Today, in the third decade of the 21st century, the Vaults, now the home of the Scotch Malt Whisky Society and of Raeburn Fine Wines, would still be recognisable to the Whytts.

Under the building, dug out of the sand, are the barrel-ceilinged vaults which give it its name. From the front courtyard, a central passage stretches back into the gloom. Off the passage on either side are two cellars, each about seventy feet long. In 1951, the Royal Commission on the Ancient and Historic Monuments in Scotland noted that this undercroft seems to have been in existence in 1587 and is therefore earlier than the superstructure, which dates from 1682. The earliest title reference I have found is dated 1586. It is a fine old building.

There are – or were in 1983, when I found myself unexpectedly celebrating my birthday in the far right-hand vault – treacherous rails running down the middle of the central tunnel, to aid the movement of barrels. On that early summer evening, I turned into the mouth of the vault to find tables covered with white linen, set with silver and glass, and lit with many candles. It was an extraordinary sight. At the time, I did not know about the connection with David, or it would have been all the more piquant.

It might seem an odd venue for a surprise birthday dinner. For some time, Pip and I had been drinking unfiltered, cask-strength, single malt whisky from a Speyside distillery, at our friends' farmhouse in Aberdeenshire, and would bring the odd bottle home. Friends liked it. The idea was born to buy in cask, for distribution in our lobby at 10 Scotland Street. This was very popular. One evening, Pip came home and said he thought we could make something out of this good whisky, and he'd found a wonderful building, and would I put the mortgage up by £10000?

If you look on Canmore, the Scottish online database of ancient monuments, archaeological sites, buildings, industry and maritime heritage, and search for the Vaults, you will find aerial photographs taken when the Back of the Vaults was excavated in 2004. The one I like best is the oblique aerial view taken from the south west which clearly shows the site of David Kedie Whytt's warehouse in relation to the Vaults and his short route to the Shore and his home.

The Vaults, Giles Street and Lang Gate Side, where David and James had their premises, had long been associated with the Thomson and Gibson families. In 1785, John Thomson and his partner Andrew Somervail completed the Vaults as the building stands today. In the Whytt's time, various combinations of Thomsons and Gibsons traded in Leith and on South Bridge where John Thomson, merchant and insurance agent, operated a few steps from the premises of merchant William Gibson. The 1797, marriage of William Gibson's daughter, Danzig-born Cecilia, to John Thomson cemented existing partnerships. Both were members of the Kirk Session of South Leith Church where the Whytts worshipped.

John Thomson and Cecilia Gibson's eldest boy, born in 1797, was James Gibson Thomson – JG. Throughout the Napoleonic Wars, as JG passed from infancy to manhood, Thomson Gibson and Company traded with varying success, sometimes from the Vaults where they operated mainly as corn factors with a side-line in the Whytts' business of selling captured ships and their cargo. In 1815, Thomson Gibson and Company, who had been engaged in some way in the West Indies trade, went through bankruptcy, and made various shifts to retain some of their property. By 1820, both William Gibson and John Thomson were in the Gibson lair in New Calton Cemetery. James Gibson Thomson, aged twenty-three, took over, and JG Thomson and Company was born.

In 1831, JG married Grace Hamilton Bell, the daughter and granddaughter of surgeons George and Benjamin Bell. They were married at JG's family home, 22 Forth Street, by his mother's cousin, the Rev. Lewis Balfour. Lewis Balfour was a son of Jean Whytt of Bennochy, and grandfather of Robert Louis Balfour Stevenson, novelist, essayist and poet, the author of, among many works, *Treasure Island* and *Dr Jekyll and Mr Hyde*. The Vaults must have seen some interesting visitors.

The temptation to trace the precise familial connection between the Whytts and JG Thomson is strong. I have managed to resist. So far.

Having steered the company to success during the long depression after the Napoleonic wars, JG Thomson became prominent in the business of the city. As a City Councillor, he sat in company with David's brother William. He became Secretary to the City, then City Treasurer and Deputy Lord Lieutenant, representing the monarch. He had many charitable interests, a number of which were shared with David and William. Like them, he was a stalwart of the Free Church of Scotland. Unlike them, he was a leading light in the Royal Association for the promotion of Fine Arts.

For forty-seven years, JG was the Prussian Consul in Leith and Edinburgh and, for his faithful service, was awarded the Orders of the Red Eagle and of the Crown by the King of Prussia. The clue to this lies in his mother's family. The Gibsons, for generations, had lived in and traded with the free port of Danzig. They were embedded in the Baltic trade, commuting regularly on business. JG was extremely well-connected.

Like David and Ann Whytt, JG and Grace sent their four sons to Edinburgh Academy, whence they made the usual journeys to outposts of the empire, both as merchants and in the army. JG died on 16 October 1886 of a cerebral haemorrhage. His death was notified by a cousin of his late wife, Joseph Bell, who is held to be the model for Sherlock Holmes.

JG Thomson's last bottling at the Vaults took place in 1964. Twenty years later, when we first looked over the building, it was a bit of a shambles, but no amount of disorder or neglect could disguise how fine it had been, and could be. The top two floors were derelict and dangerous, and therefore invited immediate exploration. The general office, two storeys high and littered with discarded equipment, was an echoing ode to 1950's bad taste. Our children saw it as a rule-free playground, with potential for un-censured destruction. It is now the Member's Room of the Scotch Malt Whisky Society. The tasting room, with its vast mahogany table and hidden swan-neck tap and china bowl, and the evocative Vintners room with its fine plaster decoration, where Guild auctions were held, had miraculously survived intact, in perfect, if dusty, condition. Underneath it all, the vaults sat cool and unchanging as they had for the previous four hundred years.

Early photographs show strings of black mould hanging from the vaulted roofs. Miraculous properties were ascribed to this mould. Any injured employee, it was said, would plaster the wound with gunk scraped from the roof, and benefit from what was said to be penicillin. In 1957, a director of JG Thomson sent off samples to the Royal Botanic Gardens a couple of miles east. Mr Henderson, a botanist and mycologist and later the Regius Keeper of the Garden, replied to the effect that the growth went by the name of Cellar Fungus and was widespread on the continent – though not in Scotland. There was no close connection between it and penicillin. It would however have been useful in promoting clotting of blood. By 1983, the black mould had retreated to a few tired traces. Today the ancient vaults are once again fulfilling their purpose and serve as fitting cellarage for Raeburn Fine Wines. The latest incarnation of JG Thomson and Company, launched from the Vaults in 2021.

I am ridiculously delighted to make these connections among the Vaults, David Kedie Whytt, and 10 Scotland Street.

Throughout and after the war, while trading with his father, being Secretary Clerk and pursering, David had a second base in London where he ran yet another business as a naval agent, assessing and distributing prize money. Many admirals and captains became very rich through prize money. I'm reminded of Captain Wentworth in Jane Austen's 1817 novel, *Persuasion,* and her first-hand knowledge of the prize system through her brothers, Admirals Charles and William Francis Austen. The latter made a considerable fortune out of the war. John Gourley, who finished the war on *Pelorus* off the coast of Ireland, does not seem to have been one of the many officers who were enriched by prize money.

David's business as a naval agent was mainly conducted from London, but he also operated in Leith. In February 1807, the Dutch frigate *Utrecht* was wrecked off the island of Sanday in Orkney. David was appointed commissioner for the sale. The officers of *Utrecht* were brought south and put into the care of John Gourley who wrote to Admiral Vashon for advice. Vashon wrote to the

Admiralty in London. What should he do with them? He recalls that when the British ship *Romney* was wrecked off the Dutch coast, the officers were returned to England with no sanctions, and suggests that it would be a good thing not to be outdone by the enemy, in the matter of generosity. All written in his Secretary David Whytt's hand. The officers were repatriated, and the German sailors on board *Utrecht* sent south to Portsmouth, and enrolled in the militia. I have no idea why a Dutch frigate would be so far from home, unless it was pursuing one of the Baltic convoys which called in at the Orkneys to pick up whale oil or other necessities. North, there are the Shetland Isles, then nothing till the Arctic. To the west is Greenland; to the east it's five hundred kilometres to Bergen.

Some years ago, I was employed on a UK-wide mentoring programme to work on a film with a group of Sanday pupils. We took the plot to pieces, analysed it, re-wrote it and with some wonderful teachers, a joyful, funny, short animation, starring doleful seals and an exceptionally brave cat, made its way onto a shortlist and to the awards ceremony in the Odeon, Leicester Square, London. The pupils and their head teacher travelled for near twenty-four hours and on several modes of transport, to arrive in time to be awarded, to their immense joy, *Best Animation*. Later, the film was part of Virgin Atlantic's offer. I'll always be grateful to the organisation which actually paid me to be part of it all and to get to know Sanday. When the weather is fine, Sanday – flat as a pancake and ringed by endless clean beaches, the air alive with birdlife – is idyllic. In February, when *Utrecht*, barely 150 feet long with only two decks – the Dutch built shallow – had to be salvaged from this faraway place, such days are rare. The notice of sale specified that the hull of the Dutch frigate *Utrecht*, grounded on the east side of the Outer Holm of the Island of Sanday, measured 149 feet on the gun deck and was around thirty-nine feet broad.

David was offering a large quantity of valuable oak timber, beams, knees and planks. There was also a lot of gear on board. As commissioner for the sale, David advertised it through his broker, Mr Grinly. A notice in the *Caledonian Mercury* called the cargo 'the largest and most valuable quantity of Naval Ordnance offered in this country for many years.' There were 'Brass and Iron Guns,

Carronades, Small Arms, Anchors, Cables, Sails, Standing and Running Rigging, Shot, Shells, Iron Ballast, Sheet Copper, Lead, Water and Spirit Casks, Iron Hoops etc.' The sale took place in a yard behind the Leith Assembly Rooms. David required buyers to pay 25% of the purchase immediately, and the rest within six days. He did have more than his commissioner's interest in this, as I discovered while rooting around in the Edinburgh City Archives. In a shoebox, I found a letter to the Lord Provost from David Whytt and Captain Nash – he of the press gangs. With several flourishes and compliments, they asked to be excused the levy of £22 11/- for shore dues, and £9 6/- for harbour dues on the hired tender *Mary*, and the merchant schooner *Anna*. As commissioners for the sale of the stores of *Utrecht*, they had hired these vessels on behalf of His Majesty, to land and sell the guns, stores and apparel on the wrecked vessel, by order of the Admiralty Court, England, on behalf of the Crown.

Whytt and Nash claimed that as the *Mary* and *Anna* were about his Majesty's business and His Majesty's vessels were exempt from tax, they also should be exempt. When this claim was referred to Bert Sandeman of the Edinburgh City Council, he threw it out, replying, at some acerbic length, to the effect that Messrs Whytt and Nash had no case, the *Mary* being private property and only His Majesty's Ships of War and yachts being exempt. Mr Sandeman remained most respectfully the Provost's Obedient Servant. The Provost refused the claim. One gets a distinct impression from this exchange that David Kedie Whytt was trying his luck.

In April of the same year, at the Britannia Coffee House, where, as we will learn, his older brother William attended meetings of the Edinburgh Booksellers Society, David auctioned the famous fast sailing Lugger Privateer, *L'Adolphe* which had been disrupting British trade in the Channel and the North Sea and evading the vigilance of the British Cruisers by superior sailing. Application was to be made to Mr David Kedie Whytt, Secretary to Admiral Vashon, agent for the captors or to Messrs James Whytt and Son. Merchants, Leith, who would shew inventory of stores etc.

THREE

WEDDINGS

On 13 September 1807, David Kedie Whytt, merchant in Leith etc etc, stood still long enough to marry Ann Henderson of Falkirk, Stirlingshire, described in the *Scots Magazine* as the 'daughter of the late Alexander Henderson, merchant.' She also had a living mother, Marion Aikman. It's always worth looking at the other entries on the page. Two below Ann and David's is the marriage of Captain Bettesworth of the Frigate, *Crocodile* to Lady Hannah Grey, daughter of politician Earl Grey, later Prime Minster and largely responsible for the 1832 Reform Act which would give David the vote. A few entries on is the birth of the only child who survived beyond infancy, of Lady Caroline Lambe, whose husband was to become Lord Melbourne on whom the young Queen Victoria relied. Caroline was a novelist and the lover of Lord Byron, credited with describing him as, 'mad, bad and dangerous to know'. A few lines later is the birth of a girl at Leith, daughter to Mrs Coldstream, and little sister to James Coldstream whom we will meet later as a trustee of William Whyte's will. This page, on which almost all of the men named are in one of the services, is perhaps more giving of echoes and co-incidences than most. But many pages provide fascinating connections and wormholes, if you are that way inclined.

Three months after David and Ann's wedding, Ann's sister, Wilhelmina, married John Padon of Borrowstoness – the Sunday name for Bo'ness – a thriving small town a few miles along the coast from Falkirk and less than twenty miles from Edinburgh.

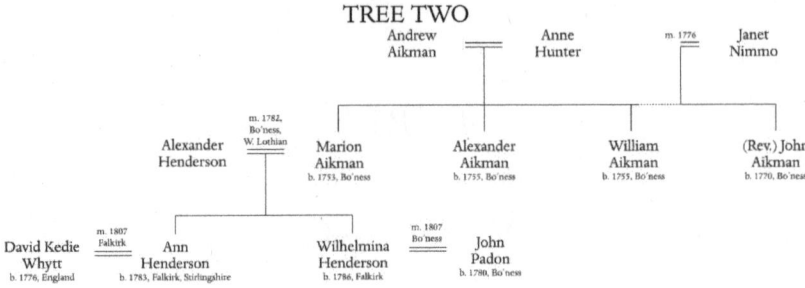

The Hendersons of Falkirk, once prosperous, had fallen on harder times. In 1782, Alexander Henderson had married Marion Aikman, daughter of Anne Hunter and Andrew Aikman, a baker in Bo'ness. Alexander, forty-five to Marion's twenty-nine, was a timber merchant – probably with connection to the timber yards in Bo'ness which had long had a timber trade with Scandinavia and the Baltic, and acted as Glasgow's access to the North Sea and Europe. A daughter, Ann was born in 1783, and Wilhelmina in 1786. Their father died in 1800, leaving debts but no will. Help had to be obtained from the widow Marion's brothers. And here is the first of this family's several brushes with slavery.

Marion had twin older brothers, Alexander and William Aikman, and a younger named John. Alexander left home at sixteen, sailed to Danzig and then across the Atlantic to Charleston, South Carolina, where he apprenticed himself to Scotsman Robert Wells, bookseller and printer. Apparently, he shared a desk with Wells' daughter, Louisa until, in 1777, as a British Loyalist during the American Revolutionary War, he left for Jamaica with his brother William who had been running a circulating library in Annapolis. Jamaica was now British, after decades of fighting among rival colonising invaders: the French and the Spanish. Louisa's father, also a Loyalist, fled for England, leaving a son and Louisa to run the business. She was banished in 1778 and wrote an extraordinary memoir of her journey to England.

Alexander Aikman bought a printing business in Spanish Town, a dozen miles from Jamaica's capital, Kingston, and sent for Louisa Wells. She set off, only to be captured by the French who kept her for three months, before returning her to England.

On her second attempt, she was detained by the Royal Navy, as she was travelling on a ship carrying enslaved persons. When she finally reached Jamaica, she married Alexander Aikman. He printed the Royal Gazette, became a magistrate and Member of the Assembly of Jamaica, made a fortune, had numerous children, and bought many enslaved people. By this time, 30% of Jamaica was owned by Scots. He and his son, Alexander Junior, controlled official printing in Jamaica for more than fifty years. With brothers William, who died young at thirty-three, and John who had joined them, Alexander ran several successful bookselling and stationery businesses. He died aged eighty-three in 1838 at Prospect Pen.

John Aikman stayed only a few years and returned to Scotland to join his two half-brothers in the bookselling trade in Edinburgh and it may well have been through them that their niece, Ann Henderson, met her David?

In London to buy books, John Aikman picked up *Cardiophonia or Utterances of the Heart*, which he thought was a novel. It turned out to be a religious work, which converted him. Now a committed Christian, he could no longer countenance holding a share in the bookselling business on the island of Jamaica – because business was done in Jamaica on Sundays. He preached his way round Scotland and returned to take up the post of assistant minister at the Tabernacle, on Greenside, at the top of Leith Walk. Sketches of John Aikman show a man with a genial, slightly-wandered look to him. He built an independent chapel described as 'dark, dingy, and comfortless' on Argyle Square by the University, and made his home at 11 Charles Street.

Many of my old friends become a bit misty-eyed at the mention of Charles Street. In the 1960s, until the University knocked it to the ground, this was a busy area of ramshackle housing, much dating from Aikman's time, where a counter-culture rubbed shoulders amicably with an old-established working-class. On the east side of the street was the Paperback Bookshop – a new concept in bookselling, with poetry and art in the basement and aromatic fumes, gratis. It was founded in 1959 by Jim Haynes, who remained a friend until his death some years ago. He and a colleague, whom I seem to remember spent some months in what he described as a 'luxurious Dutch prison', nailed a rhino head to the outside wall. The floors creaked and the stairs leading into the gloom of the dank basement were precipitous. It was undoubtedly a death-trap – and it was great. Round the corner was Kushi's, the Indian restaurant where mother cooked and children did their homework at a corner table, and the Crown Bar in Lothian Street, a hub of Edinburgh's folk-scene. There, the late Owen Hand – a gem of a folk-singer who, in white dinner jacket with red carnation and cigar, morphed into a formidable bouncer on 10 Scotland Street's doorstep at my daughter's sixteenth birthday party – was once wakened from a 'reverie' in front of an amused audience to be told he'd been tuning his guitar for fifty-five minutes. Robin Williamson, just starting up the Incredible String Band and happy to have us sitting on the floor while they tried out ideas, was living round the corner.

Students lodged in this neighbourhood and were involved in it. Dilapidated flats were abundant and available for rent for a few shillings. I was once invited to one such and offered eggs cooked on a primus stove, as there was, presently, no electricity servicing the building.

Not far to the west we would visit Mrs Smith, a traditional Edinburgh landlady. No reference was ever made to Mr Smith. She had a double upper – a top flat with attic bedrooms reached by linoleum-clad stairs. Heating was a coal fire in the main room. It was advisable to visit well-clad. She provided half-board for young gentlemen – but no ironing; they took their washing home to their mothers. Mrs Smith was tiny, gnarled and garrulous, with a cigarette perpetually hanging from her lower lip. Her boarders loved her. The last time I saw her, she gave me 'a dirty old tray'. I recently had it renovated: it's a beautiful piece of Art Nouveau brass work.

The site of John Aikman's home in Charles Street now houses the business-like Dugald Stewart Building and the School of Informatics, while Edinburgh's students are filed away in custom-built boxes, insulated from the city. But there's still a rhino head on the wall where the Paperback once operated.

Weddings

John Aikman's life was not without controversy, and he felt it necessary to defend himself against accusations that his chapel was built with money inherited from his slaver father, who was in fact a respectable tradesman in Bo'ness. His inheritance came from his brother William's bookselling business. Aikman's defence in the *Witness* of 9 May 1846 was that William owned only two people, Harry and Neddy, freed when he died, and he himself had owned only one man who looked after his horse and carriage. What is in no doubt is that John's eldest brother, Alexander Aikman, his brother's son and daughter, and his brother's grandson, between them owned 394 enslaved people across several plantations in Jamaica, and were paid £7542 13/7, courtesy of The Slave Compensation Act, which accompanied the emancipation of enslaved people on British territory. This was not the only time, as will be clear further into the story of the Whytts, that this family, like many Scots, benefited from slavery.

In 1807, with the marriages of David Kedie Whytt and John Padon to Marion Aikman's daughters, Ann and Wilhelmina, the Aikmans and the Padons joined the Whytt network. But not before David and Ann had sorted out their pre-nuptial agreement, which is given in full, along with a post-nuptial agreement, in David's thirty-six-page will.

The pre-nuptial agreement is a very old device, used to control the ownership of property and, in most cases until relatively recently, to stipulate conditions under which widows will be supported and controlled with annuities, but not with capital – even if it were originally theirs. In common with his father, David's provisions are unusually equitable for the time. He pledges himself, through an annuity and the purchase of property, to provide for Ann and any children of the marriage. He leaves her all his household goods. He and Ann pledge that this shall satisfy any claim they might have on her mother, Marion, or her estate. This is actually a reference to £3000, a considerable sum, which Ann brings with her to the marriage, and which David now acquires the right to divide, in equal shares, among their putative children. The provisions for Ann and her children are to be overseen by her mother, Marion Aikman, or her mother's brother, the Rev John Aikman.

After the marriage a further contract was signed in the light of Wilhelmina's marriage, to John Padon. A notable thing about these documents, apart from the way they control the flow of assets, is the autonomy of the widow Marion, freed to act for herself and her daughters and, on the other hand, the removal of agency from Ann as she marries David. Marion's father must have had a better head for figures than her husband, as she also had a pre-nuptial agreement which ensured she'd be cared for, if ever she had to pay back the money she'd borrowed from her brother, Alexander Aikman of Jamaica, to discharge her husband's debts. I wonder where that £3000 that Ann brought to her marriage came from.

Ann and David set up home in 3 Moray Street, nearby Leith Walk, which was, until the nineteenth century, a pleasure walk from which traffic was banned. Moray Street is now Spey Street and number 3 is long gone, but a sketch has survived. It was made in 1896 to commemorate Thomas Carlyle's Edinburgh home and can be found in Wilmot Harrison's *Memorable Edinburgh Houses*.

In a letter to his brother, Carlyle describes his lodgings. Moray Street, he writes, 'is halfway down Leith Walk and parallel to it, on the left side, just after one has passed through the Leith Toll-bar.' He is fortunate to occupy the quiet and elegant back rooms of the house at a cost of eight shillings per week. His view as he sits at his window – and therefore that of Ann and David before him – is green fields and nothing else between him and the Forth. His landlady is 'a cleanly heartsome little body who keeps a quiet, well-ordered house.' What pleased Carlyle most, and no doubt the Whytts, was the excellent convenience of the place. Moray Street, Carlyle writes, is 'within a catspring from the road our carriers follow in going down to Leith.' He is pleased that carriers deliver boxes to his door with no charge. Also delivered to him were boxes of wine from the Vaults. JG Thomson's archive contains several letters from Carlyle, ordering and commenting on quality. He is happy to be so close to the shore of Leith and Portobello, with their sea air. In the mornings, he teaches a little maths in Great King Street, in the second New Town, to two young women and one young man who are quiet, stupid people, and Euclidian geometry to a boisterous sea Captain who is not; in the afternoon, he translates from the French, and the evenings are filled with his correspondence and his own writings. At school, I loved Euclidian geometry with its clean lines and foreseen conclusions. Perhaps it should still be taught for the calming of troubled adolescent minds. Carlyle's description of Edinburgh as, 'a great monster of a place, with towers and steeples and grand houses all in rows, and coaches and cars and men and women in thousands,' made my search through his and Jane Carlyle's letters worthwhile. He is much concerned about socio-economic equality. However, my admiration was rocked on discovering his vicious racist and imperialist views in his *Occasional Discourse on the Negro Question*, which, even at the time, raised protest from friends.

I discovered Carlyle's connection with Moray Street by chance, while pursuing the Reverend Edward Irving, who had a long, close friendship and correspondence with Carlyle, and was part of the circle of the London Whytts. In 1828, he returned to Edinburgh to deliver a series of lectures on the apocalypse and stayed with Mr Bridges at 60 Great King Street. Mrs Oliphant, the novelist, in her *The Life of Edward Irving,* refers to the street as 'one of these doleful lines of handsome houses which weigh down the cheerful hillside under tons of monotonous stone.' An interesting take on the Georgian New Town. I wonder if Carlyle's two stupid children at Great King Street were Bridges.

When not long-ordained, Edward Irving became convinced of the imminent second coming, was sent off by the Church of Scotland to London and became a famous – and later notorious – preacher. Ejected from his pulpit, he founded the Catholic Apostolic Church.

The reason I was pursuing Irving is that, in the mid-20th century, a minister of the Catholic Apostolic Church, along with his three sisters, lived in 10 Scotland Street. But that's for later.

In 1808, David, now a married man with his own establishment, had become even busier. In March, with his second Admiral, Lord Gardner, Commander of the Cork Station, he was patrolling round Ireland aboard *Ariadne*, a sloop of war carrying twenty guns. Alan Gardner had joined the Navy around the same time as Vashon, and, like him, spent a great deal of time in the American and West Indian stations. While in Jamaica, he married the immensely rich widow, Susannah Gale, daughter and heir of Francis Gale, a sugar planter and owner of many enslaved people. In 1764, Joshua Reynolds painted the sixteen-year-old Susannah, who was in London for her education. Gardner took the painting with him on his many voyages. When it arrived in its final resting place in the National Gallery of Victoria, Melbourne, skilfully-mended rents and tears were noted. After a short stay in Leith, Gardner was made Commander in Chief of the Channel Fleet and left for the south. A little while ago, I was wandering with good friends, round Bath Abbey. High on a wall, I found a marble tablet memorialising Alan, Lord Gardner, Admiral of the Red Squadron of His Majesty's Fleet and Major General of the Marine Forces. Gardner died soon after relinquishing the Channel Fleet, with, according to the tablet, ' a Constitution worn out in the Service of his Country'.

In the spring of 1808, at Mr Grinly's Saleroom, David and James auctioned the fast Danish Sailing Gallias, *Christina*, at present becalmed in Leith Dry dock. She had been cut out of a Norwegian harbour by his Majesty's sloop *Childers*, and adjudged by the High Court of Admiralty as the sloop's prize. At the same time, the cargo of fish, nails, iron, stores etc. were on sale, with catalogues available. In the summer, the Whytts dealt with the beautiful, coppered Danish Privateer *Torden Dkjol*, with all her guns, shot, rigging, apparelling. She had been causing much grief to British ships in the Mediterranean and had been captured, after a long chase, by HM sloop *Ringdove*, one of the fastest sloops on the Northern Station.

Through the autumn of 1808, James and David Kedie Whytt, advertised for sale prize ships and goods, Norwegian yachts and sloops, barley meal, rough barley, sails, anchors, cables and ropes. In December, there were more prize ships, including a Danish ship captured by his Majesty's gun brig, *Basilisk*.

In 1809 their sales include 840 bags of coffee, eleven prize ships with contents of wines, fox skins, sugar and hand spokes, otter skins and a quantity of cordage, sails and small arms belonging to a Russian brig destroyed by HMS *Snake*. The Gibsons were also

Weddings

offering coffee for sale at the Vaults, remarking that coffee, 'that article', appears to be on the rise. In 1810, there were captures made by HM ships *Clio* and *Erebus* – six Danish prize vessels and cargoes, five other prize vessels and a Russian Galliot. Somewhere in all this, the Whytts found time to pursue a Mr Leask in court in the Shetland Isles for non-payment.

On 14 May 1809, at Moray Street, the Whytt's first child, Marion, was born.

In 1810, George Anderson, the builder of 2 George Place, Leith Walk, handed over the keys to David and Ann's new home, ten minutes' walk from Leith Shore, and a few less to the Vaults, to David's parents' home at Morton Street, and to the Admiralty and David's Admirals. It is a three-storey, classical, terraced, flatted tenement with a basement and attic. Eleven twelve-pane windows run across its face. David and Ann approached the staircase to their flat through a timber door with a fanlight above, reached by a stone platform over the basement area. The tenement still stands, substantially unchanged, though now a little weary and named 374 Leith Walk. Historic Environment Scotland has given it a B listing, which designates it as a building of special architectural or historical interest and a major example of its period style or type. More importantly, this may mean that it will not be allowed to fall too far into disrepair.

Ann and David's home on the second floor was described as 'a lodging or flatt (sic) of five rooms, closets, kitchens with a cellar, back ground, office and rights to the road and pump well, and to the common stair, to the passage between the sunken flats' which gave access to the drying green at the rear, and to the common sewer and the roof. The description ends with the addition of 'rights to the whole parts, pendicles and pertinents thereof and free ish and entry'. I love a good ish.

Edinburgh was a wealthy city in 1810, despite and, in some cases, because of, the war. Inventories, compiled for the confirmation of wills or on bankruptcy, were made from the early eighteenth century in Scotland. They give detailed insight into the contents of the homes of the dead and the unfortunate. At a time when the middle ranks valued visible wealth, the Whytts seem to have been more interested in kinship ties, piety and charity. Nevertheless, furniture was needed for their new home.

The war had hindered importation of hard woods such as rosewood and mahogany. Perhaps Ann and David were part of the flourishing second-hand/recycling economy of the time. They may well have followed the popular practice of renting large items and having furniture mended. In 1810, several styles of bed were around in Edinburgh. The most common was posted with curtains and I think we shall install the Whytts in one of these. A significant item would be the chest of drawers which most middle-class women acquired on marriage. This chest was the only possession of the wife of a bankrupt to which she could claim ownership without supporting legal documentation. But not the linen which it contained. The chests made in Edinburgh were reckoned to be of good workmanship, but of inferior design to the famous Glasgow chests with their distinctive, spiralled carving, known as quilled on the cann. My convict great-great-great uncle, reprieved from his death sentence for sedition, took his Glasgow designs with him to New South Wales.

The flat(t) on George Place was still in the family in 1915 when David and Ann's daughter-in-law, Hannah, was listed as proprietor. Back in 1810, brother William, setting a precedent, bought the house next door, which was occupied at one point by Mrs James Aikman, widow of Marion Aikman's half-brother by her father's second marriage. A close-knit family.

In 1811, at 2 George Place, Ann gave birth to her second daughter, Janet Davidson Whytt, named for David's mother. Down at the Vaults, Thompson Gibson and Company were selling sails and rigging in the loft which was presumably less perilous than when I explored it in 1982. Even then, it was an utterly memorable, long, wide, dusty space shot through with sunlight and perfect for storing sails.

In 1812, among other annoyances, Britain was capturing American ships trading with France, and impressing American sailors. The US declared war. Leith, the Navy and David were even busier. In April 1813, a third daughter, Wilhelmina, was born to Ann and David and a few days later James Whytt posted a notice in the *Caledonian Mercury* advertising the Danish Galliat *Splied* and all her stores. The ship was 65 feet long by 15 feet across, with a hold depth of 6 feet. To my twenty-first century mind, this is a wee boat in which to trust your life and fortune in the North Sea. Just above James' notice is one from J Thomson, Gibson and Co, selling the Danish schooner *Syerstadt* and her cargo of salt, rose copper, barley, caraway seeds, barrels and firkins of herring, stock fish, and half a barrel of tar, to be examined in the warehouse at the Vaults. Rose copper, caraway and firkins of herring . . . the lists of goods in the holds of these wooden ships at Leith Quay read to me like poetry and, inevitably in the back of my brain, produce an echo of John Masefield's 1903 poem *Cargoes*. 'Quinquereme of Nineveh . . .'

In 1814, John Murray, publishers to the Admiralty and the Board of Longitude, issued *The Navy List of Licensed Navy Agents or Petty Officers and Seamen* and there, on page thirteen, is David Kedie Whytt of Leith. If you have no interest in the problem of longitude, skip the next bit. The Board of Longitude, formed in 1714, administered a scheme of prizes intended to solve the problem of finding longitude at sea, essential for good navigation – that is, having any chance of knowing where you are. Dava Sobel wrote a book on the matter – *Longitude – the True Story of the Lone Genius who solved the Greatest Scientific Problem of his Time.* The Genius was John Harrison, a clockmaker, who built the first chronometer accurate enough to determine where exactly a ship at sea was, longitudinally. I gather that the book is contentious among historians wary of the genius theory of history. It does, however, lay out the problem and its solution for the layperson. The Board's purpose fulfilled, it was dissolved in 1828.

David's London business address was 22 Essex Street, a narrow street of elegant seventeenth century brick houses, running south from the Strand. Number 22 is at the rounded end, where the Watergate, an arched opening, leads down narrow steps to Milford Lane which debouched, in David's time, onto a wharf and warehouses, mainly being used for wood. On either side were piers, docks, more wharves – this was before the Victoria Embankment was built and the river was a field of wooden masts, most especially during the Napoleonic War. I've stood, at night, in the subdued age-appropriate lighting, looking up at number 22 Essex Street, a three-storey Georgian house, which appears little changed since David ran up the stairs. Of course, I don't know if he ran up the stairs, but it's beyond me how he could have done what he did in those years except at a run. The whole end of the street now seems occupied by law firms, specialising in crime. A plaque on the wall told me that among former residents were Henry Fielding, the novelist, and Prince Charles Edward Stuart, claimant to the throne of Britain, and that Dr Samuel Johnson established an evening club at the Essex Head in 1783. Also on this street were coal merchants – Essex Street is very near the river – a bookseller and stationer, a wine merchant and the office of the Society for the Detecting of Swindlers. If you stand at night with narrowed eyes, they are there still. David did me an immense favour by living and working in buildings which still exist, allowing me to trace him on his energetic way. I have to thank Joseph Mallord William Turner for giving me David's eyes as he went about his business. Their lifespans are almost exactly congruent. Most evocative are Turner's many drawings and paintings of ships on the Thames and at sea, and especially his painting, c.1794, of the Old London Bridge, soon to be replaced, with the wharves and warehouses stretching down to Southwark.

Number 22 Essex Street was occupied by David's partners Lark and Woodhead, naval agents. In 1816, Lark and Woodhead were declared bankrupt, and very soon after Mr Lark died. A subscription was raised for his impoverished wife and children. Mr Woodhead continued trading and his firm became part of the Royal Bank of Scotland until 1915, when the firm was dissolved.

I looked to find where David might have lodged. In London, there was a small but strong Scottish presence, based on trade and around the Caledonian Chapel where most Scots worshipped. Among a vanishingly small number of Whytts, I found Ebenezer Alexander Whytt, David's almost exact contemporary, who was trading out of various addresses near the river and Essex Street, and living in St Swithin's Lane. In the face of any evidence to the

Weddings

contrary, I think it's reasonable to suppose that he lodged with Ebenezer or another of his kin.

Ebenezer Alexander Whytt was born in Kirkcaldy in 1778, two years after David, to Dr Ebenezer Whytt, who was one of three Whytt babies born in Kirkcaldy in 1731. By 1805, Ebenezer Alexander was a merchant in London, trading with Robert Whytt, whose wedding he witnessed in February 1806. Robert returned the favour in December, at Ebenezer's wedding to Ann Gordon, the daughter of Captain Peter Gordon and Ann Phillips. Captain Peter Gordon and Ann Phillips had married in St John's, Newfoundland. where her father, Henry, was the Sheriff.

In the latter half of the eighteenth century and throughout the war with France, Captain Gordon was an officer of the East India Company's merchant service. The Company was a joint stock company, which began in the seventeenth century to trade with the east, and quickly morphed into a colonialising power with a merchant fleet and administrative service and its own security force, twice the size of the British army. Huge fortunes were made, territories looted, and many people enslaved and transported to serve its purposes. The word loot came into the English language from Hindustani slang, as India was stripped of the enormous wealth of its empire which stretched from Kabul to Madras. The Company moved into China, introducing opium and took Hong Kong as its base. At its height, political decisions which affected millions of people were taken by the company's directors, a small group of men with vested interests, often bribed by further vested interests, sitting in a room, in a London townhouse. Peter Gordon was an energetic cog in a vast wheel. In the late 1790s, he was operating out of Calcutta as the master of *Wellesley*, a full-rigged, heavily-armed merchantman, presumably named for one of the Irish brothers, Arthur and Richard Wellesley. Arthur fought his way round India, commanded the British forces at Waterloo and, as the Duke of Wellington, was twice Prime Minster. Richard was Governor General of India, before going off to run Ireland. He appointed Peter Gordon Commodore of the transports taking troops to Egypt to assist in throwing out Napoleon's army. That done, Peter set about protecting Britain's trade routes between

Britain, India and China, carrying troops, agents, government stores and trade goods out, and luxury cargoes back from the East, while avoiding his sailors being taken by the Navy. On the Cape route – crossing the Atlantic, sailing down the coast of Brazil to Rio de Janeiro, catching the winds to beat back across to the Company-owned Island of St Helena and thence to the waystation at the Cape of Good Hope – Gordon captured the French ship, *Franchise*. She had escaped the British blockade and had been on the rampage up and down the west coast of Africa. The *Franchise* was taken into the British Navy and at one point was served by my great-grandmother's cousin, Peter Hart from Helensburgh. According to his Captain, Hart conducted himself as a sober, honest, good and faithful man. He would himself become a captain before dying of cholera in Shanghai on the way back from Sydney, where he had visited his, and my, relative, Alexander Hart.

Various pieces of inscribed silver attest to Peter Gordon's value to the Company. He must have saved them a lot of money. They, in turn, may have enriched him. The Curators of the East India Company Records at the British Library provide registers of personnel who traded on their own account. A Captain might bring home 9336 pounds of tea on which he would pay 7% tax on 688 pounds, and 17% on 8648 pounds. Mates, the Purser, the Boatswain, Gunners and Carpenters also had allowances, in diminishing amounts down to the Carpenter's 246 pounds, which probably made a carpenter a rich man by his standards. Tea was a valuable commodity kept in a locked caddy. Perhaps one of the tiny keys I discovered in the corners of this house over the years was Ann Henderson's caddy key. I do have my own Georgian caddy given to me by my friend Frances Gordon. She cautioned me that it was unclear whether the word caddy was taken into English from the Malay Kati or the Chinese Cati.

Records of the Company list goods brought home for sale by a Captain Munro on *Houghton* in 1784. He shipped tea, rhubarb, cassia, dragons' blood, Nankeen cloth, bamboo fans, turmeric and sago, rattan and cane mats and half a chest of China ware. China ware was also used to make up consignments and arrived gratis

Weddings

with the tea. I have a little clay Chinese Yixing teapot decorated with calligraphy, which somehow made it into a subterranean Glasgow junk shop in Cowcaddens, before the area was destroyed by improvements. The owner shuffled out of the corner where his overcoat had blended him with shadow and offered us the teapot and an object we were told was a Malay Kris, a fearsome-looking dagger, for ten shillings. We were students and there was no such thing as a cashpoint, but I managed to borrow the needful. When we parted forty years later, I took custody of the teapot and Pip the kris. Junkshops then, in the early sixties, were littered with plunder and trophies. But no dragon's blood, which I regret to say was a kind of resin. *Houghton*, I discovered, was the ship on which William Roxburgh, apprentice Company surgeon, first shipped to India in 1772. He was a man of humble birth from Symington who became a noted and influential botanist and meteorologist. He was Keeper of both the Calcutta and the Edinburgh Botanical Gardens, and died the father of twelve children by his three wives, and one son John, the child of none of these wives, who worked with him. He is buried in Greyfriars Churchyard.

Over eighteen years, as Peter Gordon roamed on Company business, Ann Phillips gave birth to six living children. Their father came from Plymouth and Portsmouth, depending on from which part of the world he had sailed, and sometimes from the docks in London – mostly built by the Company to berth and unload their ships – where David Kedie Whytt was plying his trade. Images of the Thames at the time, spiked with masts, illustrate clearly the exertions and skill needed to extract a ship and gain the lower reaches. Gordon wrote a will, worried about his 'Lass', his partner in life, who was twenty years his junior. Lass, an old word for a young woman, is, for someone of my generation at least, layered with tenderness and meaning far beyond its definition.

Three years later, Captain Gordon was dead. The following year, his daughter, Ann Gordon, married Ebenezer Alexander Whytt. Ebenezer's marriage to Ann Gordon was one of his luckier moves, and everything looked favourable as they set up home together at almost the same time that David Whytt married his Ann.

David's business address at 22 Essex Street remained constant through the years, though he worked with a number of partners, sometimes Thomas Goode; sometimes James Sykes. They advertised in *The European Magazine* and *London Review*. In February 1810, he and Sykes dealt with the prize shares of *Vrow Antyna* and *De Hoop*, and again in, 1810 and in 1813, he's distributing prize money down the river in Greenwich. I did some of the research on David and John Gourley in the National Maritime Museum in Greenwich. The best way to travel there these days is by the same method used by David – by boat down the river.

In Greenwich, I found letters from the Admiralty praising the work of Admiral Gourley and his young son, Midshipman John Charles Gourley, lately enrolled in the Navy. I also found an exuberant letter to Admiral Vashon, on board the *Texel* in Leith Roads, from young Gourley who was on patrol off the coast between Leith and Berwick and enjoying chasing smugglers. The smuggling in wintertime, he writes, is mostly carried out 'in the first and last quarter of the Moon' when, with the assistance of the dark and 'covered with a little grain or coal, a great quantity of contraband is brought ashore'. Local fishermen then unload. If a Revenue cutter is nearby, they are warned by a speedy boat or by a fire of straw on the shore. He has noted the places the smugglers come from, and informs Vashon that he has tipped off the press gang, which he has found very useful in clearing out smugglers on the northern coast.

In 1811, as Ann gave birth to her second daughter, Janet in 2 George Place, David, in the pages of the London Gazette, was brokering the proceeds of the capture of *Tri Bergithie* by the sloop *Snake*. On the same page is a notice of the bounty earned by the sloop *Derwent*, on capturing *African*, *Maria Paul* and *Two Cousins* 'and their cargoes of slaves'. It is one of only two references to enslaved people I have found in the maritime primary sources I consulted. London was largely insulated from the mechanisms of its trade in people. What happened to this 'cargo'? I searched and, finally, on the Trans-Atlantic Slave Trade database, I found something. Captain Dupuys set sail from Freetown, Sierra Leone on *Two Cousins* to cross the Atlantic with a cargo which included five enslaved persons. This intent, we are told, was thwarted and four of them were landed in the Old World, which we know, thanks to David, was London. There's no mention of what happened to the missing fifth person. I searched for the other two ships through an horrendous catalogue of British, Spanish, Portuguese, American . . . ships in the database but could not find the specific *African* or *Maria Paul*. I hope the four people who landed in London were treated well and prospered.

In 1812, the Commissioners for the Royal Naval Asylum at Greenwich advertised in the *Aberdeen Journal* that they were taking in fifty boys and four girls, children of the widows of seamen and mariners, lost on five ships. I asked around as to why there were so few girls. The consensus was that the boys would be educated while the girls were set to domestic work. The commissioners did not know the widows' addresses and so letters telling them of their good fortune in securing a place for their fatherless children, were forwarded to DK Whytt, then secretary to Vice Admiral Otway.

David's third Admiral, William Albany Otway, is reported to have been frank and affable, with a record of indefatigable service which ultimately impaired his health. And no wonder. He entered the Navy in 1765, aged ten, and was immediately pitched into a lifetime of battles, sinkings, fevers at sea, and captures. In 1813, he dictated a flowery letter from Leith to the Lord Provost, alerting him to the fact that two French frigates had been seen and that, based on their course, he feared they were going north to intercept the Gothenburg convoy. He saw them off. He, too, received the Freedom of the City of Edinburgh.

In 1812, James Whytt lost his wife, Janet. She died of a decline at 3 Morton Street and was buried in the South Leith graveyard just round the corner. Her death was announced in the *Scots Magazine* and *Edinburgh Literary Miscellany*, among a sad litany of dead infants, drowned mariners and victims of disease in the West Indies.

On 5 January 1815, six months before the Battle of Waterloo, which would make the seas safe for cargoes to Leith from mainland Europe for some time, *Janet* docked from Oporto carrying many 'pipes', that is barrels, of Portugal red wine. James and David took

10 Scotland Street

delivery of two of these. *Janet* also bore boxes of plums. On 3 April, Ann's daughter, Grace, named for her paternal aunt, was born at 2 George Place.

Soon after the Treaty of Paris, which formally ended the war, the Admiralty announced that from 16 March 1816, no more convoys would leave from Leith. David returned to civvy street and his four daughters, Marion, Janet, Wilhelmina and Grace.

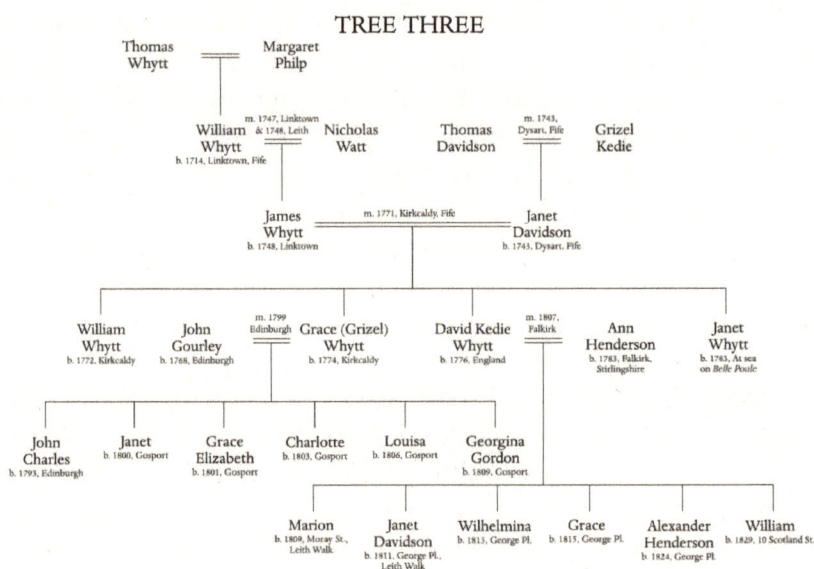

FOUR

TO SCOTLAND STREET

The family's relief at the cessation of hostilities in November must have been shattered when young Lieutenant John Charles Gourley was drowned on 18 December 1815 while trying to rescue a boy in trouble on the half-frozen Loch End near Edinburgh. The funeral left from his father's house at 28 Gayfield Square and carried young John to the Whytt ground, in the South Leith Churchyard. Lieutenant Gourley's provenance is a bit of a mystery. His father married Grace Whytt in 1799. I have been unable to find John Charles' birth record, but the South Leith record is quite clear. John Charles was 22 when he died and so his birthdate must have been around 1793. He entered the Navy in 1805, when he was twelve, as a Jewel Boy third class and rose quickly to Midshipman and then, in 1814, to Lieutenant. His father's memorial records that his son, having saved three youths who had fallen beneath the ice, drowned when trying to rescue a fourth. Gourley went on half pay till his retirement, thirty years later.

Was Admiral Gourley widowed when he met Grace? I can find no further information. Whatever the truth of it, his son appears to have been very much integrated into the Gourley/Whytt family. I think on young John Charles as I walk through Lochend Park.

A year later, in 1816, a notice in the *Caledonian Mercury* intimates that the Whytts are giving up the wine and spirit trade, and offers for sale at their warehouse at 61 Giles Street 'Casks, Bottles, Gauntrees, Weighing Beams, Stoups, a Hand Cart etc, all in excellent order and worthy of attention'. Though James and David now

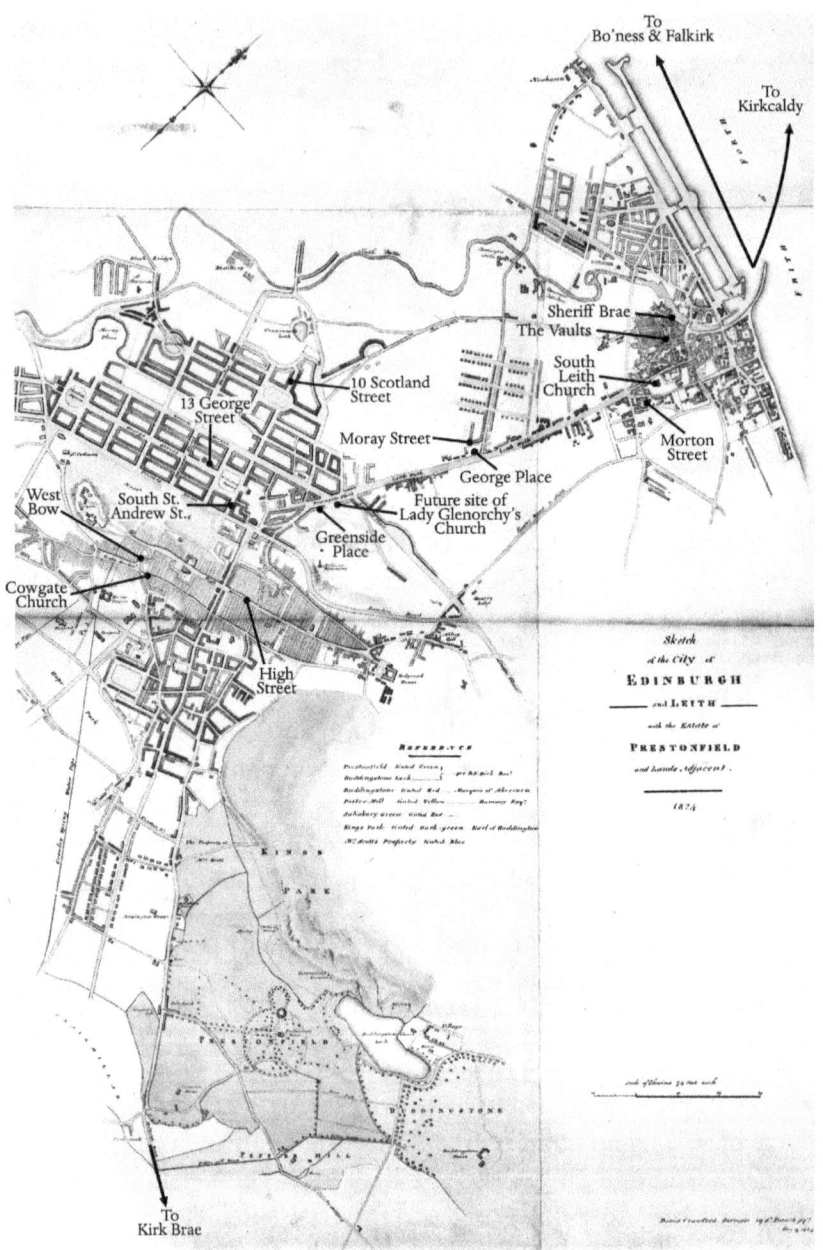

MAP THREE Sketch map of the City of Edinburgh and Leith with the Estate of Prestonfield and lands adjacent. David Crawford, Surveyor, 1824. Reproduced with the permission of the National Library of Scotland.

turned their attention to bookselling, David continued to work as a naval agent from George Place and Essex Street. Long after the official end of the war in 1815, he was still selling captures and distributing prize money. In April 1817, he gives notice that the proceeds of two brass guns captured in 1809 by HMS *Seahorse* and £300 retained for *Seahorse's* share of a captured enemy ship will be lodged in the High Court.

Later that year, Ann gave birth to her namesake, Ann. The poor mite lasted only four months before succumbing to water on the brain. In 1820, Ann's first son James, named for his grandfather, was born and lived only two years before he, too, made the journey to South Leith Graveyard. Of the fifty parishioners' deaths recorded for the month of James' death, more than half were under thirty years of age, and six were under five. They died of decline, inflammation, bowel hives, teething, gravel, whooping or chin cough, stoppage of the bowel, croup, water in the head and six more were stillborn. So many stillborn. Stillbirths were registered in most parish records in Scotland for a further thirty-two years till, in 1854, the Registration Act mandated central registration of all living births. Stillborn babies had no legal existence and were not registered. Not until 1939 were they again included. I had two stillborn aunts and a stillborn cousin among the unregistered.

David ended his work as a naval agent and, by 1822, was listed in the directories solely as a Bookseller at 2 George Place. In 1824, just before the move to 10 Scotland Street, Alexander Henderson Whytt, named for his maternal grandfather, made his entrance. Ensconced in Scotland Street, with her four daughters and her wee son, Ann must have felt that she had made port.

The Second New Town, of which 10 Scotland Street is a part, followed the rubric of a uniform exterior. From the road, which was laid with stone setts as Scotland Street still is, one crossed the footwalk of irregular large stone slabs, to pass over a sunken area which gave access to the basement. The builders had to work with a steep slope on Scotland Street. The problem was solved by varying the structures under the ground floor flats. Sometimes the basements are two deep. David would walk from his business in the town, down Dublin Street and cut round Drummond Place to reach his home. There, before mounting the half-dozen steps to the door, he would clean his boots on the iron scraper – as do I. In his eighties he would, I think, have been grateful for the railings which bound the steps, using them as an aid to reach the platform in front of our door. There he would use the mechanical bell-pull – which today bemuses contemporary delivery people – to call the servant to turn the key in the huge iron lock, with its brass handle and bolt and a forbidding interior. I have it repaired regularly, every ten years or so.

The door has four panels and a central *faux* split with a glazed panel above, as do most in the New Town. Beyond these standard house doors, however, one might find a three- or four-storey town house, a main door flat with basement(s), a main door flat with a stair down to a basement and stair up to a second storey, or a stair cutting through the main door flat to give access to the two or three upper flats. Sometimes the two top storeys are one house, named a double-upper, and sometimes the top flat is split into two. In all my years nosing around, I cannot remember two interior layouts which were identical.

My deeds for 10 Scotland Street speak of a main door flat of six rooms, with a light bed closet, a water closet and other conveniences. The light bed closet is the small room with a window, off the main bedroom. Number 10 originally included the basement, now numbered 8A, which sits under numbers 8 and 10. It consisted of two rooms, a scullery, a water closet, or toilet, and other conveniences, three cellars at the front and the ground at the back. The basement area, reached by steps from the street, was and is well-flagged, with good cellars under the pavement – none of which were a water closet, as was the case in some streets. David and Ann's servants had an indoor toilet, and two fair-sized bedrooms looking out onto their drying green at the back. The kitchen stretched the length and width under Ann's dining room, with a deep fireplace, inset with a black iron range for cooking. Tucked in at the front and carved out of number 4, with which number 10 shares its southern wall, is a scullery with a window. Through the years, I spent quite a lot of time in that basement, which was bricked off from my flat long before I arrived. If I had been able to transport myself through the bricks and take the steps which spiralled on down, I would come upon a small door and beyond it one of these other conveniences – a dark, cold-cellar, curving downwards, carved deep into the bedrock. Three owners, since my original basement friends left, have made changes. Friendly builders let me in, to look up at the underside of the stair leading to my house, and at the wall, breached for the first time since it was built. From the foundations, I acquired a beautiful piece of stone, seeing the light for the first time in 200 years. It sits on my kitchen table and is contemplated, while I decide what to do with it.

I can guess which surfaces of my home David touched. Much is unchanged. On my front door is the massive lock, operated only from the inside. Some years ago, my small granddaughter and I were stranded on the step, unable to open the door. A locksmith let us in, pointing out that 'someone' had pulled the chain which released the bolt. 'Sorry Gran,' said my granddaughter. She owes me £90. Above the monster lock is the distinctive New Town lock with its many fragile leaves, and elegant long key, which I use daily. And, for the avoidance of who-knows-what, above that, a very secure modern lock.

The clapper on my doorbell rings on its casing in the inner lobby, when a cord, fed through a system of levers, up and through the outer lobby, is activated by pulling the brass knob on its plate, just to the right of the door. All the interior lock escutcheons are original, as are most of the doorhandles; black wood for principal rooms, and a mixture of brass and wood for the cupboards. The linen cupboard has an unusual spring-bolt closure, which bears a French maker's mark, almost worn off by use. I can be fairly sure where Ann laid her hand. The doors, certainly, the wall-mounted bells which called the servants, the door to the toilet, the door to the narrow, dark, dogleg staircase to the servants' quarters below with, to the left, the cupboard and butler's sink for the maids. She used, and I use, the key which miraculously still lives in the lock of a lobby cupboard. In her dining room, there is a cupboard which has not been decorated since last she placed her napery on the shelves, and locked the door with the key which I now use. I stand before the windows and close the shutters, placing my hands on top of hers.

In what was Ann's drawing room and is my drawing room – though its name segued into the Green Room, when I painted it after a 1983 visit to Leningrad and the Winter Palace with its distinctive colouring – there is a mirror. The mirror is large, extremely heavy, and embellished with gold curlicues. In 1974 we were young enough to move it, and our friends young enough to help us, for some lunch and a beer. Removing the mirror revealed that it had been above the fireplace since the walls were distempered, and before the Victorian addition of the picture rail which stopped on either side. It must have been Ann's. When I stand in front of it, she is just at my shoulder.

When we moved in, the curse of the plate glass window had struck Scotland Street, but only on the street-facing windows, and the characteristic twelve-paned astragals were soon restored by a friendly engineer who saw the potential in a rundown street, and set up as a renovator. Much of the glass of the rear windows was original, and some still is, with tiny flaws and bubbles and a liquid feel to it.

A long lobby leads from my front door into what estate agents now call a dining hall. At the south-east corner is my office. This room was Ann's dining room, in which she would have had a large, extending, dining table, surrounded by chairs. As the time of dinner slid inexorably from noon to six o'clock, the dining room became more important, a centre of hospitality. It often housed the family's pianoforte, played by the young women of the family. It was a useful skill, as hours could be filled with practice, and was proof of the ability to pay for expensive lessons. Warmth was provided by a coal fire which mostly heated the four storeys of chimney above. The fire basket sat within Ann's black marble fireplace. White marble was reserved for the drawing room. Between the dining and drawing rooms, there is a door to what was once the sunken toilet venting onto the stair of number 8, which must have been less than ideal. When I arrived, this closet was full of coal, the coal cellar having gone with the basement. In the upper flats, coal was commonly kept in a bunker in the kitchen, into which it was dumped from a sack carried up the stairs by the coalman. As we moved from one flat to another, each less-improved than the former, I cleaned out three coal-bunkers in succession. It is not a pleasant task.

For Ann and David, that toilet under the stair would have spelled luxury. For the servants, the water supply and drains, installed by the builders, must have been a boon. This sweet water supply and efficient drainage and sewerage was the culmination of a long process of research, advocacy and invention, which began with the threat of bubonic plague in 1720. The link between living conditions and pestilence was made, and gradually incorporated into improvements and the new buildings on the northern slopes of Edinburgh. The original, southern part of the New Town drained off to the east in open sewers down to Holyrood, where it joined the East Foul Burn carrying the effluent from the Old Town, and then to the irrigated meadows of Lochend. Here fodder was grown for the town's horses and dairy cows. It was quite a feat of engineering. Through the nineteenth century, effluent progressively moved underground and into a big sewer, but the irrigated meadow system in part remained until the 1920s. The second New Town drained into the Water of Leith, which progressively ran more slowly as industry and mill laids hampered the flow.

Next to Ann's drawing room is a bedroom, the smallest, overlooking the lane leading down to stables. A friend and I have one of the last of these, with their uneven stone floors and ancient roof beams, marooned in a sea of conversions. We are resolute unimprovers, though we do maintain the fabric. In David's time, my bit of the stable housed the horses and my friend's bit, with the high doors, the long shafts of the carriages and carts.

I have decided that the bedroom overlooking the stable lane was the boys' room. The bedrooms have austere granite fireplaces, in contrast to the embellished drawing room effort. Directly opposite the front door, a small corridor housed a large linen cupboard, now fulfilling itself in other ways. To the right is the door to the main bedroom, which would have been Ann and David's – light and airy, it is on the north-west corner and is an ice-box in winter. The fireplace recess is blackened with smoke, but I fear the air was seldom better than chilly. Sometime in the early twentieth century, someone bricked and rubble-filled the fireplace and installed a gas fire. I dug it all out, over several weekends, with a monstrous crowbar, a lump hammer and a trowel, and carried the heavy, filthy detritus in many bags, one of which burst, through the lobby for disposal. The revealed hearth space is worth the effort. From it, the chimney rises those four storeys, veers to the western corner and sucks heat. The mantelpiece, laboriously restored to original granite, still has socket traces of the device which held an oil lamp or candle. This room, in my time, became the nursery, and has an early-Georgian iron cot in one corner. On the morning I gave birth to my elder daughter, her reeling father spotted a pile of old iron, which he thought might be a cot, in Lyon and Turnbull's Lane sale. He had to leave but mentioned it to an antique-dealer friend, and the cot was waiting for our baby when we brought her home. This Georgian cot has held both my daughters – and their father, passed out beside them – and all my grandchildren. When our elder daughter first left Scotland Street, the room became home to my mother-in-law for some years, serially to my son and daughters and to various young people in need of a bed. As the earth turned, it became again a nursery for another generation. My friends, family and colleagues are spread across the world. David and Ann's bedroom is seldom empty for long.

Off this room was Ann's bed-closet. At some point before 1906, it was converted into a bathroom complete with a novelty – a water tank, which also supplied the basement. Not long after I moved in, I idly pulled a chain hanging from the bathroom ceiling, to see what would happen. What happened was my introduction to the woman who would be my good neighbour for nearly four decades. I had turned off her water supply. The basement had no bathroom until the beginning of this century, though at some point a short bath was installed in the scullery. I've seen this kind of workaround in a number of homes over the years.

In the centre of the back of the house is the third bedroom. Two girls in here, I think, perhaps the two younger, Wilhelmina and Grace. Off the little corridor leading to the basement is another room, perhaps a bedroom for Marion and Janet. But this sequestered room at the end of the little corridor, at the top of the stairs to the servants' quarters, may have been used as a family parlour. This is where the sun falls in the afternoon. The four girls may well have shared one room. All rooms have a traditional Scottish press and, off the main lobby, there is yet another deep press, Ann's key still in its lock.

Press is the word my grandmother and mother used for a cupboard. I wondered if it were comprehensible and turned to *A Guid Scotch Dictionary*, printed in Glasgow by David Bryce and Son, and by Frederick Stokes and company in New York. I have kept it in my range of dictionaries, not, perhaps, because of its utility, but because it is inscribed with his name, in pencil, by the neat hand of my maternal grandfather, who died four years before I was born. My gran died when I was ten and I was given a box containing my grandfather's books. He was 'taken from school at twelve', his words, when his father died, leaving a young widow with numerous small children. My grandfather went to work, first on the railways and then as a mineral sampler with Tatlock and Thomson, the Glasgow City Analysts. He spent what spare time he had at Workers' Educational Association classes and meetings of the Independent Labour Party and taught himself to play the violin and make use of shorthand. In his leisure time, what there was of it, he read poetry. His books reflected his values and his tastes. For me, they more or less changed everything. His little dictionary came to me when my widowed mother died. On its gilded edge, in ink, are the squared-off initials of my draughtsman father, dead these forty-five years. I like the conjunction of the marks of serial ownership of these two self-educated men. The work is by Cleishbotham the Younger of the Manse of Gandercleuch. Taste those names. It measures sixteen by seven centimetres, and is intended, wrote John G. Ingram, the producer of the second edition of 1879, to be cheap and portable and to familiarise the English scholar or the tourist with the nervous force and clearness of the Scottish language. I like nervous force. He used a quotation, from the English poet Cowper, on the work of Robert Burns, 'His candle is bright, but it is shut up in a dark lantern', to illustrate the necessity of this little blue linen-bound book. This made me reflect on the everyday Scots speech of the Whytts, in and out of 10 Scotland Street. David, working in London, would have learned, like many Scots, to be bi- if not multi-lingual. In all probability, he would have had some childhood Gaelic, Scots of course, English when needed, and would have been able to operate in French, with perhaps some German and a bit of Spanish. That would not have been unusual for a Scottish merchant of his time. Scotland had strong links with Europe. Trade, of course, but also in the fields of learning, architecture and the arts. *The Edinburgh Evening Courant*, of April 1828, announced French teacher Mr Espinasse's annual distribution of prizes, and Miss Wilhelmina Whytt, of 10 Scotland Street, received third prize for conversation and literature. Below the list of young ladies, there is a further long list of the prizes awarded to gentlemen.

Francois Espinasse was married in October 1819, in St Andrew's Church on George Street, to Janet Cruikshank, daughter of a London merchant. Co-incidentally, the entry for Francois is directly below that of Joseph Liddle, Solicitor to the Supreme Court, who was to play a large part in the lives of the Whytts and bring his new bride to live in William Whyte's property at 12 Scotland Street, when it was brand-new. Francois Espinasse, son of Augustin Espinasse and Marie Delagrange, teacher of French, and Chevalier de la Legion d'honneur, taught the good people of Edinburgh for six decades. He died in 1870, at 1 London Street, at the top of Scotland Street. If I turn, I can see it now. In this town, in this place, I do feel I walk with ghosts.

The second New Town was built with commercial and retail establishments on its streets. Many were for the convenience of maids and housekeepers, newly-faced with running large homes with dedicated kitchens – and stairs. Lots of stairs. You had to be strong to be a servant in an Edinburgh home, though perhaps 10 Scotland Street was an easier billet. Nearby on Broughton Street could be found plasterers and poulterers, boot and shoemakers, grocers and spirit dealers, bandage-makers and ironmongers, tobacconists and bonnet makers, candlemakers and feather dyers. A wide variety of goods were on offer on Princes Street, in shops converted from houses by paving over the basements and altering the interiors – all recorded in the Dean of Guild Court. There were grocers, from which Ann might order store apples, marmalade oranges, oats, a peck of pears, of cherries, of figs. At 75 Princes Street, Thomas Stevenson offered Berlin Wool, stays, buttons and trimmings. At the Sign of the Golden Bull, for ready money with no discount, one might buy gilded ornaments, while, at 12 Princes Street, close by William Whyte's first shop, William Renton and Company were Wedding, Baby Linen and General Outfitters; Silk Mercers, Shawlmen, Drapers and Haberdashers, who would also see to your Family Mournings, Cloaks, Furs and Millinery. In January, they offered three kinds of Flannel, and in June, Summer White Tulle and Stiff Net. Mrs Brown of Perth was Embroiderer to the Queen, the Empress Eugenie, the Duchess of Kent and the Royal Princesses, and not above embroidering pinafores and baby feeders. The number of establishments offering repairs is striking: dresses taken in and out, shortened and lengthened, dyed and embellished; trouser cuffs turned, elbows patched. Clothes were an investment, made to last. And often sold on. All of these establishments would deliver to Ann's door. Scotland Street had its basement dairy and grocers, two of which lasted until I arrived; and when Ann and David moved in, below the north side of number 10 was a baker's premises. It covered two storeys and consisted of a shop, a bakehouse, an oven and a dwelling house of four rooms, a kitchen and other conveniences, which presumably means it had a toilet. Mr Boyd was the first baker, followed by William Calderwood and then by the Scotts, who were still there a decade after David's death.

The Scotland Street builders, William and Alexander Lewis Wallace, a father and son partnership, were remarkable. Alexander's sons moved to London in 1862 and founded Wallace and Company, import/exporters, with Framji Patel. One set up a business in Burma that became the Bombay Burma Trading Company, and expanded into Thailand – then Siam – and into Java, south India, Borneo and Africa. They traded in timber, tea, coffee, rubber and tapioca and, later, cotton for the Lancashire mills. The Wallace family retained a controlling interest till 1989, when the company was dissolved. It could stand for an exemplar of Imperial capitalist ventures.

Scotland Street, like Drummond Place at its head, was designed by Robert Reid, who worked with Robert Adam on Charlotte Square. Each block of the second New Town is a single architectural composition, resulting in clean lines, which have been little altered, compared to the ravages inflicted upon the first. Apart from the conversion of shops and basements into separate homes, and the addition of two wee second floor ornamental balconies, Scotland Street is much as Reid intended. Till recently, our street lamps were a mish-mash of styles, cracked and listing, casting a lurid orange hue. Surrounding streets have appropriate lamps and after nearly thirteen years of dogged correspondence with the Council, historically-appropriate lamps are now installed.

Appropriate needs defining. When Scotland Street was built, there was no street lighting. Traces remain of six basic railing-mounted private oil lamps. Number 10 had none. In 1817, the Edinburgh Gas Light Company, of which JG Thomson was a director and proprietor, and William Whyte a shareholder, applied to the Dean of Guild Court for permission to lay their pipes through the Streets and Closes of the Town, under the oversight of the Superintendent of Works. Ordnance Survey maps from 1849 to 1905 include the siting of lamps and show that there has never been a uniform scheme of lighting across the city, or even in adjacent streets. Gas standard lamps eventually arrived in Scotland Street in the 1860s. For Scotland Street, the Council and Edinburgh World Heritage worked with us towards a replica of the 1860s scheme. This was greatly assisted by the miraculous survival of a contemporary globe, in the possession of my next-door neighbour, a civil engineer. Many of the restored nineteenth century lamps in the city are the product of her and her late husband's work and skill. To produce replicas, a papier mâché form was made of the original glass, and from that a polycarbonate copy. The prototype was a thing of beauty. The lamps are now sited in Scotland Street at their original locations, one of which is happily outside my window. The lamps are energy-efficient and centrally-controlled. David, with his candles and oil lamps and lanterns, would have looked on in wonder.

In my research, I was blessed with an abundance of scenic and resonant resources across the globe. They are listed hereafter. The most useful: the National Library of Scotland and its mirror across George IV Bridge, the Edinburgh Central Library, built by Carnegie – the many floors of which descend to the Cowgate and the church built by William Whyte, brother of David Kedie Whytt, for David's son-in-law Thomas Smith – and the National Records of Scotland at New Register House and General Register House, on my doorstep at the east end of Princes Street.

David Kedie Whytt and I acquired 10 Scotland Street by the grant of an instrument of Sasine, the means by which we registered property ownership in Scotland until very recently. The first Sasine, dated 1617, is written in Latin in a floral cursive script, in the world's first national land register. It is lodged in the National Records of Scotland, the repository of a record of every person in Scotland who was born, died, divorced, made a will, took a case to court, and so on, for several centuries. Lately, the records for genealogists were brought together in Scotland's People, where, for a small fee, you can spend a day mining. Again, for a fee, you can pursue online the long-dead long into the night, in the comfort of your own home, wherever in the world that might be. I remember the crumbling microfiches and clumsy fiche readers, and am grateful. The service is run by a group of helpful, knowledgeable people. Upstairs is the Historical Search room in which, for free, you can access a trove of documents and people who know what they are about, and who are pleased to help. Register House has been providing the service since 1787 and is among the first purpose-built national record repositories.

It was built on the proceeds, some of which were given to the city, of the sale of confiscated Jacobite estates by King George III. In 1774, the foundation stone was laid at the head of the recently-completed Leith Street, and opposite the almost-finished North Bridge. Robert Adam, the original architect, specified locally-quarried stone and brick vaults underneath flagstone flooring to protect the documents from fire and flood. Various trials, mostly financial, delayed its completion and in 1778 the money ran out. The shell became a magnificent doss house, while the rotunda was used for the assembly and take-off of hot-air balloons. In the mid-1780s, the bookseller William Creech deemed it 'the most magnificent pigeon house in Europe'. When Scotland Street's Robert Reid took over to finish the project, the money men were no doubt glad of his restrained style. But the central cupola is a wonder.

Finally, in 1787, Scotland's Public Records, which had been exposed to damp and vermin in the basements of Parliament House in the Old Town, were transferred by cart down the High Street and over the North Bridge to their permanent home. Several decades of argument about how the registers should be controlled and administered commenced. Meanwhile, as far as I can ascertain, in the basement, a Mrs Weir and her skilled staff set about restoring the documents which had been damaged by time and neglect. Finally, in 2011, disparate departments came together in the National Records of Scotland. The last piece of the jigsaw – the Land Register – should be completed by late 2024.

Thirty years after Register House opened, the front wall and double staircase were pushed back. In the lost nine feet, placed inconveniently on the pavement, stands a large equestrian statue of the Duke of Wellington, the victor of the Battle of Waterloo – though of course in Germany and hinterland the victor is the commander of the Prussian and allied army, Gebhard Leberecht von Blucher, a letter in whose hand to the Emperor of Russia was among JG Thomson's possessions when he died. The realignment of the front wall created a public space that nowadays is used, to make their case, by an array of organisations and protesters, from obscure sects to Greenpeace, to Women in Black.

Tucked in behind, and to the left of the main building, is New Register House, with its glorious circular Reading Room. A garden sits hidden between the two buildings and is planted with fifty-seven plant species, all associated, some in fact and some imaginatively, with Scotland's past. There are benches, it is quiet, and in summer it is a haven.

To the left of New Register House is a small path called Gabriel's Road. Riding ancient boundaries, it cuts across the symmetry of the New Town, emerging on St Andrew Square, to the right of the Royal Bank of Scotland. This Palladian villa was built in 1772 for Sir Laurence Dundas, who made a fortune as Commissary General and contractor to the army. With the Jacobite Rebellion confiscations and a major European war on the go, he became one of the wealthiest men in Scotland. The official website of Historic Scotland remarks that he was a man well-versed in the shady dealings of Georgian politics and commerce. But he and the Royal Bank must keep their gates open, as Gabriel's Road is an ancient right of way for such as I, who use the path to cross from Princes Street onto St Andrew Square. Heading for Scotland Street, I follow the line for much of the way. If I could continue on Gabriel's Road, under and over the intervening buildings, I would pass to the west of Scotland Street, and finally reach a flight of stairs, boldly signed Gabriel's Road, leading down to Glenogle Road. If I then continued down Collins Place and forded the Water of Leith, Gabriel's Road would take me all the way to Inverleith House. Collins Place is one of the rows of stone, terraced houses, known as Colonies. These iconic homes were built by the Edinburgh Cooperative Building Company, which was formed in 1861 to provide decent housing for working people. We lived in Collins Place in the late sixties, in the second of our five Edinburgh homes, as we moved ever-nearer to Scotland Street.

FIVE

PROBLEMS AND THE PADONS

David and Ann's move to Scotland Street was surely marred in October 1825 by the death of their brother-in-law, John Padon, which was to cause a great deal of bother. Padon, with a partner, Andrew Vannan, had taken up distilling in Bo'ness. His widow, Wilhelmina Henderson, in the eighteen years of their marriage, had borne nine children. When I first looked into what had become of the family after John Padon's death, I found Mrs Padon on the 1855 valuation roll at 15 Hart Street, close by Scotland Street. I traced the trajectory backwards.

Wilhelmina was thirty-nine when she was widowed, and became solely responsible for eight children, ranging in age from seventeen to two. Her eldest son, Thomas, was fifteen. Wilhelmina packed up and took her tribe to 15 Hart Street, an upper flat a few minutes' walk from 10 Scotland Street and her sister, Ann. It's a fine house, turning the corner of Broughton Place. In the absence of records of the sisters out in the world, I imagine these two women, both with a gaggle of children, living a short distance apart, providing each other with essential support.

David took over his sister-in-law's affairs. In the newspapers he placed a notice to the effect that the family of the late Mr John Padon, Distiller of Borrowstoneness, had no further interest in the co-partnery of Padon and Vannan. If only. David, from his business address at William Whyte and Company, 13 George Street, then set to work to sell the distillery. He described the property as 'a well-situated distillery' which had undergone extensive repair and the installation of a new mashing machine in 1824. 'In addition, it is close to the Union and Grand canals through which track and luggage vehicles pass daily for the east and the west and to Ireland. There is abundant cheap coal close by.'

This last attribute I came to know very well. Bo'ness is a small town on the southern banks of the Forth, at almost exactly the place where the Romans gave up, built another wall and turned their backs on Scotland. It has recovered, to some extent, from many decades of relying on coal hewn from seams, pushed out under the river, and its roaring iron foundry and woodyards, in which both men and women toiled. Bo'ness now celebrates the Hippodrome, a beautifully restored 1912 cinema, a wee steam train, and a fine Art Deco fish and chip shop. My late mother-in-law, Bess, was born and brought up there, the youngest of five whose father died in the slaughter on the Somme on the first of July 1916, when she was two years old. Advancing on the enemy, he was armed only with his bagpipes, which he played until cut down. From Bess I learned about the women who laboured in the woodyards, one of them her widowed mother. Her older sister was taken from school to run the home. Her brothers, at twelve, crawled deep under the earth and the river and bore permanent scars on their backs from the narrow coal seams. For two brothers, the army offered an escape. Another found his end in 1964 when he fell over 500 feet from the Forth Road Bridge, which he was helping to build.

Bess grew up in extreme poverty, in a two-room house on Foundry Square, in some of the worst housing in Scotland at the time. None of this dented her optimism and generosity. I got to know the Bo'ness of the early twentieth century through her eyes. She remembered crowds of masts in the harbour, and falling into the river aged three, weighed down by her petticoats and over-large tackety boots. The last of the Arctic whalers out of Bo'ness sailed and returned with the seasons. The distillery, down by the Forth, was still operating. 'It smelled,' Bess said, 'like witch hazel,' and was a pleasing building, but there was little work to be had, as it was run with only a few men and no women. Her son was born in a fine inter-war council house, on one of the terraces of the hillside above the town, nearly twenty years after the closure of the distillery. He remembers the pagoda roofs of the malt house that he saw as they passed in the bus on the way to visit his grandmother and step-grandfather, a lovely man, an ex-miner, who cultivated vegetables and tobacco in their long back garden.

The fact that the pagoda roof was still there for them to see from the bus was, to an extent, down to our David Kedie Whytt, whose first attempt at selling the distillery failed. He tried again. And again. Finally, he announced, rather crossly, that the upset price of the distillery, which he had already described in great detail in the *London Courier* and *Times*, the *Edinburgh Courant* and *Mercury*, and the *Advertiser*, had been reduced. The adjourned sale would resume by public roup, a Scots word for an auction, at Mr John Gibson's saleroom on Princes Street. David's desperation, on behalf of his sister-in-law and her family, is palpable. 'The distillery,' he repeated, 'is capable of distilling above 4000 gallons of spirit weekly, with a STEAM ENGINE of twelve-horse power, Feeding Byres for 114 head of cattle, and Stables for six horses . . .' There is commodious accommodation for the foreman – who even has a garden – and lots of machinery, utensils and casks.

In addition, there was a lease for the ground on which the whole caboodle sat, which would run for eighty-three and a half years. This, I conclude, was the source of his desperation. David becomes almost lyrical. Few distilleries have such natural advantages. It's on the seashore right next to the harbour of Borrowstoneness. It's close by canals. There's lots of cheap coal and an inexhaustible supply of water. He ends by saying that it is, 'highly deserving of the attention of capitalists, or others, who propose to start up in the distillery business.'

In 1828 he dropped the price to £2400. It didn't sell. It may be that he dropped the price because his mother-in-law, Marion Aikman, had died on 3 June 1828, in Hart Street, without having made a will. Ann sorted out her estate, which consisted of personal effects and books worth £132 17/8, and a debt of £350 owed to her by her deceased son-in-law, John Padon. When the estate was settled in December 1830, this debt was 'not considered worth anything and so not included in the inventory'. John Padon does not seem to have been much of a businessman and surely, of the sisters, Ann had made the better choice.

Andrew Vannan, John Padon's former partner, made the best of things, and he and his family ran the distillery with some success, until it was sold in 1874. In 1912, it was turning out 25000 gallons of spirit a week, duty paid, before it closed forever in 1925. In one of the slightly improbable coincidences which have slid into this narrative so often, the foreman, when the distillery closed, was my great-uncle, who had lost a leg at some point in his long life. He lived a few hundred yards from my future mother-in-law, though whether they were acquainted I will never know.

One hundred years previously, David had clearly had a problem. He solved it by taking upon himself the burden of John Padon's part in the distillery. It took me a long time to discover this. David's will, having dealt with 10 Scotland Street and 2 George Place, then bundles all the rest of his real estate together. In his brother William's will, I finally found the reference. In William's long list of bequests, he comes, near the end, to his share of the property of the late John Padon, distiller at Borrowstoneness; the land and property he had acquired with his brother David to help out his friend's family. Not for the first time, I decided I would have liked these men.

The Padons remained in Hart Street. When I looked at the 1841 census, I was taken aback to see that there were three sets of twins – until I remembered that, in this census, ages were rounded up and down to the nearest multiple of five. In 1851, Wilhelmina Henderson Padon was still in Hart Street, living with all eight unmarried children and a servant. Of the male offspring, Thomas was a solicitor of the Supreme Court, three were clerks and Alexander was a bookseller and stationer. Did he work for William Whyte on George Street? After their mother's death, her offspring stayed on in Hart Street. The 1871 census counted all eight of them, still unmarried, and now with two servants. By 1881 there were seven. In 1891, and 1901, there were four, and in 1911 there were none. Anne was the last to die, in 1906, aged eighty-six. A single generation had lived together, in the same house, for eighty years. In the will of David Kedie Whytt's youngest daughter, I discovered that, for all these years, the Padon home had been rented from David, and latterly, his heirs. He had done a sterling job.

SIX

DEATHS AND A SECRET

When he moved into Scotland Street, David and his father were working with William at his newly-enlarged shop at 14 South St Andrew Street, a five-minute walk from Scotland Street round Drummond Place and up the steep slope of Dublin Street. I have been told that tackling that slope undoubtedly adds several years onto lives. In 1825, the business moved to fine new premises at the east end of George Street, next to St Andrew's Church.

In 1828, Ann – I surmise unexpectedly at forty-five – found herself pregnant, and in her sixth month, had to bear the death of her second daughter. Janet, aged seventeen, died of a fever at 10 Scotland Street, and was buried in the Whytt ground, in South Leith churchyard. She was the first to die in my house. Her brother William, arriving three months later in April 1829, was the first to be born here.

He arrived at the end of a tumultuous decade. The war which had taken up so much of David's time was long over but had led to years of austerity and hunger for the poor. Edinburgh was still an intellectual, artistic and thriving music centre which rivalled any in Europe and had deep European connections. At the same time, there was great unrest. Agitation grew for annual parliaments and a widening of the franchise to include all men. The Government reacted to rebellion, some fomented by Government agents, with violent repression. I can find no evidence of Whytt family involvement – on either side.

James Whytt was still living at 3 Morton Street, with his daughter Janet and his granddaughter Margaret. I realised I still had not found any information about this granddaughter. All three dutifully attended both South Leith and Lady Glenorchy's Church. David does not appear, at this point, or indeed any other, to have been quite so pious. In the 1830s, David and William signed several petitions urging the end of chattel slavery. William paid his dues to the very influential Edinburgh Ladies Emancipation Society, which set out its objects in its constitution in 1834: *That this Meeting be of the opinion that Slavery is contrary to the Word of God, and subversive to the best interests of mankind, resolves itself to form itself into a society to promote its universal extinction.* This, the Society continued to do at least until the end of the century, meeting regularly and campaigning worldwide. Their close correspondents include the writer Harriet Beecher Stowe. The Ladies, led by Eliza Whigham, were very well-informed and articulate in their demands. The Misses Thomson, Gentlewomen, of number 8 Scotland Street, were members. I am struck however, by a donation of a few shillings by Laura S. Haviland, of Michigan. A widow and mother of eight children, Haviland was deeply involved in the Underground Railway, helping escapees. She made several journeys south to escort fugitives to safety. Enraged plantation owners took her to court and she received many death threats. Undeterred, she set up schools and orphanages and used various disguises to frustrate her pursuers. She lived to be eighty-nine and somehow found time to send, from her often-meagre funds, a few shillings to the Edinburgh Ladies.

On 2 January 1834, David's sister Janet, she who was born on *Belle Poule*, died of a decline and was interred in that plot in South Leith Graveyard.

Later that year, the Reverend John Aikman, Ann Henderson's uncle, went to his maker. He had married a widow, Sarah Dallas, and left a trust which was to be the subject of a most-un-Christian dispute, for many years. David and William Whytt would have attended his first burial in his own chapel in North College Street – but his exhumation, and subsequent re-burial in Dean Cemetery to make way for the National Museum of Scotland, was too late for them.

However odd John Aikman seems to me, he was clearly well integrated into David Whytt's family, for he appears as witness and trustee in several Whytt wills. His younger brother, James, whose life was almost contemporaneous with David and William, was a bookseller and printer. They must have been colleagues as well as family. He worked out of premises at 6 Charles Street, a few doors along from the rhino head, give or take 150 years.

Perhaps, on Janet's death, her father lost heart for, nine months later in September 1834, aged eighty-six, he died of water in the chest. James' will is written in closely-packed script on thin paper, so that the writing on the reverse shines through. It is very difficult to read. There is a codicil and a codicil to the codicil. But I persevered.

James' overriding concern is the welfare of his daughter, Janet Davidson Whytt and of his granddaughter, Margaret Whytt, the natural daughter of his lawful son, David.

And here we have it. The mysterious granddaughter, Margaret, was born around 1796, when David was twenty, and living in the West Bow with his family and the servant, Margaret Sinclair, for whom his father paid a servant tax of 2/6d.

Was there a relationship between David and Margaret Sinclair? I can find no trace of her after she is noted in the servant tax register, nor reference anywhere to the birth of Margaret Whytt. David would not marry Ann for a further eleven years. His natural daughter, Margaret, pops up in all the records, a fixture in the Morton Street house. To put James' concern for her in context, his granddaughter, Margaret, lived with him for thirty-eight years, until his death, longer than any of his children except Janet. James ensured that both women were secure for their lifetimes. He brings into the equation his granddaughters, Janet Davidson Whytt, and Janet Davidson Gourley, and any future daughter who might be named for his late wife. And then he must have had to watch, as, in succession, his daughter Janet and his two granddaughters, Janet, pre-deceased him.

William inherited all of James' property in Abbotshall and his Morton Street home. Mr Robert Reid, a bail agent, moved in, and Margaret packed up her inheritance of James' bed and silver, his poker and his silver watch inscribed No 553 James Blackborow London, and went off to Dalkeith. Her uncle William took over her care.

Deaths and a Secret

James Whytt was interred in the family plot, in South Leith Churchyard. He joined the three Janets and the infants, his first grandson James, and his granddaughter Ann. Though the parish records tell us he was buried 'one grave's length from the southern boundary of JWD' – James, William and David Whytt's ground – the plot is nowhere to be found. Between James' death and 1848, the South Leith Church was a building site and many gravestones moved or used. The graveyard still has some intriguing stones, among them, that of a Mr Pew. I think of Robert Louis Stevenson's youth in Edinburgh and his family connection to The Vaults, and wonder if, on his wanderings, he noted and stored away Mr Pew, until he found the name perfect for the malignant Blind Pew, who fascinated me when I first picked my way through *Treasure Island*. James is the last of the family to be put in the Whytt ground. No doubt, when JWD bought it, they thought their plot would be tended by them forever. However, in 1843, the Church of Scotland, so central to their lives, split in two. The family left for the new Free Church and the South Leith graveyard was lost to them.

On James' death, the family's focus swung back from Leith to an Edinburgh which was expanding fast and was strikingly cosmopolitan. Among a Register of Aliens, instituted at the beginning of the French wars, were Samuel Robinson, a chemist from Philadelphia, lodging on Richmond Place – though mainly living in St Petersburg; Mr Stregman, a merchant from Riga, born in Lisbon, staying at Hamilton's Hotel, on Princes Street; Sally from Amsterdam, come to marry Leon David, an umbrella maker in the Canongate; Count Piper, a Swedish officer lodging in Infirmary Street – though usually resident in Vienna; and five doctors from St Petersburg are in Buccleuch Place, hard by the University.

10 Scotland Street, in 1834, housed three grown daughters. Were they accompanied to the social occasions in the Assembly Rooms on George Street and to the many concert halls, lectures and theatres, now available in Edinburgh? Ann's two small sons would soon make their way down to the newly-built Edinburgh Academy, in fields by the Water of Leith. The eight Padon cousins lived close by, and William over the shop at 13 George Street where he and David were in a co-partnery.

An address delivered by the very elderly James Thin to a meeting of booksellers' assistants, in October 1904, gives a glimpse into the working life of David and William in 1836, the year that the twelve-year-old Thin became an apprentice bookseller. He worked Monday to Saturday, from nine of the morning till nine at evening, and was granted one day's holiday per year. One hundred and five booksellers, several living in Scotland Street, provided services to the 136000 inhabitants of Edinburgh. Twelve booksellers were also stationers, as was William. Combining bookselling with literary auctioning, as James and David Whytt did, was fairly common.

Newspapers, James Thin tells us, were not sold in shops. Proprietors enrolled subscribers and delivered weekly or bi-weekly. In some districts of the New Town, they were sold in the street by a man blowing a horn. Speech criers supplied the news today provided by the popular media. James Thin's father founded a bookselling dynasty, operating on the corner of Infirmary Street and South Bridge, opposite the Old College of the University, and making benevolent donations to good causes, including, in 1854, one to the Edinburgh Ladies Emancipation Society. I spent many hours in that bookshop, where the women who ran the children's section were legendary. It closed in 2002.

We have arrived, more or less, in the vicinity of 1836, when David Kedie Whytt wrote the letter which I found in Kew, and which was the inciting incident for decades of obsession. As I've said before, it's beautifully written, and I speak as one with a handwriting certificate, awarded to me in the early 1950s for an exercise in writing with a steel-nibbed dipping pen. I believe that would have been the kind of pen used by David as he sat in my house but – and I am plagued by this question – in which room? Well, for some reason, as I sit with my back to the window of my kitchen, I feel him by my shoulder; which is of course complete nonsense. I formed many of my opinions in the sixties, when we studied philosophy and were determinedly rational. The superstitions of our parents were to be mocked and discarded. I've since grown up, but I still have no truck with the likes of spirits and fairies, demons and deities. Nevertheless – such a useful word – and I find this difficult to articulate – Davy is sometimes in the air. Davy, he is, and his brother, who is Mr William

Whyte in the world, is Willie when he comes to tea at number 10. If I am totally honest, behind my eyes, Davy is not so tall and is fair of hair and complexion, genial and hospitable. Willie, however, is lean, black-clad and spare in demeanour and attitude. This, I have gathered, not from full-length mental portraits, but from furtive glimpses, when I'm not looking. I suspect my mental images owe something to *Modern Athenians, a series of original portraits of memorable citizens of Edinburgh, 1837–1847*, drawn and etched by Benjamin W Crombie. They are wonderful, characterful, almost caricatures and well worth seeking out. Ann is mistier. I can see her leaving Falkirk with her new husband, oddly unbalanced with her skirts above the ankle, and a large, ungainly bonnet catching the wind. In Leith, she would climb the stair to the family home in Morton Street, and there meet Margaret Whytt, James' granddaughter. How was that explained? And then all those babies. One of the clearest notions I have of Ann concerns her mourning for Janet; watching her daughter's slight form being carried through my hall, and out of my front door, for the last time. Did she raise the window, her hands on the same brass bar I used this morning, to let out her daughter's spirit? However, living with the Davy of my imaginings, there must also have been laughter in Ann's life.

William Whyte and Company was a thriving concern but David had growing children. He may have needed the pension he applied for. When we left them in 1834 on the death of grandfather James, Alexander was in Class II at the Edinburgh Academy. On 2 August 1834, he won the first-class prize for scholarship. William was an infant and the three girls were twenty-five, twenty-three and nineteen.

In 1834 the Church of Scotland drew up registers of male heads of households. These lists testify to Edinburgh's wide social mix. David and Ann and their family were enrolled, a quarter of a mile to the west, at Playfair's 1828 St Stephen's Church. Many of the congregation were affluent, but the first minister found it necessary to set up literacy classes in the vaults. The building is now deconsecrated. It has a fine, large, basement hall, which in the 1960s and 70s was home to regular Saturday jumble sales, where miraculously-preserved garments of long-gone eras, the treasured possessions of dead parishioners, were sold for pennies. They were competitive, violent affairs. You had to be quick, with sharp elbows. A pushchair/battering ram was useful. I once found two men scrutinising an ancient brass and copper object with a handle, which looked a bit like a lamp. I told them it was a car radiator heater, and claimed it. We ran several old motors with that sort of radiator, until road conditions rendered it impossible, sustainably and practicably, to run a car with the stopping distance and turning circle of a small liner. I passed my test in a 1947 vintage, 1.5 litre Riley, with running boards and flip-flop indicators. I still have the radiator heater. Soaring above St Stephen's, the forty-nine-metre tower has Europe's longest clock pendulum. However, the chime which rang out for so long is now silent due to the sensibilities of twenty-first century neighbours.

In 1837, the bells of the town rang out for the young Queen Victoria's ascension to the throne. David was into his sixties and still working hard.

On 17 March 1839, Grace, the youngest Whytt daughter, married Thomas Smith. Ann's happiness at this union may have been tempered by the knowledge that, ten days earlier, Smith had been ordained as a minister, and, as the Church of Scotland records have it, 'set apart for the mission field,' and would take her daughter halfway round the world. David gave Grace £200, perhaps for clothes: the stays, bonnets and petticoats and long drawers she would wear in the heat of Calcutta. Grace and Thomas deserve a chapter to themselves, and that they will get.

A month after the wedding, Ann Henderson Whytt applied to the courts, on behalf of herself and her sister, to be recognised as heirs of their father, Alexander Henderson. Until 1868, land and buildings were not heritable without a record being made in the retours. This means that a jury heard the case and the sheriff retoured, or returned, the information to the Record of Retours. The record established the applicant's right to inherit. Ann made a Special Service, specifying exactly the property in question. Why had she waited till then? Her mother Marion had a liferent on her late husband's property. It would have made more sense if Ann had applied when Marion died.

Deaths and a Secret

I ordered the documents. They were easily obtained and are written in a reasonable, if sometimes illegible, hand. However, I had forgotten that until 1847, except for a short break in the seventeenth century, such retours were in Latin.

My studies in Latin ended in 1962. They would have ended in 1960 had not the head of my school's classics department, said yes when I asked her to give up her free time to teach me when I was scheduled for religious studies and the hated PE. I spent some years teaching in a High School and I wonder now at my cheek and at her kindness. I passed the exam, but it was a long time ago. I engaged a translation agency, paid a not-inconsiderable sum and tinkered a bit with it, while I waited. When the translation arrived, I read it with interest. A few paragraphs in, I began to feel uneasy. Vice-Count? Fatherland? *Jacobus* translated as Jacob rather than James? Then the line, 'the adjoining land belonging to the crown.' This puzzled me until I realised that the translator thought *occidentali* meant crown, rather than western. I re-translated, and what emerged was, 'the adjoining land on the west side belonging to the late James Grey.' The translator had clearly discarded James Grey because he didn't fit. And then there were the goats: 'The plot called Gracy's Acre for the grazing of goats belonging to Alexander Henderson.' Grazing goats? Where on earth did they come from? The correct translation is: 'An acre of the Land known as Gray's Acre disposed by the heirs of the late Alexander Henderson to the deceased Peter Bell.' How did the translator get from heirs to grazing goats? *Heredes/hircus* perhaps . . . but context? And what happened to poor Peter Bell?

To my surprise, I found that my Latin was up to it. It turned out that what the courts had to consider was the ownership of several dwellings, parcels of land, gardens and structures, walls, workshops and so on. The Courts decided that they did indeed belong to Alexander Henderson, who had bought, somewhat indiscriminately, but failed to register, a considerable amount of property. It was then necessary to establish that Ann and Wilhelmina were Alexander's heirs. This threw up a sad little tale of two dead infant brothers. The court found in the sisters' favour.

The first real census of the British Isles took place in 1801. It was a headcount enabling legislation, a tally of men available for the army and navy, projection of food needs, and was of great interest to the emerging life insurance industry. The first census which recorded names and data for each household took place on 6 June 1841. David and Ann are listed with their two daughters, their son Alexander, aged fifteen and now a bookseller's apprentice, and two servants, Isabella Forby and Agnes Liddell. This census solved a mystery. I had searched high and low for David's birth or baptism record. The census told me he was born in England. I assume his parents were in London visiting London Whytts and on bookish business but the record of his birth is nowhere to be found.

The 1841 census gives us, for the first time, a snapshot of the world of Scotland Street. The street was home to lots of children. On census night, more than one hundred families were counted. There were eight uninhabited houses and ninety inhabited, in which lived 590 people, of whom 222 were male and 378 female. Without a wearisome trawl, my guess is that the gender disparity is due to daughters living at home, while young men were allowed to strike out; and to the many female servants. There were solicitors, bookbinders, a gardener, a music teacher, a physician surgeon, several school teachers and preachers of the gospel, booksellers, a newspaper editor, masons, bakers, coachmakers, an engraver, a carpet weaver, a meal dealer, a dressmaker, advocates, accountants, bankers, an artist's colourman, a mathematician, a genealogist and Mr Charles Black, the C of A & C Black publishing firm which, in 1851, had the foresight to buy the copyright of Sir Walter Scott's Waverley novels for £12000. Adam Black lived at 38 Drummond Place. The firm moved to London in 1889 and was acquired by Bloomsbury at the start of the present century.

If there was need of the law, Drummond Place, at the top of the street, was inhabited mainly by judges and advocates, with a large proportion of Writers to the Signet. These were to be seen, in the early days of the square, hailing the sedan chair, carried by two Highlanders, which stood for hire at the corner of London Street, and within calling distance of David's front door. These Highlanders, drawn south after Culloden, also ran messages, carried goods up stairs, beat carpets and polished tables, tableware and cutlery. Fully one in six of employed men were engaged with the law and other professional activities. An English observer commented that in Glasgow it was pig-iron, in Liverpool and Manchester, cotton, but in Edinburgh it was quarrels. But by mid-century, around 50% of the male workforce was employed in industry. One third of employed women were industrial workers, while the rest were in domestic service. Unlike other cities, however, industry was not concentrated in large plants. Rather, it was to be found down lanes and alleys, behind the tenements and churches. When I arrived at Scotland Street, potato and egg merchants had only recently vacated the Lane. The main industries of Edinburgh were brewing and publishing, with Edinburgh's publishers attracting work from London and further afield. The population of the street reflected well the wide variety of Edinburgh's occupations and professions in the second half of the nineteenth century.

At number 7 Scotland Street lived Felix Horetzky, music teacher and composer, who was born in Poland and studied in Vienna, where he taught guitar to the archduchesses of the imperial family. He toured Europe before settling in Scotland Street and marrying Sophia Roberton from Roxburghshire. The internet has a number of virulent squabbles going on about Felix. To sum up, he was very successful in Edinburgh and all the best people came many miles to be taught by him. Or, he was unstable, bad-tempered, a reformed drunkard and envious of others' success. Number 7 is directly opposite number 10; he must have looked into David's windows and perhaps sold his music through the shop on George Street.

At number 34 lived the family of James Smyth, an officer of the Customs in Leith, whose son Charles Spelman Smyth was a surgeon. His other son, Spelman James Smyth, also a customs officer, lived at number 22 with his Leith-born wife. This family appears to have been the one English-born family in the street. James Smyth was, according to his headstone in St Cuthbert's Cemetery, a paragon of amiableness, benevolence and Christianity. James may have worked in the Customs House in Drummond Place. It was a Robert Adam building, originally built around 1775 in open country for Major General Scott. Two engravings show the Custom House in Drummond Place Garden in 1819, with a clear prospect to the Forth, and in 1829, when the road around the garden was laid with setts and Scotland Street erected in the background. The building was demolished in the 1840s for fear that the Scotland Street railway tunnel might have made it unstable.

Scotland Street Railway Station, at the north end of the street, opened in 1842, the same year as the very useful Glasgow-to-Edinburgh line. The line from Waverley Station to Leith and Granton, entailed the extraordinary engineering feat of safely digging a double-track tunnel, forty feet under more than half a mile of prime real estate, on a steeply sloping site. No buildings were damaged, but a number of the tunnellers were drowned when water escaped. The gradient of the tunnel is one in twenty-seven. Wagons had to be pulled, as their engines could not be used. It was deeply impractical.

On 18 July 1845 it was announced in the press: 'To bathers. A carriage leaves Scotland Street Station of this Railway at SEVEN o'clock Morning returning at EIGHT, and will continue to do so during the Bathing Season. Fares Threepence. The Edinburgh Leith and Granton Railway.' I do wish I were able to board that northbound train, arriving early on a fine morning to take Scotland Street residents to the sea. The station closed to passengers in 1868, though the route north through the Rodney Street tunnel remained in use for some time.

When I first arrived in Scotland Street, the Rodney Street tunnel was blocked with rubble and unnavigable. The southern end, leading up under Scotland Street to Waverley Station, which had been used to grow mushrooms and as an air-raid shelter, was ineffectually closed up. I've traversed it both legally and by stealth, and can report that it's a tunnel. It's now securely bricked up. The northern end of the railway line, leading down to Leith and Granton, has become a very useful part of the city's cycle network. When my children were young, the former station and coal yard was a waste ground, with a few swings. It's now a busy, well-equipped playground, thanks to the efforts of a few dedicated locals.

The *Index of Booksellers* lists David Kedie Whytt's bookselling business at 17 Hopetoun Crescent between 1844 and 1846. Hopetoun Crescent is five minutes' walk east from Scotland Street. It was used as a way-station in 1823 for some of the plants

– including trees of twenty, thirty and forty feet in wooden barrels on horse-drawn carts – of the Botanical Gardens of Edinburgh, as it moved its home over a mile from Leith Walk to Inverleith. The Hope family had feued – a very old term for a perpetual lease, now abolished – some of the Crescent, and building started and then stopped for nearly 200 years. This left a nice wee garden opposite two forlorn blocks of houses. Numbers 17 and 18 were built together, in lonely splendour, in 1827. The architect was Patrick Wilson, later the architect of the Cowgatehead Church, which William Whyte would build for his nephew, Thomas Smith. Numbers 17 and 18 are substantial houses of thirteen rooms over two storeys, water closets on each, and servants' quarters, a washhouse, a scullery and a larder in the basement. They also have ionic columns. Why did David need so much space? Perhaps he was having gas lighting installed in 10 Scotland Street and moved his family and business away from the mess. Number 17 is now a hostel and 18 is run as a refuge and soup kitchen by the blue-robed nuns of Mother Teresa's Missionaries of Charity. Most gap-sites in Edinburgh have been filled over the last twenty years and the Crescent now has its full smile.

By late 1847, David was back in Scotland Street. It occurs to me that the move might have had something to do with the fever epidemic which raged in Edinburgh in 1847. Perhaps the household had put members in quarantine.

In the 1851 census, David is seventy-five and Ann, sixty-seven, living with their four unmarried children. Alexander, in the column headed: Rank, Profession or Occupation, is a bookseller's agent and William is a bookseller's clerk. Against Ann, Marion and Wilhelmina's names, this column is blank. In the basement are Elizabeth Barton and Catherine McLeod, who had come, like many young women, from Assynt in Sutherland in the far north, to look after the Edinburgh bourgeoisie. In addition, I imagine to their grandparents' delight, there are two children, born in Calcutta, the eldest of Grace Whytt and her missionary husband, Thomas Smith. John Smith is eleven years old, and Annie nine. And in this household of two elderly parents and two young children, the unmarried women had no occupation?

How did John and Annie Smith get to Scotland from Calcutta? There had been various attempts, in the late eighteenth century, to open up the old medieval routes from Europe to the East – all foundered on shifting alliances and enmities, mainly between Britain and France, and Egypt and Turkey. These children may have sailed, possibly by clipper, across the Indian Ocean, round the Cape of Good Hope, stopping at St Helena, and finally to Leith, to be met by their grandparents and taken to 10 Scotland Street. However, it is possible they were pioneers of the overland route through the Red Sea, with its arduous journeys across the desert, and seasonally perilous voyages across the Indian Ocean. I think they came by the Cape, accompanied by an ayah or chaperone. It was a lot cheaper before steamships became common. Thomas Smith, some years later, gave a lecture on the overland route to an audience gathered in Inverleith House, a fine mansion in the Royal Botanic Gardens. By whatever means these children arrived, for a time, in his last years, David had almost all of his family around him. We find him in the poll books of 1850–1854, doing his duty as a voting citizen. In 1851, he placed his crosses against Mr Morris and Mr Saunders. They didn't get in. The Padon men in Hart Street voted for Mr Fyfe and Mr Blackadder, who did. Naturally, I believe that David was voting for the more liberal alternative.

It is 1851. Grace Whytt Smith had been married for twelve years. When I first read the 1851 census I was, by chance, in Ann's drawing room, and I tried to sit in her head through the decade since Grace left. Tracing Ann's story is a matter of generalisation and conjecture. She speaks out in her marriage contracts, her application to be her father's heir, and in her will. In her elder daughters' cases, it is only in their wills we hear their voices. Everything else is conjecture. But one can imagine what Ann felt, waving Grace off, knowing that she would not be with her daughter through the inevitable pregnancies, births and infant deaths; always, scraping along just underneath Ann's daily thoughts, the fear that she might never see her daughter again. She must have felt, sitting there in our drawing room, powerless. Two of mine, and their families, live on mainland Europe and, despite our constant electronic communication, not a lot of imagination needs exercised on my part to enter Ann's mind.

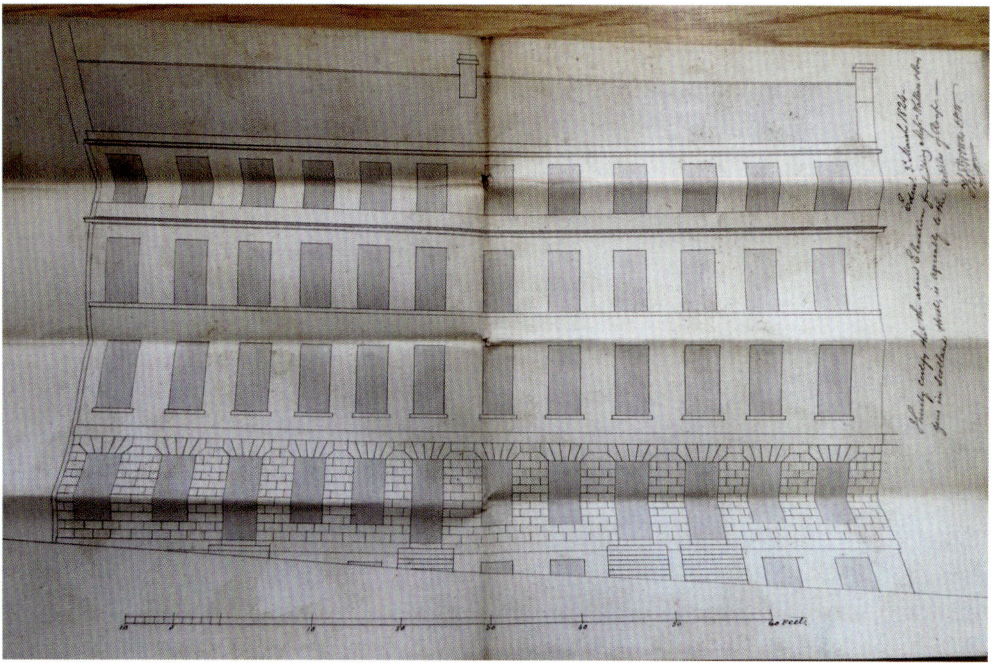

<u>Builders' Sketch and Petition for 10 Scotland Street</u>. On 23 June 1823 the Edinburgh City Fathers invited prospective buyers to view plans at the City Chambers for a block of 140 feet in Scotland Street. The builders, William and Alexander Lewis Wallace, submitted this plan. Their petition was successful. They built quickly. On Friday 8 April 1825, David Kedie Whytt and his wife Ann Henderson took possession of 10 Scotland Street.

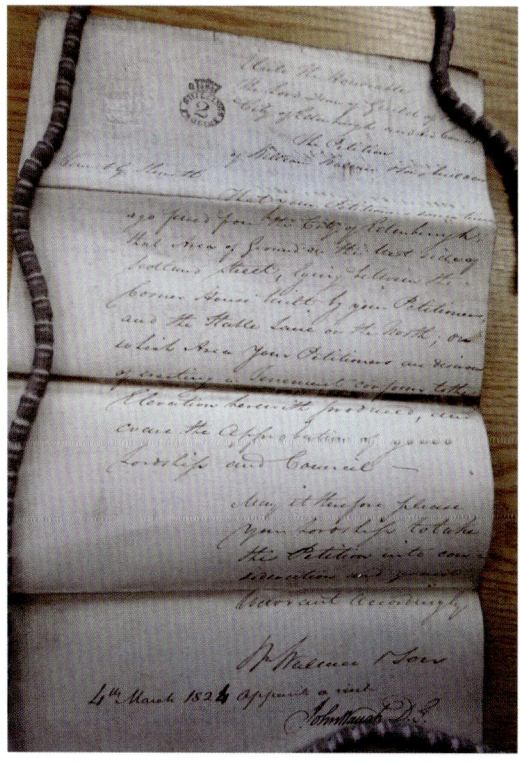

<u>Grassmarket and Bow.</u> At some point in the mid-1780s, David's family had crossed the River Forth from Fife and made their first home in Edinburgh on the West Bow, just off the Grassmarket and close by the Cowgate. Here David's father James Whytt set up his book-binding business – a short hike up the Bow to the booksellers in the Luckenbooths.

<u>The Reverend Robert Dickson of South Leith Church.</u> The Napoleonic Wars offered opportunities. The Whytts moved down to Leith, set up as wine and spirit merchants, joined South Leith Church and bought a lair in its graveyard. I found this ancient copy of a Raeburn painting, done in oils on a bit of wood, in one of my favouritet haunts, the Leith auction house run by my friends at the top of Scotland Street, Susan and Martin Cornish.

<u>Water's Close.</u> David and James Whytt ran their businesses in Leith from various addresses, especially after David became a Purser/Paymaster in the Royal Navy and a Naval Agent in Leith and London. For the Admiralty, they sold by auction, enemy ships and their cargoes. One of their business addresses was ancient Water's Close. The name still remains, but little of the fabric. In September 1807 David married Ann Henderson.

 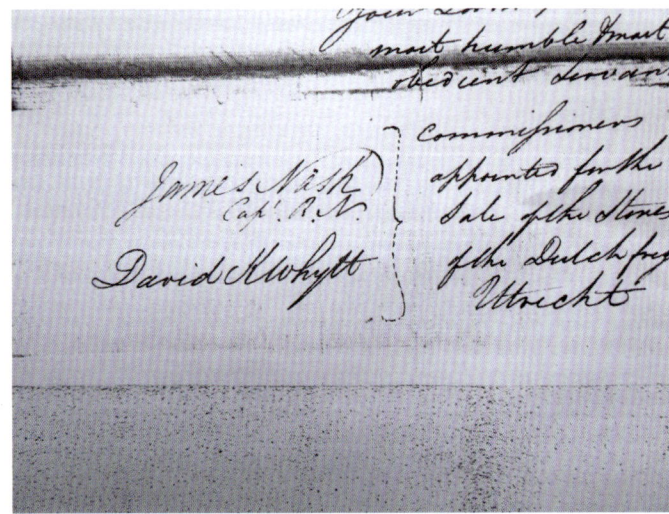

Ann Henderson's Mirror. When we moved into 10 Scotland Street fifty years after David and Ann's grandson sold the house, this mirror, large and extremely heavy, sat in Ann Henderson's drawing room, above the white marble fireplace. We moved it and discovered the mirror had been in place since Ann had followed contemporary fashion, and installed it there. When I stand in front of it, she is just at my shoulder.

<u>The Vaults, Leith</u>. When JG Thomson finally sold the Vaults in 1983, Benjamin Tindall Architects remodelled the venerable building for the twentieth century while keeping its essential nature intact. You may see across Scotland the fine work of Ben and his colleagues in the most illustrious of venues to the most humble – including 10 Scotland Street.

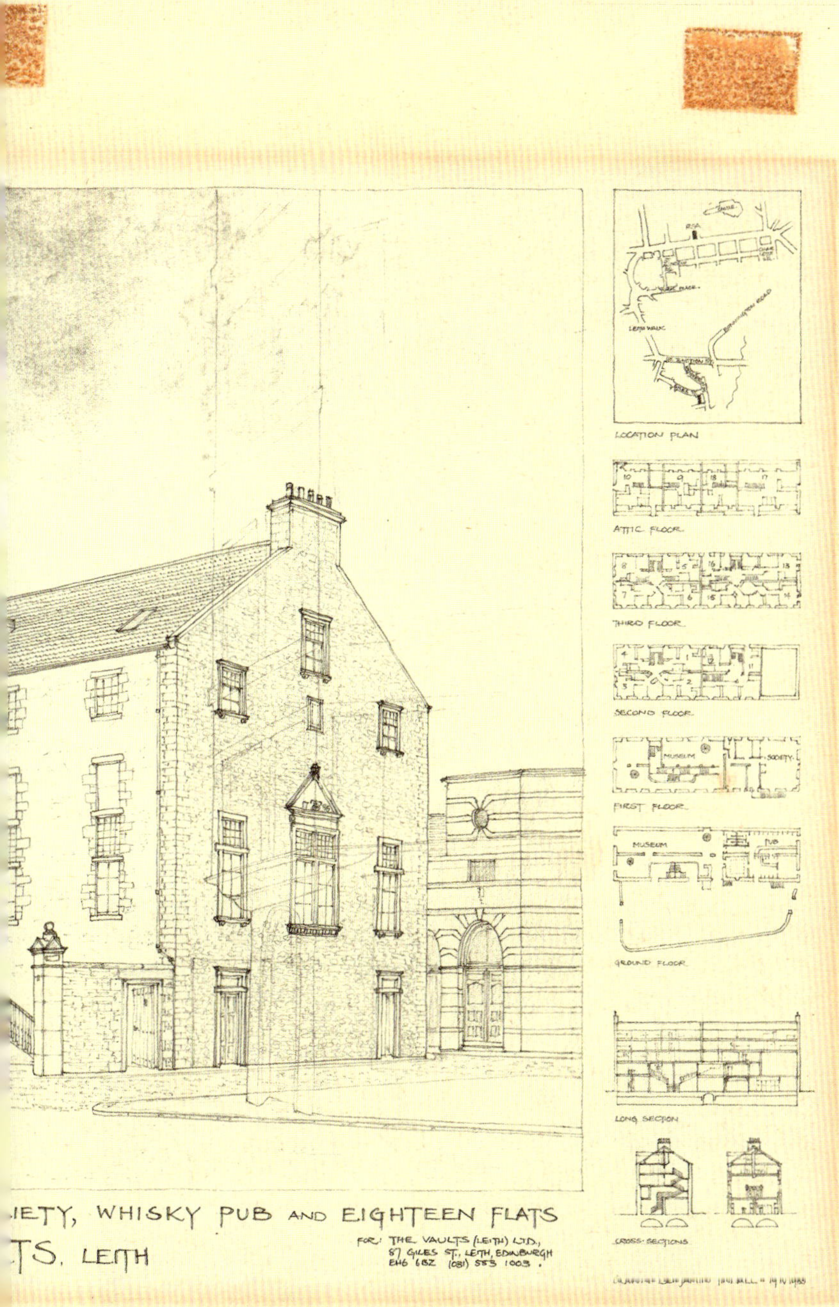

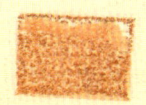

LOCATION PLAN

ATTIC FLOOR

THIRD FLOOR

SECOND FLOOR

FIRST FLOOR

GROUND FLOOR

LONG SECTION

CROSS SECTIONS

...IETY, WHISKY PUB AND EIGHTEEN FLATS
...TS, LEITH

FOR: THE VAULTS (LEITH) LTD,
87 GILES ST, LEITH, EDINBURGH
EH6 6BZ (031) 553 1003

<u>JG Thomson Ink Stamp</u>. In 1983, the fine bones of The Vaults were in good order. Internally, the building was a mess and most of the contents were the tattered and battered remnants of its early-twentieth-century glory. Among the detritus, I found a handful of stamps from a much earlier era, and preserved them. This one is a favourite.

<u>Bell and Bradfute Doorstep</u>. Not long ago, I climbed the Mound and stopped by the portal of the Bank of Scotland to look across at the magnificent frontage of the eight-storey tenement, built by James Brownhill in 1723, before the Mound was conceived of. It sits on the curve as Bank Street heads down from the High Street, and at the turn of the eighteenth century, housed Bell and Bradfute, booksellers. This fine tile work was rescued from decades of oblivion by the present owner.

> 302
>
> N° 10, Scotland Street
> Edinburgh, 26 May, 1836
>
> Sir,
>
> I have had the honor to receive your Letter of the 11 instants transmitting by Command of the Right Honorable The Lords Commissioners of the Admiralty an Extract from His Majesty's Order in Council of the 15° April 1836 directing an increase to the Half Pay of Pursers of the Royal Navy, with certain exceptions and under certain regulations; and signifying their Lordships directions that if I consider myself intitled under the said order in Council to the addition which His Majesty has been graciously pleased to grant, that I will transmit my application to you to be laid before their Lordships for their decision.
>
> In reply, I respectfully request you will be pleased to acquaint the Lords Commissioners of the Admiralty - that I am not in receipt of any Official Salary, or Pension - and that I did not decline - nor shall decline, to serve when called upon - and to solicit that their Lordships will be pleased to place my Name on the increased Half Pay List accordingly.
>
> And I have the honor to be with the greatest respect,
>
> Sir
> Your most humble
> and most obedient Servant
> David K. Whytt
> Purser of the Royal Navy
>
> C. Wood Esqre M.P.
> Secretary of the Admiralty,
> London

<u>David K Whytt's Letter to the Admiralty</u>. When I was handed the deeds for 10 Scotland Street, I read that David had bought the house from the builders. I was interested but parked the idea of investigating further. Some years later, in the National Archives, Kew, I found this 1836 letter, oilskin-wrapped, in an old, grubby box and read it. I left Kew knowing that after that crystalline moment in the archive, I'd committed myself to pursuing David Whytt properly.

<u>Number 10's locks</u>. On my front door is the original huge iron lock, operated only from the inside. It has a brass handle and a bolt and a forbidding interior. I have it repaired regularly, every ten years or so. Above the monster lock is the distinctive New Town lock with its many fragile leaves and elegant long key, which I use daily.

<u>The Whytt Grave 2021</u>. David and his brother, William, after they left the Church of Scotland for the new Free Church, and the Whytt lair at South Leith was lost to them, reserved for themselves and heirs, twelve square yards of the Calton Burial Ground. When I found their grave in 1997, bits of the panels were missing, but traces were left, and from these and from memorial inscription records, it was possible to reconstruct the names and relationships of the family beneath the stone.

Ann would hear of public affairs from newspapers and journals. News of Grace, would come, many months in arrears, along with reports of epidemics and the journey of so many a young Scot to the Scottish Cemetery on Calcutta's Karaya Bazar Road. In today's Kolkata, the Scottish Cemetery, which was established in 1820, is under a gradual process of renovation. There are many, many graves and the average age at death is pitifully low. Private news would have arrived in Grace's letters, none of which are archived, as far as I can discover. The press regularly published reports from the missionary societies which did not concern themselves with the doings or welfare of their employees' wives, though these women often played an energetic and central role in their husbands' work. Thomas Smith wrote to his sister about his life, and to an extent that of his wife, and Miss Smith passed on what news there was. Some of these letters are in the care of the National Library of Scotland, and we will come to them.

I try to imagine the last five years of David and Ann's life in Scotland Street. They had been married nearly fifty years, had lost at least three children and missed the early years of their grandchildren, and had lived through wars and hard times. There must have been, however, consolation in the family close by, and in their relative prosperity. David's last charitable donation of a guinea was recorded, on 9 May 1855, in the *Witness*, an evangelical publication edited by the geologist, Hugh Miller. Failure of crops in the West Highlands the previous year had left the crofters without seed, cash or any means to obtain credit. A subscription was raised to buy seed and to provide families with boats, barrels of salt and nets so that they might feed themselves.

On 3 January 1856, Ann's sister Wilhelmina died.

Exactly eight months later, on 3 September, David Kedie Whytt's death was announced in the local press and in the *London Chronicle*. He died of *ramollissment cerebri*, suffered for several years. The term is obsolete. The first definition I found was softening of the brain. This led to a scan of mid-nineteenth century research. The poor man had dementia. My mother suffered the awful disease for seven long years. I feel for David's wife and daughters, and hope his torment was not long. He died aged eighty, at six thirty in the morning, at number 5 James Place, Portobello, now a suburb of Edinburgh, on the shore of the Forth. Perhaps Ann had hopes of the sea air; and by this time, Grace, returned from India, was living with her brood just along the river. Alexander notified the death and the undertaker, John Boyd, certified David's internment in the Old Calton Burial Ground.

The Calton Burial Ground was established in the eighteenth century, mainly for families associated with the incorporated trades of Calton. It was not territorial, and so ideal for those who, after the Free Church of Scotland had left the parent ship, found themselves without a cemetery. The free churches were built on in-fill sites, with no room for burials. The burial ground was formerly a bleaching green with unimpeded access to sky and sun, high on the hill on which sheep and cattle roamed, with a panoramic view of Edinburgh. It is approached through a wall on the south side of Waterloo Place, a road which was cut through Calton Burial Ground in 1815, leaving a stump on the north side much-used for trysts. One passes through the tall iron gate to climb a flight of steep, enclosed steps. Ahead is the Martyr's Monument, a tall needle commemorating five late-eighteenth-century reformers who were transported for wanting universal male suffrage. To the right, at the top of the hill, is the monument to the philosopher David Hume, who died in 1776, just as David Whytt was emerging into the world. Hume specified that his tomb bear only his name and dates – and absolutely nothing to do with religion. For some time, it had to be guarded to repel Christian objectors. His niece later joined him, and in his absence had 'Behold, I come quickly, thanks be to God which giveth us the victory through our Lord Jesus Christ' inscribed on her panel.

In the late 1960s, Edinburgh University's Philosophical Society would congregate by Hume's memorial, on 7 May, his birthday, to read his work and then repair to the pub – in this case, the Café Royal, close by his last home. I seem to remember wearing velvet breeches and a lace jabot under a long red cloak lined with turquoise. My garb was not at all the most extravagant. Since the discussion of Hume's now-infamous racist footnote to his essay *Of National Characters* I doubt such gatherings take place. Nearby is a statue of Abraham Lincoln, atop the American Civil War Memorial, commemorating the six Scottish soldiers who fought for the Union. Down in the south-east corner are the remains of Calton Jail, whose governor was grandfather to Charles David Murray, a tenant of 10 Scotland Street at the turn of the twentieth century; the prison which briefly held my great-great-great-uncle, condemned on much the same charges as the men commemorated on the Martyr's Monument.

Interred here, in the Old Calton, are many publishers, booksellers and men of the law, but also merchants and tradespeople. The cemetery attracted numerous shoemakers, including a heel-maker, John Morton, who has one of the most elaborate graves. He died in 1728, aged fifty-four, and there is a long description of his works and worth. The decoration is striking, topped with two lions rampant and flanked by two, near-naked, young women. Nearby is John Haig, who more or less invented the blended whisky industry when the wine and brandy trade declined, in the latter years of the nineteenth century. He also gave us – some might say unfortunately – Field Marshall Lord Douglas Haig. Many hold Haig responsible for, among other routs, the 1915 battle that killed Edwin Eyre Gulland, of 10 Scotland Street.

There are no naked ladies on the grave of Reverend Robert Candlish, one of the ministers who formed the Free Church of Scotland in 1843. David's brother, William, published his writings. His father was a friend of Robert Burns and his mother, Jean Smith, was one of Burns' Belles of Mauchline.

Peter Williamson, whom we met earlier setting up the penny post, is also to be found on the windy hill. He was born in Scotland, kidnapped and put on a ship bound for Virginia. It was wrecked near the Delaware River. Peter survived and was captured and sold in Philadelphia. Freed after seven years, he bought a plantation which he built up until he was taken by Native Americans, who destroyed the plantation. Presumably it was on land from which they found a living. He escaped and enlisted in the British Army, but was captured by the French and taken to Canada. Finally, he arrived back in England and was drafted into a regiment, but was discharged because of wounds, and given six shillings to get home to Scotland. On his return, he sued Aberdeen Town Council, who had been complicit in his kidnap, and the resulting pay-out enabled him to set up his enterprises in the Luckenbooths and then the Exchange on the High Street, across the square from apprentice James Whytt. After his early life, setting up a penny post must have seemed a walk in the park.

The cemetery holds several artists including, just inside the wall at the top of the steep slope, Julius Von Yelin, a fellow of the Royal Academy of Science of Munich. His stone told me he died in 1826. He was seized with illness while addressing the Royal Society of Edinburgh and died six weeks later in Edinburgh's Royal Hotel, despite the efforts of the best of Edinburgh's physicians and two German doctors. The Chevalier Von Yelin was the Principal Finance Councillor to the King of Bavaria and an internationally admired scientist. He had come to Edinburgh to witness the spirit of Enlightenment and legislative improvement which he hoped to promote in his own country. I found the resting place of Herr Von Yelin many years ago. Just before I handed over this manuscript, I discovered that the ground in which he lies was purchased by James Gibson Thomson. JG bought Yelin a lair and attended the funeral with the great and the good, including the Lord Provost, several professors and Sir Walter Scott. Scott's attendance at his friend's funeral was his first venture out after his financial ruin. *The Scotsman* records that Scott wrote, 'His funeral is the first public place I shall appear at. He dead, and I ruined; this is what you call a meeting.' One hundred years later, on 1 October 1926, *The Scotsman* reported that in, 1922, JG's granddaughter had decided to place a memorial stone on Chevalier Yelin's Grave. Unfortunately, she died in January 1926, and so it was her niece who finally placed the stone on the grave bought by JG a century previously.

I searched long for David's gravestone, and finally, in late 1997, Pip and I found it a few steps from Yelin's, east of the main path, near the summit. On the pediment is carved 'THE BURYING GROUND OF WILLIAM WHYTE AND DAVID KEDIE WHYTT'. From the cemetery's register of purchased ground, I discovered that Messrs William Whyte, Bookseller in Edinburgh, and David Keddie Whyte, Merchant in Leith, 'fewed (sic) for themselves and heirs Twelve square yards of the Calton Burial ground for a Burial place . . . bounded on the East Three yards North West, from the North West cornerstone to Mr James Butler's ground and on all other sides by unpurchased ground,' and paid £1 7/6 sterling per square yard. There is no date on the entry but as David was still a merchant in Leith it seems that, once again, they were planning far ahead.

The stone was erected by Alexander Henderson Whytt, David's son. William had specified a plain marble tomb. Alexander interpreted his wishes loosely. It is a granite slab onto which two narrow panels were placed side by side. William was named at the top of one, David at the top of the other. Stewart McGlashan, sculptor and stonemason from Campbeltown in Kintyre, supplied the gravestone. McGlashan and Company made many public monuments, some of which were sent to the edges of the growing British Empire. In the 1920s, one of his employees, Matthew Moyes, a sculptor from Fife lived at number 23a Scotland Street from where it was a short walk down through the park to McGlashan's. The yard and office survived at Canonmills Bridge until 2019.

Alexander chose well. His family's monument is plain and pleasing and looks north over the river to Fife. When I first saw it, parts of the panels were missing with bits scattered around the base. Some years later, they were widely scattered. There is little left, but from the notes I took I can reconstruct the names.

To the left, we see that the stone is erected to the memory of William Whyte, bookseller. Below him are his parents, Janet Davidson and James Whytt, and his sister, Janet Whytt. Just below is William's other sister, Grace Whytt, Relict of John Gourley. The *Record of Mortality Calton Burial Ground March 1857-January 1863* confirms that she is buried 'in the Old Ground 2nd lair from N-side in Messrs W & DK Whytt's lot'. On the right side is our David, followed by Ann Henderson. Beneath them are listed the names of their children who died young: Ann, James and Janet. Just under this is the poignant record of Janet Helen Gordon, who died in London, on 5 November 1861, aged twenty-one. Finally, there are the names of David and Ann's daughters, Marion and Wilhelmina and their last-born, William. So there – according to the records of South Leith Parish which stretched all the way to Princes Street – lies

David Kedie Whytt, in the old ground, in the middle of his own ground and of his family. He has a fine view, captured, incidentally, by my friend and one-time boss, the late Jack Firth RSW, who made a pencil drawing of that view and, when he heard my tale, delivered it to me.

When I took my grandchildren to see David's grave, they politely heard me out, but were more interested in ascertaining whether there were any vampires around. I visit David from time to time, usually of a fine morning when I am feeling optimistic. I believe he led a good life.

Ann Henderson registered David's will, which is prefaced by their nuptial contracts. The will itself consists of a Trust Disposition and Settlement. Because of this, we have his complete description of his homes at Scotland Street and George Place. Unfortunately, he lumped the property acquired through his wife's family with 'All and Sundry other lands and tenements, tacks, steadings, heritable bonds and other heritable subjects'. Alexander had to resort to a retour to prove his ownership of the Bo'ness properties when his mother died.

When I read David's will, made in good time, thirty years before his death, I was struck immediately by the phrase, 'equally between and among them, share and share alike.' His three daughters and two sons, with a few caveats, should inherit equally. David's decision seemed most unusual for his time. Then I remembered the equal shares in Ann's pre-nuptial agreement, overseen by her mother, Marion, who surely knew what she was doing, after marriage to the feckless Mr Henderson. David's trustees were his wife, his brother, and the Reverend John Aikman, who had protested so vehemently that he had no profit from slavery.

To Ann, David leaves the liferent on the house on 2 George Place, his Purser's pension, and everything specified in their nuptial contracts. To his natural daughter he leaves five hundred pounds. The rest belongs to his five lawful children, 'share and share alike'. This family looked after David's natural child– but they made a distinction between her and the ' lawful' children. Illegitimate children were specifically excluded from provisions in the pre- and post-nuptial contracts. In Scotland now, all children, whatever their perceived status, have equal inheritance rights. David's trustees are to decide whether the co-partnery with his brother William should continue. In effect, however, the business ceased with William's death, eighteen months later.

The family's lawyer, Joseph Liddle, of 12 Scotland Street, drew up the will and, with two of William Whyte's clerks, witnessed David's signature. The inventory of his belongings at his death is short. All his furniture, his seals and clothes, his gold watch and his cash estate of nearly £900 and the arrears of his purser's pension have to go to Ann.

On 6 March 2013, in search of that pension, I returned to Kew, sixteen years after I had unwrapped that letter from David to the Admiralty. I had searched for specific records on the National Archives website and found they were not digitised. The estimated cost of copying the records was several multiples of the advance saver rail return to London. I set off, and found that two trips out to Kew on London Underground cost more than the journey from Scotland.

In 2013, registering as a researcher had become more complicated. The National Archives, London Metropolitan Archive and the University College London Library, where I also went that day, required two forms of identification. I produced my driving licence, an ancient, tattered green paper thing with no photograph. Eyebrows were raised, but in combination with my bus pass it proved acceptable. Two photographs were taken four hours apart. In one, I am a sweet, if slightly-deranged old lady and, in the other, a conscienceless poisoner of multiple wretches.

At Kew, the geese were still there, but the pathway was now poo-free. I have no idea how they managed that. My documents were on microfilm. I was given a reader and a magnifying glass, and started to plough through. Very near the end I found him, or rather Ann. On 20 September 1856, Ann applied for David's pension, as his widow. The form was on flimsy paper and the sheet, tattered. The script and abbreviations were difficult to decipher. But Ann's signature is clear. It is not a practised hand, rather that of someone who has carefully learned their letters, but has had little occasion to use the skill. A medical certificate attesting to David's death on 3

September was noted, as was his will and his half pay officer's pension arrears of £25 15/8. By 10 November, the request had passed through the Audit office and the continuation of the pension granted. I was struck by the speed by which her claim was resolved.

The other document I had asked for proved to be a large box of papers from the Court of Chancery, which was a Court in English Law, set up to avoid long cases and provide equity when the common law could not. It may have succeeded in the latter aim, but many cases dragged out over many years. My only knowledge of Chancery was Charles Dickens' Jarndyce v Jarndyce in *Bleak House*, which did not bode well. This box told the long sad tale of Peter Gordon's war with his family. It was gritty and filthy with undisturbed, archival grime, the writing was atrocious, and there was a lot of it. I took the coward's way out and ordered a scan. This resulted in nineteen pages of tiny, closely written script, sometimes faint, on faded and browned paper. An heroic friend transcribed it. Ebenezer Alexander Whytt was at the heart of this case. He made various more or less unfortunate partnerships, mainly with Robert Whytt, and was bankrupt several times. His saviour on many occasions was his mother-in-law, Ann Phillips Gordon, who housed him and gave or lent him quite large sums of money. The money came from Peter Gordon's estate which he had specified should be shared among his children, one of whom was his namesake, Peter. This Peter was a mariner, missionary, militant reformer and compulsive litigant. Wherever he went, from Irkutsk to Sydney, he distributed tracts and bibles, fell out with almost everyone he met and was frequently imprisoned. He ended up back in London, in douce Barnsbury Street, living with his mother. He waited till her death before accusing her, his widowed sister Ann Gordon Whytt and all her children, his mariner brother, plus their legal representatives, of taking his late father's fortune. At the heart of Peter Gordon's case, which rumbled and bickered on, was the money given to Ebenezer Whytt, the opacity of the doings of various financial advisers, the inability of anyone to find any paperwork and the untimely deaths of several of the principals – including Ebenezer Whytt, whose funeral must have been an interesting occasion.

Widowed Ann Henderson moved to 28 Howard Place, a four-storey house in a row close by the Royal Botanic Gardens, a few minutes' walk from Scotland Street, and a few steps from the birthplace of Robert Louis Stevenson at number 8. In 1861, Ann was seventy-seven years old, and, I fear, already not in good health. With her on the night of the 1861 census were Marion, Wilhelmina, Alexander and William. Alexander, at thirty-seven, was now an Inspector of Insurance Agencies in London. The family was looked after by two teenaged domestic servants, Margaret Mitchell from Moray and Elizabeth Cargill from Forfar. The house at 10 Scotland Street was lying empty. Below it, the bakers' premises were home to George Scott, master baker, his wife, Mary, who kept the baker's shop, three apprentices, Allison Willison, a domestic servant, and two unmarried Scott children.

SEVEN

ALEXANDER HENDERSON WHYTT

At the beginning of August 1861, banns were called at the parish church of St James, Clerkenwell, Islington, and also in Perthshire at East Dron Church, for the marriage of Alexander Henderson Whytt, aged thirty-seven, and Janet Helen Gordon, aged twenty-one. I looked for Janet Helen. At times it seemed that every second person in the north-east of Scotland was named Gordon. They are everywhere, and range in rank from William Gordon, Duke of Sutherland, to the lowliest milkmaid and pauper – and Captain Peter Gordon's family.

Janet Helen's father, the Reverend Donald Gordon, was born at Stoer, a scattered township on the far and windy west coast of Sutherland. He made his way to Kings College, Aberdeen, before becoming a school teacher in the village of Farr, where he was ordained as a minister. He and Donaldina Ross were married in Scourie, by his brother Charles, the minister in beautiful Assynt, and they lived for a while in Eddrachillis, where his brother William Gordon was the doctor, a few miles south of Scourie and Badcall. These wonderful names are anglicisations of Gaelic. A glance at a modern map of where they are to be found, way, way up the scribbled western edge of Scotland, shows lots of empty land. In Donald Gordon's youth the land was neither empty, nor its inhabitants isolated. The roads which crossed Sutherland were good for their time. Two hundred years ago, the mountains and moorlands of Sutherland were actively managed, in a system of transhumance – moving livestock onto the hill in summer – which supported thousands of people in the Straths, and on the mountains and moorland in summer. The Reverend Donald Gordon was transferred from one busy church to another and ended up in Edderton Kirk, a scattered parish on the Dornoch Firth, where the climate and eastern landscape were more bleak than beautiful. Alexander Whytt's bride, Janet Helen, was born there in 1840, as potato failure and consequent famine began their ravages. In 1843, her father joined the Free Church, and four years later he was dead. Donaldina took her family to the town of Tain.

They may have had to leave the manse, but they were not destitute. The Reverend Donald Gordon had hedged his bets on the providence of the Lord and taken out several insurance policies. If he had stayed in the Church of Scotland, his widow and children would have been entitled to a pension. In 1672, the Scottish Parliament had passed an Act to ensure that a bereaved minister's family would receive half of his stipend. The problem of funding this scheme was solved by Alexander Webster, a hellfire preacher who was able, because his wife was very rich, to indulge his taste for alcohol and ventures which caught his interest. With Robert Wallace, a mathematician and the minister at Greyfriars church in Edinburgh, he devised a scheme. They collected mortality statistics from every parish in Scotland, and worked out how many ministers were liable to die per annum, and therefore how much was needed in the funds. Then they worked out how much ministers should pay in, and how much interest would accrue. The scheme finally passed the General Assembly of the Church in 1743, and the apparatus of the Scottish Ministers' Widow Fund was put in place. In essence, they had invented pension funds and the actuarial profession. In the end, Donaldina was reasonably comfortable. Along with her husband's insurances, money owed, his furniture, apparel, cattle, his gig, etc., the estate was a healthy £1500. This is the more surprising considering that his yearly stipend at Edderton was £230, including grain.

There was also money due from his brother William Gordon, who, on Whitsunday 1849, had become the first doctor at Bonar Bridge in the huge Highland parish of Creich, which I happen to know quite well. Before the opening, in 1991, of the magnificent

Dornoch Firth Bridge which carries the A9 north up the wild coast to the end point of Scotland, we took the route through Bonar Bridge on the last stretch of a long drive to our rented cottage at Dalnamain, in Strathcarnaig. Latterly, the A9 took us quickly to our road end where we turned into the hairpin-bend, single track which zigzags up the strath from the coast to Lochbuie and thence back to Bonar Bridge. On the right is a dense alder wood, which gives way to rough ground through which the little River Carnaig runs, edged with primroses in the spring. In the dark, it is an interesting drive.

Our cottage was foursquare and basic, unseen from the road where one car a day was traffic. Nights, save for starlight, were bible-black and full of silence – punctuated, if our cat Milo was in residence, by the dying cries of sundry small creatures, found laid in tribute at the foot of our bed in the morning. Light came from an array of oil and paraffin lamps. The water came off the steep hill behind us and, on occasion, I had to organise earth-moving equipment to keep it flowing. But the sum paid annually to the factor was modest. At the front was a little porch, which led by the right to the kitchen and a tiny scullery with weeping walls and a lean-to where we trimmed and cleaned our oil lamps. To the left was a sitting room furnished with assorted old armchairs, and two single beds which were very useful in the winter when we retired with the coal fire blazing. The first to emerge in the morning got it going as fast as possible. The walls were boarded with wood, installed, we were told by the carpenter's grandson, around 1930. Upstairs was the coldest bathroom in the world, ceremoniously heated by a paraffin heater on the odd occasion anyone dared to have a bath, and two bedrooms. If you could get it started, an ancient generator rattled, groaned and occasionally shrieked and powered three lightbulbs. It had a vicious flywheel. Twenty steps away was an abandoned byre and a number of distressed stone dykes. As long as you didn't go round the back where an electricity pylon loomed, it was out of reach of the twentieth century. Our nearest neighbour was a cycling nun, some miles up the road in a similar cottage. It was a place for quiet, good food and whisky, and peace. It had not always been so.

Nearby is a standing stone which is held to be Neolithic to Late Bronze Age; around 4000BCE to 551CE; and two hut circles, along with a corn-drying kiln. Below the cottage, there is evidence of medieval rig-cultivation. Along the valley, with the light falling low along the slope, the remains of a township can be seen. We walked across it occasionally, tripped over the remains of walls and ditches, and wondered.

After the 1745 Jacobite Rebellion, British Army Quartermaster William Roy produced a military map, which provides a snapshot of the Strath before everything changed. All names were anglicised. Dail Na Mein, the dale of the minerals, became Dalnamain. Roy recorded a considerable settlement at Dalnamain. It was mainly self-sufficient with strong links out into the wider world. Dornoch and the coastal ports were within easy reach. People and goods moved from and to the Strath and the southern industrial towns and across the sea.

The *Scots Magazine* lists several deaths on His Majesty's Service of young Dalnamain men of the Caithness Highlanders. In 1803, James Sutherland of Eveliket at Dalnamain is listed. As always, I looked at the other entries. This page was excellent and yielded the announcement of a death at Rotherhithe, of a Mrs Giles, a maiden lady, who had been first pronounced dead five years previously. Mrs Giles' servant was putting her in her coffin when she noticed signs of life and transferred Mrs Giles to a warm bath. A surgeon was called and bled her but, despite this intervention, Mrs Giles survived a further five years and wrote her will in favour of the maid. The will stipulated that Mrs Giles be kept in the house for two weeks after death, and not buried until her head had been cut off. Understandable, really.

While the Caithness Highlanders were abroad, at Dalnamain, the community was silver-smithing, coppicing and willow-weaving, growing food and keeping animals, cooking, building and thatching, working with wool, leather-crafting and making music. Dornoch archives holds a diary, written by John Matheson of Dalnamain. From his description of their lives, it is clear that the people of Dalnamain were educated, bilingual and outward-looking, who, if they made it past infancy, lived complex, connected, long lives. The settlement at Dalnamain was one among many.

This is Sutherland country, most of it owned by the Dukes of Sutherland, an immensely rich and powerful family. Before the Strath was cleared, there were at least ten families living and working at Dalnamain. The Sutherlands' agent, Patrick Sellar, entirely legally through the courts, in five weeks in April 1820, drove six thousand Sutherland people to coastal smallholdings, incapable of sustaining them. Many emigrated. There is no doubt that a growing population had been relying on too little productive land. It would seem obvious that a remedy might be more land. Not to the landowners. The fate of the people of Dalnamain was mirrored throughout the Highlands and Islands of Scotland from mid-eighteenth to mid-nineteenth century. My own great-great grandfather, Duncan MacDougall, was one of the luckier ones. He was evicted during the clearance of Torosay on Mull, left his family and all he knew and, avoiding the emigrant ships awaiting the desperate, made his way to Laggan in Badenoch, speaking only Gaelic. There he met Isabella Kennedy who, I'm told, spoke only English. They had a along productive marriage.

By 1834, the hinterland of Sutherland was more or less empty of its people. Potato blight and famine finished the job. In 1841, there was one estate shepherd's family living in our cottage at Dalnamain, and, in the outbuildings, four workers, hired and housed to look after the sheep that had displaced the people. Now the cottage is derelict, and, after several thousand years, Dalnamain is home to no living person.

The clearance of the people from the land had consequences for professionals. Sheep don't need doctors, teachers or ministers – or seamstresses, laundry women, midwives ... In the populous pre-clearance Highlands, there was plenty of work. Then quite quickly there was not. Dr Gordon – I can find no other Dr Gordon in the region and conclude that this was Janet Helen Gordon's uncle, William – recorded the grievous injuries inflicted on women who were resisting the men sent to clear them from their homes in Strathcarron, not much more than a mile, as the crow flies, from

Dalnamain. He then took himself and his family to Kincardine, on the Dornoch Firth, where he was counted in the 1861 census, living in the manse with his wife and five children, and a governess named Mary Kennedy. He died in 1877. There is no record of whether he ever paid his brother's widow the £378 he owed her.

On 16 August 1861, his niece, Janet Helen Gordon, of Tain, married Alexander Henderson Whytt, at East Dron Farmhouse, home of the bride's sister Mary and her husband, John Richmond. His father, Thomas Richmond, a prominent landowner and wealthy merchant, had five daughters; Eliza, Ann, Hannah, Louisa and Jane. He had business with the Whytts in London. Is this how Alexander met Janet Gordon? I imagine Ann Henderson, with her family, making the journey across the Forth to her son's wedding, and her anticipation of this new marriage, and the grandchildren it might bring.

After their wedding, Janet Helen Gordon journeyed south with Alexander to 25 Albion Grove, Barnsbury, her new London home. There, on 5 November, she died of phthisis–pulmonary tuberculosis. She had such a short life, and a marriage which lasted less than three months.

Not two years later, Alexander travelled to Edinburgh to marry Hannah Richmond. For three weeks, banns had been published at St Mary's, Islington, and at St Stephen's Church, Edinburgh, for Alexander Whytt, widower, and Hannah Richmond, daughter of Thomas Richmond who had recently died. He left a very healthy estate with an inventory that gives a detailed and, to me at least, fascinating picture of life on a large Perthshire farm. Hannah was nineteen and Alexander was exactly double her age.

Alexander and Hannah were married on 23 March 1863, at 8 Forres Street, Edinburgh, the home of his kinsman, James Aikman Smith, by the minister of St Stephen's. I wonder at what time they were married, and I hope Ann Henderson, who died at fifteen minutes past six that evening at Howard Place, was able to attend her son's second wedding. Certainly, she was alive when the marriage certificate was signed. According to her doctor, she had suffered from ovarian dropsy for several years. There are harrowing contemporary accounts of surgery for this condition. Alexander, who must have left the altar for her deathbed, signed her death certificate.

Off the couple went to 25 Albion Grove. With his mother's death occurring on his wedding day, and so soon after the death of his first wife and of his second wife's father, Alexander must have wondered what was coming next.

Ann Henderson had made her will immediately after David's death, when her widowhood gave her the agency to dispose of property. Alexander, her executor, quickly dealt with her moveable estate. If Alexander was unable to deal with her wishes, she nominated her daughters Wilhelmina and Marion. Her youngest son William, forty-four years old, was not appointed.

Alexander's task was not arduous. Ann lived in a house with eleven rooms, but had very few possessions, and left them all to her daughters Marion and Wilhelmina. Ann was careful to note that she was only performing an act of strict justice. When her daughter Grace had married, their father had given her £200. He had offered the same to Marion and Wilhelmina, but they turned him down. Since then, they had had nothing but their board and clothes. Oh dear.

As for Ann's sons, they were now men and able to provide for themselves. There was no mention of David's natural daughter, Margaret. The document was drawn up by Joseph Liddle's son Thomas, of 12 Scotland Street, and witnessed by Ann's son William and her grandson John Smith.

Ann had £31 in the house, £192 in the National Bank of Scotland, and interest of £67 on the large sum, on which she had a liferent, from her late brother-in-law William Whyte. The value of her possessions rounded up to a total of £568. Alexander followed his parents' wishes by transferring equal shares of all property among his siblings – apart from their brother William.

There was also estate in England which I puzzled over, until I realised it was the £12 due to her, in arrears, of David's Purser's pension. In 1864, Alexander made a Special Service to his deceased father David Kedie Whytt for his share of several houses in Bo'ness. That achieved, he signed off his mother's estate and went back to his new, young wife in London.

Alexander's second bride, Hannah Richmond, was less than a year in Barnsbury before giving birth to Margaret Stewart Whytt. The London Whytts had left Barnsbury for Highgate and on the matriarch's death the unmarried offspring moved to South Grove, close to the home of Andrew Wark, a man who was to do great service for Alexander and his sisters. Perhaps feeling a need for family support with their infants, Alexander and Hannah followed and moved north, where their son David was born.

Almost simultaneously, on 8 August 1865, and probably without Alexander's knowledge, Margaret Whytt, his half-sister, died of dropsy and heart disease at Buccleuch Street, Dalkeith. She was sixty-nine, twenty-nine years older than Alexander. Her death was registered by Robert Wilson, a neighbour. Thanks to James, David and William, she was comfortably off, but with the death of William Whyte, her connection with the family seems to have ceased. Her will, made just a fortnight before her heart failed her, has William's voice running through it, and is basically a list of bequests to the Free Church of Scotland. Her minister and her candlemaker neighbour distributed funds to the Church, the Foreign and Home Missions, the Gaelic schools, the Conversion of the Jews, the Highlands and Islands, Female India Mission, Medical Missionary Society, Colonial Fund, Continental Evangelism Fund, Dalkeith Congregation and the National Bible Society. Her estate came to £450, including money in the bank, clothes, books, desk and her watch, which was, presumably, grandad James'. To put this into perspective, £450 in 1865 had purchasing power of £57000 in 2020. Entirely down to the Whytt men. Margaret's half-sisters and their mother seem to have had no contact with Margaret after she left Morton Street. We might assume that this signalled the more repressive moral codes of the latter half of the nineteenth century. Those concerning perceived illegitimacy became particularly strong, and lasted a long time. In 1950s Glasgow, one of my relatives 'got a girl pregnant' and 'had to get married' amid shame and secrecy. The whole episode was made a million times worse by the fact that 'that girl' belonged to the Catholic Church. I remember the whispers and the shaking of heads – though not on the part of my mother. Born in 1913 and a woman of her time and class, she could surprise me. The scandal went on until another family member disgraced themselves in some way, and the tongues turned on them.

In 1866, Alexander came north to commit Wilhelmina to Saughtonhall Lunatic Asylum. The General Register of Lunatics in Scotland records this fact but the detail is missing. He came north again in 1875 when five men signed Wilhelmina over to Superintendent Mary Thompson of Whitehouse Asylum. This time, there is more detail. It is recorded that for a week Wilhelmina had been incoherent and labouring under religious melancholy. The admission papers describe her as a single sixty-two year old gentlewoman who is neither suicidal nor a danger to others. She is, however, of unsound mind and a proper person to be detained. Two physicians reported that she talked incessantly of being such a grievous sinner that she had no hope of forgiveness. Her mental state is a judgment for the enormous sins she has committed and her eternal punishment has already begun. Unless by some violence, she will not find death in this world or any other. Poor soul. There is no record of how long she was confined on this occasion. It occurs to me that her malady may have persisted for some time and could no longer be contained in the home after the death of her mother. Marion left for 52 Grange Road, close to Grace and Thomas Smith.

In 1868, Hannah Richmond had a second son, Graham Weir, born at 5 Scotland Street. The family was back in Edinburgh and renting until they could take possession of number 10, a few feet down the hill and across the road from 5. Alexander was now Secretary to the Edinburgh Life Assurance Company, at 22 George Street. He busied himself with golf and good works and became a director of the Edinburgh Society for the Relief of the Destitute Poor. He quickly discovered they had been running down their capital instead of providing relief out of interest. It appears he had an excellent head for business.

Very soon he was appointed Secretary to the Scottish Widows Life Assurance Society and took his family off to Birkenhead where, on 5 October 1871, Hannah gave birth to her third son, Alexander. A few months later her daughter, Margaret Stewart, was dead, aged eight. The death notice is heart-rending. She was the eldest child and only daughter, and at home they called her Amy. There was smallpox in Liverpool in 1871. I hope it was not responsible for Margaret's death. Nor for that of Graham Weir, aged four, who followed his sister to the grave a few months later.

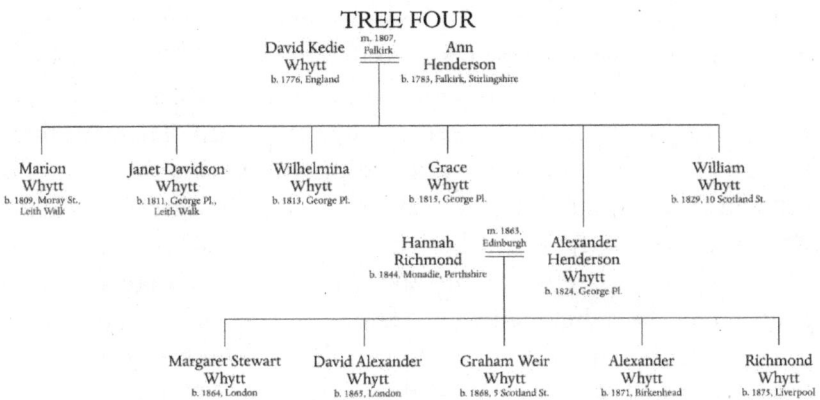

Alexander became captain of his golf club and secretary to the Liverpool Caledonian Society, whose main object was to help poor Scots. In 1878, the *Liverpool Mercury* records his presence at the annual soirée of the Liverpool and Birkenhead Liberal Association. Apparently, tea was served and speeches warmly welcomed. By 1881, the family were in Oxton, and Alexander is a Scots Life Insurance Officer. With him are David, Alexander and a new son, Richmond, aged six. These four males are looked after by a cook, a housekeeper, and by his sister Marion. Hannah Richmond is absent. She was five minutes up the road from Scotland Street at 16 Albany Street, where her sister, Jane, with her husband, a child and a nursemaid, were lodging. It looks as though Hannah had come north, to be with Jane, after a difficult birth. Perhaps she went to visit Wilhelmina who was now in Inveresk asylum.

In 1885 Alexander lost his three remaining sisters: Marion, the eldest, succumbed in April to congestion of the lungs, with Thomas Smith by her side; Grace, in November, of rheumatic gout, and, in December, Wilhelmina died of bronchitis, debility and old age at Inveresk.

Grace died intestate, but there were sons and a husband to see to things. Her sisters had nominated Mr Andrew Wark, stockbroker of London and Ayrshire, to be one of their trustees.

I had searched, and found nothing to tell of the lives of Wilhelmina and her sister Marion save their birth and death dates, mentions in family wills, their moves around a small compass with family, Wilhelmina's incarcerations, and that one French prize so many years ago at M. Espinasse's class. They had lived together or with their mother almost all their lives, and, I discovered from the inventory, shared one bank account. Their mother, in her will, had said that, after Wilhelmina and Marion had refused their father's offer of £200 to match that given to Grace on her marriage, the sisters had 'got nothing since but their board and clothes.' It occurs to me that Wilhelmina's state of mind cannot have been helped by her lifelong lack of agency. I expected meagre wills, forgetting that this family built up property, put it in trust and passed the capital down the line, while reaping the rewards of rents and annuities.

This is where Andrew Wark, of South Grove, Hornsea, came in. He was Marion and Wilhelmina's stockbroker, and a highly successful broker at that. The sisters had, between them, an impressive portfolio, in Britain and in the United States. Wilhelmina had shares in the Manchester, Sheffield and Lincolnshire Railway and stock in the Colchester Stour Valley, Sudbury and Halstead Railway. She had mortgage bonds on the Chicago, Milwaukee and St Pauls Railway Company, Hastings and Dakota Division. This line reached St Pauls just too late for my aged great-great-grandparents, who, in 1870, had to take the stage to St Paul's and then a cart to join their daughter, into the woods, in Dakota country. They bitterly regretted having left Glasgow, but there was no way back.

Marion's will told much the same story, with a bit of a bias towards holdings in the Caledonian Railway, and shares in assurance companies, debentures and consuls. Both had income from property – a tenth of Marion Aikman's Falkirk property, which housed numerous tenants, one fifth of 10 Scotland Street and of 2 George Place, one half of Howard Place. Each had moveable estate of almost £5000. They were, in theory, very wealthy women. In practice, however, they neither controlled nor had the use of that wealth, unless their male trustees so decreed. It is a recipe for depression and delusion. All they possessed, apart from small bequests to their younger brother William and to their niece, Annie Smith, went to their brother Alexander.

Alexander and their solicitor wound up their estates, for the sisters' second trustee, stockbroker Andrew Wark of Hornsea, was dead.

He was born in Irvine, Ayrshire, in 1827, went to London, prospered, returned to marry Margaret Cuthbertson in 1859, and kept contact with his roots all his life, spending his holidays in Ayr. Home was Old Hall on Highgate's South Grove, where the London Whytts, and for a while, Alexander and Hannah, were neighbours. Old Hall was substantial, built on the remains of a sixteenth century building. The house backed onto Highgate Cemetery, and had a convenient door in the garden wall giving access. Andrew was a rich man and philanthropic with it. His church was, of course, Edward Irving's one-time charge, the Scotch Church in Regent Square. Wark had many charitable causes, and actively helped young Scottish men in London to make their fortunes. In 1870, he retired from superintendence of the Somers Town School, an outpost of Regent Square. The church gave him a copy of The *Pilgrim's Progress*. At Old Hall, the Wark family grew quickly, until by 1873, there were David, aged twelve, Thomas, ten, Margaret, eight, and Alexander, aged three.

In June 1873, off on their holidays to Ayr, the family boarded the Scotch Express, known in the summertime as the Tourist Train. It left London just after 8pm, unusually heavily-laden with twenty-three carriages and several guards vans. It was pulled by two engines, belching smoke. In the early hours of the morning, approaching Wigan station at between 35 and 40mph, the train passed over a set of points. The first sixteen carriages crossed without incident. The last seven jumped the rails. The Warks were in one of these carriages, in two different compartments. Andrew, his wife, their eldest son, David, and a governess, were in a first-class compartment, while next door, in second-class, were the other three children and two nurses. The carriage behind rammed into theirs, completely destroying their compartment. Two of the Wark children, Thomas and Margaret, were killed instantly, as was their nurse, Alice Minnet. The third, Alexander, had a broken leg and internal injuries. Their mother was pinned between the sides of her compartment, and suffered a broken thigh. David was trapped beside her. Andrew Wark, unhurt, hunted high and low for a saw with which to cut out his wife and son. Margaret was taken to an hotel, along with Alexander who did not survive the night. In all, eleven people died and thirty-five were badly injured. There was extensive damage to the station and nearby premises. Parts of the destroyed carriages were used to build fires to give light to the rescuers. It must have been a ghastly sight. The dead were laid out in the Wigan Station waiting room. Margaret Wark was taken to the local infirmary, while her husband had to identify the bodies of their children, Thomas, Margaret and Alexander and Alice, their nursemaid. He then must relate the events of the previous evening at an inquest. The funerals took place from Old Hall, leaving from the rear entrance, directly into Highgate cemetery. All three children and Alice Minnet were buried in the same grave. In the newspaper account, no mention is made of the children's mother, in hospital in Wigan. It is difficult to imagine her pain.

Eight years later, her son David, aged twenty-three, was buried alongside his siblings, closely followed by their father. Margaret lived on for another thirty years. She did not remarry, though Andrew's will, unlike any other I have come across, specified that she would lose nothing if she did so. She died in April 1911, at Old Hall, with a niece in attendance and a moveable estate of over £37000. This is one of the saddest stories I have come across. Unusually, I can find no evidence of the family directly profiting from slavery.

Having sorted out his sisters' estates without the help of Mr Wark, Alexander Henderson Whytt returned to Cheshire. On 28 March 1887, he read a paper before the Cheshire Presbyterian Office Bearers Association entitled '*On some of the aspects which the modern church of Christ presents to the world*'. It is held in the Edinburgh University Library. I am afraid I have not read it. Very soon afterwards, Alexander retired to Scotland. He and Hannah and their three boys made their home, not in Scotland Street, but in 10 Morningside Place, not far from Thomas Smith.

Morningside/Grange is and was an area of solid respectability, with houses to match. In terms of the precise Edinburgh class gradations, it was a long way from the West Bow, Sheriff Brae and Morton Street. 10 Scotland Street, no longer quite the right address for a man in Alexander's position, was rented out, and was presently tenanted by Mr Roden Hogg, who was in business as an early version of an estate agent, with a bit of auctioneering on the side.

Alexander again involved himself in golf and became a founding member of the Insurance and Banking Club of Edinburgh. In April 1891, his son Alexander, at nineteen, was a medical student, and sixteen-year-old Richmond had left Merchiston School to become an apprentice in an insurance office. The eldest boy, David, at twenty-five, was a solicitor in London, living with a Mr Hornblower, a friend from Birkenhead. He operated out of Old Broad Street, not far from the erstwhile premises of Ebenezer Whytt and Andrew Wark.

Alexander did not enjoy a long retirement. On 26 August 1891, at Marine Cottage in Leven, he died of intestinal obstruction, pneumonia and pleurisy. He was sixty-seven. His trust estate was Andrew Wark's masterpiece. There were securities in the United Kingdom, the British Colonies, the United States and on loan to the Indian Government, bonds and debentures, stock in railways in the United Kingdom, the United States and India, mortgages and bonds over estates in England, and stock in banks and insurance companies. An extraordinary imperial list, but perhaps not uncommon for a man in his position at the time. He leaves all the revenue from the trust estate to his wife, Hannah Richmond, for her lifetime – but only as long as she remains a widow. If she remarries, all she will get is the restricted annuity, provided for in their pre-nuptial contract. Additionally, if she remarries while the younger sons are minors, she will lose all curatorship of them. This is harsh even for the time, and especially so, as Hannah, at forty-seven, is twenty years younger than he.

His extensive inventory is classic Andrew Wark – until we come to Alexander's shares in steel sailing ships – *Forteviot, Balmoral, Buckingham* . . . and in two iron sailing ships, *Falkland*, built on the Clyde, and *Holyrood*, a Liverpool ship. Perhaps Alexander regretted his rather circumscribed life. His estate falls not much short of £13000 – and that's without the houses. From the list of his debts, we find that opening up the Whytt grave in Old Calton Cemetery to let him in will cost £20.

EIGHT

THE FINAL YEARS

Hannah embarked on a long widowhood. Soon after her husband's death, her eldest son, David, left for Australia. On 25 March 1893, he sailed back to Britain from Sydney on *Oroya* via Hobart, Melbourne, Adelaide, Colombo, Port Said, Naples and Gibraltar, arriving in London on 13 May. David passed the time on board by founding and co-editing with Albert F Calvert *The Oroya Gazette*. Four editions are bound in a booklet which is available in the British Library. It gives a fascinating account of a voyage of the time, in a tone reminiscent of a boys' public school magazine. It is slightly arch, with deep seams of English exceptionalism and casual racism. Numerous amusements are listed. At one fancy dress ball, David was dressed as 'Hymns Ancient and Modern' and in a production of *Claret Cup*, he played Major Rattan. There were religious services, formal dances and poetry competitions. Visits ashore are itemised. The description of some hours in Port Said is particularly interesting, with its evocations of a town built out of the mud excavated during the building of the Suez Canal. What was a *Salon à Louer* which several of their number attended? His comment was 'Ah Father, how could you?' There is a piece about *Oroya*'s electric lights, in which he is struck by the fact that there were almost seven hundred lamps, all of which were serviced by two wires. He marvelled at the hidden work this had entailed.

David did not stay long in Britain. On 19 December 1894, at St James Church of England, Croyden, New South Wales, he married Nellie Antill Howell. Their home in Yass, New South Wales, was built in 1861 using convict labour. David named it Bennochy, harking back to the family history in Fife. Bennochy is one of the oldest buildings in Yass and is listed on the heritage register. It does look quite beautiful – although it appears that an indoor bathroom was only added in 2012. Nellie bore five children, only three of whom lived to adulthood. The second was David K. Whytt – but in this case the K was Kingsley. They also had a son whom I was delighted to see listed, on the electoral roll of 1930, as a jackeroo.

In November 1896, David's brother, Richmond Whytt, sailed from London for Sydney on the Orient Steam Navigation Company's ship, *Ormuz*.

Ormuz was a steam ship with auxiliary sail, built at Fairfields Yard on the Clyde, a yard I came to know quite well. There, in the early years of the first world war, my uncle started as a 13-year-old spanner carrier. He rose to Manager and died suddenly in 1961 on HMS *Blake*'s sea-trials, holding a whisky, a cigar and a good poker hand, I am told. His death was notified by Captain Clutterbuck. In Glasgow, at that time, across all social divisions, many sang and read music, and membership of a choir was relatively common. At my uncle's funeral, the Fairfields men filed in at the back in their working clothes, took off their caps and sang the 23rd psalm in harmony. The memory moves me still. And then I remember that Captain Clutterbuck was followed in the command by Captains Plugge and Butt, which my uncle who had a ripe sense of humour would have relished.

Back in 1896, when *Ormuz* docked in Sydney, Richmond Whytt may well have said farewell to one of the mess stewards who, in one of the many coincidences in this narrative, was yet another of my relatives.

Richmond went to Bowral, a summer retreat for the well-off of Sydney, and set up a golf club and a wine and spirit business. Soon he was appointed the first paid secretary of the Royal Sydney Golf Club, and became an importer of high-quality golf clubs.

On 12 May 1899, Mr Richmond Whytt, son of the late Mr Alexander Whytt of Edinburgh, married Miss Nellie Frances Jones, second daughter of Mr and Mrs Jones, of Bowral. I don't know what Mrs Jones did to get a mention, when Hannah did not.

The Final Years

According to the press, the church was beautifully decorated with chrysanthemums and autumn leaves. Nellie wore ivory duchesse satin, trimmed with orange blossom, and carried a bouquet of chrysanthemums. The bride's travelling dress was a coat and skirt of blue cloth, with a white tucked chiffon vest and toque of turquoise mirror velvet, set off with shaded pheasant feathers. The gifts were many and munificent. The Bowral Association band played on the lawn. The Australian papers of the time did love their society pages. The bride received a diamond brooch from the groom, and an emerald bracelet from the bridegroom's mother. That would be Hannah Richmond. Did she travel to Australia? I can find no mention of her having done so. In October that year, David, with Nellie and a child, returned on *India* for a visit to Scotland,

Only Hannah's youngest son, Alexander, was left living in Scotland. He was a GP in Stirling, and, in 1897, wrote a paper on the merits of re-vaccination, taking apart the *Report of the Royal Commission of 1896*, which he felt did not delve deeply enough or reach tenable conclusions. His judgement was that smallpox re-vaccination of twelve-year-olds should proceed.

On 17 August 1898, the *Teesdale Mercury* reported a 'Pretty Wedding in Teesdale. Dr Alexander Whytt, M.D., of Stirling, and Miss Florence Emily Ford, third daughter of the late Rev. C. H. Ford, Vicar of Bishopton, Durham, were married . . . at the Parish Church of Middleton-in-Teesdale'.

This bride also wore ivory duchesse satin, but chose chiffon trim. She was attended by three bridesmaids, all her nieces. They wore cream Indian muslin over silk dresses and cream-coloured hats, trimmed with chiffon and feathers. They carried bouquets of pink carnations, and wore lace pin brooches with the bride and bridegroom's initials, the gift of the latter. There is a very long list of the guests. Hannah was there with her brother-in-law William Whytt, the last of David and Ann's children, and two of Hannah's sisters, the Misses Richmond. Also, there were several of Alexander's cousins, the offspring of his late aunt, Grace, and Thomas Smith, of Calcutta.

The report ends with a list of the many and costly presents. I'm a bit bemused at the thought that a person, contemplating a present, would know it was going to be listed, for the world to judge. Hannah gave the bride a bracelet, but there is no mention as to whether or not it was set with emeralds. The Smith family gave the couple a framed picture of Durham, a carriage clock and a claret jug. A photo frame came from Mr and Mrs Richmond. I'm assuming this will be Hannah's brother, John Richmond, and Mary Gordon. I'm struck by the next gift of teaspoons and sugar tongs, sent from Tain, by the very elderly Mrs Donaldina Gordon, the mother of the groom's deceased father's first wife, poor young Janet. Donaldina survived her daughter Janet by forty years and died in 1902 at East Dron, aged eighty-four.

A toast rack came from Miss Cooke, whom we will meet later – a cousin, of the line descending from Grace Whytt and Admiral John Gourley. The gifts I like best, as they seem to me to cover all the bases, came from Mr William Johnston, who contributed a bicycle, a cheque and an escritoire.

There is no mention of a present from Ann Henderson and David's Whytt's only surviving offspring – the groom's uncle, William Whytt. He is a bit of a mystery. In this tight knit family, he was cared for but given little responsibility. After his mother's death, he lived in boarding houses around a small compass of Edinburgh, on income from the rents of 10 Scotland Street and George Place. He may not have been solitary. Although by 1891 his siblings were dead, Hannah, his brother's widow, still lived and so did four of the Padons, and two nephews at university and school in Edinburgh. Then there were all the Whytt Smiths and the assorted descendants of Grace Whytt and John Gourley. Perhaps William was a good uncle, but I fear he was a sad soul.

By 1901, he was lodging with a Miss Jane Whyte from Portmoak, at 3 Leven Terrace, a small three-roomed house. There were no other boarders. There is no evidence they were related. He died there, the last of David and Ann's children, on 13 October 1916. He left £500 for an annuity for Jane Whyte and £200 each to his Cooke cousins, Grace and Marion. His books, jewellery, gold watch and chain, writing desk, dressing case, silver mounted canes, bookcase with supporting table and tobacco jar, went to his grandnephew,

The Final Years

Thomas Whyte Smith. His framed portrait of Dickens and his Dickens memorabilia went to his minister, whom he held in esteem, and all his other pictures and odds and ends, to his grandniece, Margery Whyte Smith. I hope she liked the model of the Taj Mahal. All the rest was divided among his nephews, David Whyte Smith, and David, Richmond and Alexander Whytt. The contrast between the value of his estate and that of his siblings is striking. There is no indication that he ever travelled further abroad than Teesdale, for his nephew Alexander's wedding. His presence there is the one time, other than in official records, that he is recorded as having set foot on the planet.

After the wedding, Alexander and Florence honeymooned in Scotland. In the 1901 census they were counted at 20 Clarendon Place, Stirling, with their three children, Christopher Richmond Whytt, Joan Mary and Rachel Dulcibella. I wonder where the name Dulcibella came from. Much later, Christopher would marry a Mary Dulcibella Ford.

In 1911, Dr Alexander Whytt was elected to the British Medical Association. In 1913, he was involved in an accident in which, *The Scotsman* reports, one man lost his life and another was seriously injured. It appears that a large car was being driven by a Mr Dupont, some miles east of Linlithgow, on the Edinburgh Road, when a farm cart emerged from the roadside and collided violently with the car. Mr McKenzie, the owner of the car, was thrown into the path of Dr Alexander Whytt, who was driving in the opposite direction. The large car overturned and came to rest on top of Mr Dupont. The article states that it is not known whether Mr McKenzie died from being thrown, or from being run over by Dr Whytt, who attended to the seriously injured Mr Dupont. By chance, the Procurator Fiscal i.e., the official who would investigate the accident, was driving home and came upon the scene. He arranged for the body to be seen to and for Mr Dupont to be taken to Edinburgh. Late into the night, we are told, the Fiscal, aided by a policeman, was making enquiries. There were no consequences for Alexander.

Less than eighteen months later, Britain declared war on Germany and both Alexander and Richmond joined up. Alexander became a lieutenant and then captain, in the RAMC, and Richmond, a private, in the 19th battalion of the Australian Imperial Army Expeditionary Force. He sailed from Sydney on board HMAT *Ceramic* on 25 June 1915. Prudently, he made his will, leaving his all to his wife. He was bound for Gallipoli.

On 23 July he disembarked at Alexandria and was promoted to lance corporal. His brigade then embarked and landed in what would later be called Anzac – Australian and New Zealand Army Corps – Cove on 21 August. They walked into hell. Winston Churchill, First Lord of the Admiralty, had cooked up a plan to remove Turkey from the war. He catastrophically underestimated the disciplined and well-trained soldiers under Lieutenant Colonel Mustafa Kemal, later Ataturk, who, in 1923, would found the Turkish Republic. Lord Kitchener, in charge of the army, did not want to move British troops from France to Gallipoli. The landing force was made up of British colonial troops, including Indians, and French colonial troops from North Africa. They spoke a babel of languages. Communication posed problems. Landing crafts were swept from the designated beaches by strong currents, to fetch up under precipitous cliffs. Many soldiers had been issued, in addition to their heavy packs, with bicycles.

The Turkish soldiers were dug in, high on the slopes, well-armed and reinforced regularly. The Anzac soldiers were pinned to shallow trenches, in the few hundred metres of ground they had taken, and had little protection from Turkish guns, many sold to Turkey by British armament manufacturers. The living were plagued by suffocating heat and swarms of flies buzzing round ubiquitous rotting corpses. Fresh water distribution was patchy, though when the trenches flooded, men drowned. Dysentery and other forms of pestilence were rife. Eight thousand Anzac men died of wounds and disease, before the commander was replaced and the order to retreat given. Too late for Richmond Whytt, who, on 1 November, died of dysentery on the hospital ship *Rawa*. He was buried at sea off Malta.

There then followed a series of unfortunate events, documented in paperwork held in the Australian military archives. The least of these was that his effects were sent in two different consignments. The worst must have been how his wife was informed of his death.

The Final Years

The news had been transmitted by cable in a series of reports, which started off in Alexandria from the intermediate commander to the Governor in Malta, who transmitted to the Australian High Commissioner in London, who sent it on. Each communication was accompanied by a different army form. Nellie Frances received the original stark cable. Pains were taken, thereafter, to ensure that proper procedure was put in place. On 13 November 1915, *The Scotsman* announced that Richmond, son of the late Mr Alexander Whytt and Mrs Whytt, had died of dysentery. In January 1916 his father-in-law announced the death in the *Sydney Morning Herald*. Later that month, his brother David received official confirmation and advertised this, also in the *Sydney Morning Herald*. Some time elapsed before it could be confirmed that he had been buried at sea. None of the announcements mentioned Nellie Frances Whytt.

Then Richmond's possessions began to arrive. In January 1916, his effects were listed by the Australian Imperial Force. He had on him, when he died: his field service pocket book, a writing case, two notebooks, letters, a belt, two testaments, two knives, two pipes, a holdall, two razors, a hairbrush, shaving soap, nail brush, toothbrush and strop, mirror, pouch, badges, housewife – a small sewing kit – a whistle, braces, two handkerchiefs, a strap, a cup, coins and two pencils. Chillingly, the parcel was numbered 5,852.

The strop tells me he had no truck with the new-fangled safety razors, and favoured the open cut-throat razor, and possibly, as my father did, shaved himself two-handed. The sound of razors being sharpened on the strop was part of my childhood. My father was born in the east end of Glasgow in the early years of the twentieth century. He bought his razors in his early twenties in Chicago. They are bright Solingen steel. I have them still.

Nellie received a full list of Richmond's effects. Then a parcel arrived with half missing. Some time later another parcel arrived without explanation. Nellie then had to establish her right to inherit. Eventually, in July 1916, the army sent a death certificate to her solicitors. Unfortunately, they mistyped Richmond's surname as Wyatt, and the whole process had to be started again. Poor Nellie.

A shambles.

Richmond Whytt is commemorated on the Lone Pine Memorial, on the peninsula bounded by the Aegean and the Sea of Marmara. Lone Pine Memorial commemorates more than 4,900 Australian and New Zealand servicemen who died in the area, and whose remains could not be identified, or who died of wounds and disease on a hospital ship. The Lone Pine is a few miles north of the Helles Memorial, where three young men from Scotland Street are commemorated. Richmond is also remembered on panel six, in the Merchiston School Memorial Hall. Nellie remarried. I hope she was happy.

Hannah, still in Edinburgh, had lost her only daughter, one son very young, her husband and now Richmond, dead of illness like so many British soldiers and sailors over the generations. She had two sons left. David was in Australia, but Alexander was with the RAMC in France, where Richmond's battalion was sent, after what remained of them was rescued from Gallipoli. She must have feared for her doctor son. Somehow, he survived, and returned to Stirling and Allan Park House. But Hannah did not have him close for long. By the time Alexander's medals were awarded in 1921, he was in Surrey. In 1923 he came north to bear witness on his mother's death certificate. Hannah Richmond, the last surviving of the generation below David Kedie Whytt and Ann Henderson, died at 59 Braid Avenue, of heart failure and senility.

She left everything to her two living sons, David and Alexander, and to Richmond's widow. I was glad to see that. There was the usual cash in the house, furniture and effects, some shares in Lever Bros, war bonds and treasury bonds, along with the income from the liferent of the trust funds of her late husband, and her father, Thomas Richmond – a total of just under £1500. Thomas Richmond's trust had been set up almost one hundred years previously. It was time for closure. An action of poinding was raised, by Alexander, David and Nellie. Poinding was a way of having a one-off payment made to all claimants.

David and Alexander Whytt had one last task. In 1924, one hundred years after their grandparents had bought the house, they sold 10 Scotland Street. David Whytt, died on 6 March 1927, at

The Final Years

Bennochy, Yass, NSW, and Alexander, in London, in April 1936 – David and Ann's last grandchild. I will end this strand of their story with his death, outside the range of living family memory.

And so to the story of David's pious bachelor brother, William, which I assumed would be less packed with interest. I was wrong.

NINE

'OBSCURE MUSIC SELLER'

My pre-conception was that brother William would be a staid bachelor in his small corner of the New Town; the older, boring, possibly solitary and desperately pious foil to his swashbuckling younger brother. And then I came to know him.

He was born in Linktown of Abbotshall, Kirkcaldy, Fife, on 5 March 1772, four years before David, and two and six before his sisters, Grace and Janet.

His parents, James and Janet, and his siblings, David and Grace, we can trace in the records as they marry, give birth to children and, too often, bury them. Bachelor William's life must be extracted piece by piece from street registers, lists of booksellers, charitable donors and committee members, the odd newspaper article, a few surprising websites – and from his long and detailed last will and testament.

By 1788, when he was sixteen, his family had crossed the River Forth to Edinburgh and established their bookbinding business on the West Bow at the western end of the Cowgate. The Cowgate is – and was – a canyon, where little light finds its way to the depths. At least in the twenty-first century there is refuse collection and clean water, and a distinct absence of the cholera and misery that was rife in the eighteenth and nineteenth centuries, and which William, as he became prosperous, did what he could to alleviate. Around 1830, much of the upper part of the Bow was destroyed to make way for Victoria Street, which was built to join the Grassmarket to the newly-constructed George IV Bridge. The original Z line of the Bow can still be seen in the steps leading to the Upper Bow and the Castle. Some of the houses at the Grassmarket end survived and there are still two lintels bearing the dates 1616 and 1720, and one tall, slender house, restored and lived in, which can occasionally be visited. It dates to William's youth and his long black-clad legs, clattering down the narrow steep stairs on his energetic, urgent way. At least when I am there.

We pick up traces of William in his late teens, now styling himself Whyte, apprenticed to a publishing company at the centre of Edinburgh's lively music scene of the 1790s. Since 1728, the Edinburgh Musical Society had brought the best performers from Europe. In 1771, they welcomed Domenico Corri and his wife Francesca Bachelli for their concert series and changed the course of musical life in the city.

As we've seen, the idea for the Edinburgh New Town was first mooted early in the eighteenth century. The Old Town, rising precariously up the ridge to the Castle, was crowded, rickety and insanitary though the further one penetrated down the hill towards Holyrood, the more one would come across fine houses with well-laid out gardens. Nevertheless, they were crammed together. There was no more room. Printing, brewing, button and feather boa making, wig, perfume, hat, glove and shawl and garment making, starch manufacturing, wood and metal working and distilling – many of these trades producing smell and effluent – and the domestic sphere of all classes, ranks and sorts, crammed the wynds and closes. In contrast, the buildings of the New Town, gradually covering the slopes down towards the Water of Leith, were mostly residential with large drawing rooms where cultural events could take place. Formerly, the music of Scotland had been mostly oral and traditional. With the coming of gentility and faster commerce with mainland Europe and beyond, there came the desire to play the fashionable music of international composers in one's own home. Pianos, teachers and sheet music were needed. By the mid-1790s, there was a busy trade and a goodly number of music publishers and sellers. Many of these, such as John Corri and his son Domenico, also mounted concerts and musical seasons. William Whyte served his apprenticeship as a clerk with Corri. His ears must have rung with music.

As his fortunes rose and fell, John Corri traded variously from 1779 until 1800 as John Corri, John Corri and Sutherland, Corri and Dussek, at several addresses, hard by the premises of Gibson and Thomson on the newly built North Bridge Street. Corri's firm failed in 1799. Dussek fled the country, leaving Corri in jail and his son Domenico to seek his fortune in London.

William struck out on his own. *The Edinburgh History of the Book in Scotland* tells us that at the end of the eighteenth century bookselling and publishing had declined in the city, and that the booksellers operated in the Old Town around the Tolbooth – with the exception of 'William Whyte in the New Town who appeared to sell music'. A further reference to him comes, perhaps unwisely, from the publisher George Thomson, who called him 'an obscure music seller'. There is a distinct whiff of *de haut en bas* here. William was indeed young to have set up for himself. And unlike the venerable and established booksellers whose families were from the Old Town and the professions, William came from Fife and trade. However, it would appear he knew very well what he was doing.

At the turn of the nineteenth century, William was listed as a music publisher and instrument seller, with an address on South St Andrew Street, a few steps from Princes Street. Although a consecutive street-numbering scheme was being put in place, and by 1811 the whole of the New Town was numbered, William, as he started up, advertised himself in the old manner, *At the Sign of the Organ*. Already a canny man, he had his finger in the wind, adding stationery, drawing materials and globes to his core stock of music and musical instruments, mainly violins, flutes and pianofortes. These were carried by sea from London to Leith and thence by cart to Edinburgh, surely helped on their way by his merchant father and brother. William also published musical scores of popular folksongs arranged for piano, ballads – *Tak our Auld Cloak about Ye, Shepherds I have lost my Love, Nobody's Coming to Marry Me* – and Scots melodies arranged for instrumental ensembles. In 1805, he published an instruction manual for the piano and harpsichord. Did he sing as he went about his work? Did he play the instruments he sold?

He employed a travelling salesman, John Blake, who tuned pianos throughout Scotland and took orders. John Broadwood and Sons, of 33 Great Pulteney Street, London, on 2 January 1810, felt it necessary to inform the public that while counterfeit Broadwoods were being sold in Edinburgh, the real thing was available from William Whyte. John Broadwood, incidentally, was a joiner from Cockburnspath, just south of Edinburgh, who travelled to London in the mid-eighteenth century, joined the harpsichord firm of Burkat Shudi, married his boss's daughter, Barbara, and by 1776, had taken over the business which still bears his name. The Broadwood became the piano of choice because Broadwood, being a joiner, knew what was needed and strengthened the case, basically, with more bits of wood. Whyte and the other Broadwood dealers guarded their privilege and protested when their monopoly was threatened.

In the trade directories, we can trace William operating at various addresses round the St Andrew Square end of the first New Town, a short, steep walk to the book sales in the Old Town. In his later years, he kept a horse and brougham, which was perhaps not such a luxury, given that John Boyd Dunlop, a Scottish veterinarian, did not invent pneumatic rubber tyres until 1887.

According to the Book Trade Index, from 1799 until 1808, while his shop was at 1 South St Andrew Street, his home was 24 Greenside Place, huddled under the bulk of Calton Hill at the top of Leith Walk. Number 24 is part of the tenement block of spacious homes, still standing, though much changed, numbered 23–25 Greenside Place. It was built by John Baxter around 1798, so William was its first owner. His next-door neighbour was Robert Stevenson the lighthouse engineer, grandfather of Robert Louis Stevenson. William would have close connections with Greenside until the end of his long life.

1 St Andrew Street was one of the first tenements to rise on the plan of the New Town. It was built by Sir William Forbes, founder of the private bank which bore his name, which, through mergers and alliances, became very powerful, developing a new form of banking in Scotland, whose influence would last for several centuries. Though Forbes was active in the Edinburgh Committee for the Abolition of the Slave Trade, a mortgage was granted by him to a Helen Watt of Jamaica, and the bank is mentioned in

University College London's Legacies of British Slavery database. He was a force in the land, a member of Samuel Johnson's Literary Dining Club, a co-founder of the Royal Society of Edinburgh, a philanthropic benefactor involved in almost all Edinburgh's charitable enterprises, and consulted by Prime Minister Pitt. Much of his efforts were aimed at recovering the lands of Pitsligo, forfeited by his Jacobite forbears after the Battle of Culloden. His portrait by Joshua Reynolds hangs in the National Gallery of Scotland. He looks every inch a banker. John Kay's later sketch gives him a lean figure, a finely-turned ankle and the legend, Friend to All. On his marriage, he moved to 1 South St Andrew Street from Carrubbers Close, a narrow, stepped lane, leading up to the High Street from Canal Street, which now houses Waverley Station. In Carrubers Close, he may well have rubbed shoulders with Allan Ramsay, the poet, and James Young Simpson, the discoverer of chloroform, as he went to and from his dispensary. The first of Forbes' thirteen children was born at 1 St South Andrew Street, and, as his family expanded, he moved to the more lately-built 3 George Street and rented the ground floor of his former home to William Whyte.

At the close of the working day, when William left his place of business, he would walk a few yards down to Princes Street with its open prospect to the castle. Turning left, he would see the original North Bridge, a rickety structure built in 1763, and the Theatre Royal on Shakespeare Square, reportedly mean in architecture and disreputable in reputation. Below and behind them was Lady Glenorchy's church, his spiritual home until the end of his days. Past the Square, the ground dropped steeply to Low Calton and its scattering of poor streets. Waterloo Place and Bridge, which would be built in 1820 to provide a fitting entrance to Edinburgh from the east, did not yet cut through the Old Calton graveyard. On his left, he would pass Register House, and head off north down steep Leith Street to Greenside Place on its eastern side. A walk of perhaps four minutes for a fit young man in his late twenties.

In the Post Office directory of 1804–1805, Whyte is still a music seller and stationer, but the trade was declining, perhaps through boredom with the perennial argument as to what constituted authentic Scottish music. On the one hand was the purist antiquarian faction. On the other were those who commissioned new music from European composers for the verses of poets, pre-eminently Robert Burns, to make them suitable for drawing room recitals. Burns visited Edinburgh frequently until his death in 1796, when our William was twenty-four and working with Corri. The town was small. They surely knew each other. Eight years after Burns' death, William commissioned an arrangement of a selection of Burns' songs from the composer Haydn. To do so, he had to lure the composer away from the august George Thomson, who had dismissed William as an obscure music seller.

Whyte doubled the fee offered by Thomson. Haydn was apologetic to Thomson, but times were hard in wartime Vienna. He was old and would soon be too frail to compose. These lovely arrangements he made for William Whyte are arguably the late flower of his work. Thomson, needless to say, was raging, and even more grumpy than usual. In Benjamin Crombie's *Modern Athenians, a series of original portraits of memorable citizens of Edinburgh, 1837–1847,* Thomson is pictured unflatteringly on page 164. You can see him online in Internet Archive. The text is even less kind. Mr Thomson's ruling weakness was said to have been avarice. Around 1776, at the age of seventeen, he was appointed to a well-paid sinecure at the Board of Manufacturing, which he retained until his retirement at the age of eighty. His duties were light and gave him plenty of time to pursue Burns for poems. His actions after the poet's death, when others tried to help Burns' family, were widely condemned. Walter Scott was incredulous that Thomson could have put to paper statements about his actions which did not in any way concur with his actual actions, i.e., lies, and shocked that Thomson should have demanded back and edited his letters to Burns before they could be published. Nevertheless, in 1847, one hundred gentlemen subscribed to a silver vase in his honour and a eulogy was given by Lord Cockburn. He died aged ninety-four in 1851. Thomson's granddaughter was the unfortunate wife of Charles Dickens.

Whyte's first folio of Burns songs was produced in 1804. The two volumes, *A Collection of Scottish Airs Harmonised for the Voice and Piano Forte with introductory and concluding Symphonies and*

Accompaniments for Violin and Violincello By Joseph Haydn Mus. Doct, were rather elegant. They were hugely successful. Once again, Thomson was not at all pleased. These arrangements are still on sale in a fine recording by Jaimie McDougall, Lorna Anderson, and the Haydn Trio Eisenstadt. Some years ago, on a beautiful summer evening, I had the pleasure of filming McDougall singing William Whyte's Burns songs in the perfect setting of Princes Street Gardens, under Edinburgh Castle.

So here is our man, in his early thirties, in the middle of a European War, commissioning, from an Austrian musical genius, new and innovative music for Scotland, and cocking a snook at one of the most influential music promoters/publishers of his time. Defying my pre-conceptions once again, he dedicated the first volume to the famous beauty, Lady Charlotte Campbell, his near-contemporary. In the National Portrait Gallery in Edinburgh, there is her portrait, made in Naples by Johann Wilhelm Tischbein, who described Charlotte as more perfect than the best artist can imagine. There are roses and fawns. My granddaughter says she looks cool. I think she looks strong and beautiful which may, across the generations, be the same thing. The National Gallery also holds a portrait, in the title of which she is described as a writer. She looks out at us with an intelligent, appraising gaze. I think she may have preferred this version.

Charlotte Campbell was the daughter of the Duke of Argyll and Elizabeth Gunning, another beauty who had been a writer and briefly an actress in an effort to relieve her family's poverty. Her portrait hangs beside her daughter's. In 1796, Charlotte, aged twenty-one, married Colonel John Campbell. In the thirteen years before Campbell's death in 1809, Charlotte bore nine children, of whom only two survived her. According to contemporary accounts, Charlotte's extensive network of connections in Edinburgh, was political, intellectual, extremely social, and to a degree, democratic. Her salons were the place to be seen. Walter Scott was a friend. She was an early influence on the enormously successful novelist Susan Ferrier, who spent much of her childhood in Charlotte's sister's home at Inveraray on Loch Fyne. Ferrier's *Marriage* was bowdlerised by the Victorians but has been restored and edited by the late

'Obscure Music Seller'

Dorothy MacMillan, who did a great deal for women in Scottish literature. She was my contemporary at university and her quiet scholarship is missed.

In 1809, on her husband's death, Lady Charlotte Campbell left Edinburgh and went south to be Lady in Waiting to Princess Caroline, who was battling her libertine husband, the future George IV. Very soon, Charlotte crossed the Channel. Travelling in Italy as part of Shelley's circle, she engaged Shelley's college friend, the improvident and extravagant Reverend Edmund Bury, as her sons' tutor. In 1818, four months' pregnant with Bury's child, she married him. He was fifteen years her junior. He died in 1832, leaving her to soldier on for thirty more years as an impecunious widow living by her pen. On the Register of Mr Chambers' Circulating Library at 84 Hanover Street, Mr Stirling, a Writer to the Signet, of 16 Scotland Street, was recorded as having borrowed a copy of *Flirtation* bks 1,2,3 by Lady Charlotte Campbell Bury. She died at her home in Sloane Street, Chelsea, in 1861, four years after the man who had dedicated to her his collection of Burns Songs, half a century before. I wish I knew what lay behind that dedication. Was it deep feeling for the woman herself? Or an eye for profit and frustrating the sneering Thomson? It must have been, for a little while, the scandal of the town. Whatever the motive, William's fortune rolled out very differently from Charlotte's, and some of it must have been based on the enormous and lucrative popularity of the collection.

Let us return to him as he makes his way in the book trade. In the eighteenth century, booksellers were also publishers and largely financed their books. As the trade grew towards the end of the century, and titles proliferated, the term bookseller was more commonly used, and The Edinburgh Booksellers Society was incorporated. Their minutes record that in December 1792, at an occasional meeting of the booksellers of Edinburgh, William Creech, publisher, magistrate and Lord Provost of Edinburgh, suggested that it might be a good idea ('attended with beneficial consequences') to have a considerable number of trades united as 'a Body Corporate under the title and designation of Booksellers and Stationers of the City of Edinburgh, suburbs of Edinburgh within the royalty and Leith'. A fund was started. This was the Creech who published Burns and had a somewhat cavalier attitude towards paying him. Burns responded with a sonnet that begins: 'A little upright, pert, tart, tripping wight.'

William Creech was apprenticed to the Edinburgh booksellers, Kincaid and Bell, before setting off to improve his knowledge in London and in Europe, as was common at the time. He established his own premises at the heart of the business, in the Luckenbooths on the High Street in 1773, and remained there, holding what were basically salons, till his death. One of his partners for a short time, as none lasted very long, was his former master, Kincaid. Kincaid's erstwhile partner, Mr Bell, seems to have had an *insouciant* attitude towards copyright. That is, he printed books to which others held the rights. Mr Bell went into partnership with his nephew, Mr Bradfute, and the pair went on to have a highly successful business for many years, much spent in contention with Creech and others of the trade. Legitimately, they re-published works by many of the leading figures of the Enlightenment, and later by Jane Austen, Mary Wollstonecraft, Shelley, Henry Fielding, Tobias Smollet . . . They also published foreign language books and works from the Americas, including several by James Fennimore Cooper, whose dashingly romantic novels dealt with the early colonial days. If you climb the Mound and stand in the portal of the Bank of Scotland, you will find opposite you the former premises of Bell and Bradfute, a shop whose magnificent frontage sits on the curve as Bank Street heads down from the High Street to the Mound. James Brownhill built the eight-storey building in 1723 before the Mound was conceived of, though of course there was a path from North Bank Street up to the Lawnmarket and the High Street, a section of which is visible from the warren under 12 Bank Street. Back above ground, on its doorstep is a fine tile work.

This lovely doorstep was covered up for many years until the owner set out to remove layers of carpet and glue. The premises at 12 Bank Street currently house Makar's Gourmet Mash Bar, a very popular, award-winning hostelry, in which, with its emphasis on locally-sourced Scottish produce, our eighteenth-century booksellers might well feel very much at home. The first meeting of the new Booksellers Society, held close by in Hunter's Tavern, in the Exchange, on 27 April 1793, reported that their petition seeking incorporation to the magistrates of Edinburgh had been granted. In December of 1793, we find Creech proposing a motion that the city magistrates be congratulated on suppressing the meetings of 'a certain class of people who called themselves the British Convention for Universal Suffrage and Annual Parliaments'. They wanted universal male suffrage and annual parliaments. How dare they? It seems Burns was right in his estimation of Creech's character. Creech is astonished that anyone would want to change the best constitution ever. This was a time, during a war with France, when everyone should be supporting the interests of the country and opposing the enemies of God and Man. Creech's language is intemperate. They were meeting in a tavern which may have had some bearing on his register.

In a record of a sale by Creech, we find: 'Catalogue of books in quires, which will be offered to a select company of booksellers, at Hunter's Tavern, on Tuesday, October 21 1794.' The lots varied greatly in size, from a single copy to several multi-volume works and were sold unbound, in quires, a practice which was dying out, though we might remember young George Sandy buying his books in quires. The sale of over 300 items, arranged alphabetically by author or title, commenced with dinner on the table at three o'clock. Creech offered buyers generous payment terms. Perhaps he had had the lots for some time and needed to shift them. In the light of his chaotic finances, he may well have been trying to improve his cash flow.

In 1796, again in Hunter's tavern, the Society was censuring George Mudie and Son for selling books below the approved retail price. They decided to cut off co-operation: no member will attend a Mudie sale until the Mudies desist. But in December, Mudie was still selling medical books for ready money at greatly reduced prices. The might of the committee tried to reason with him. Mudie said it wasn't him, his son did it. And presumably ran away.

Moreover, Mudie said, he would do as he pleased. He would make an apology to the trade but wouldn't stop. He threatened to take the Society to court. They responded by passing a motion which was basically a form of price-fixing. Mudie refused to sign it, but they wore him down. In 1797, Mudie wrote to the Society that he would observe their regulations and accept their censure. This, the Society accepted graciously, till Creech stepped in and persuaded them against Mudie. In March 1800, it would seem that Mudie was in the ascendant. He was the secretary and Creech was out of office, but later in the year Mudie was bankrupt. Creech, back in charge, expelled Mudie, despite the pleading in mitigation by the publisher Constable – he who brought Walter Scott's finances to grief. Creech again became president, and failed to pay the lawyer who had worked for him against Mudie.

At a meeting in early 1803 at the Britannia Tavern on the Shore, Leith, we find William Whyte petitioning for admittance to this bickering bunch. The petition passed unanimously and, according to an account signed off by Creech, the rest of the evening was spent in innocent mirth and festivity. Whyte was present at the meeting held in the Britannia Tavern in compliment to the brethren in Leith, 'at which many excellent toasts were given, many excellent things were said and the company parted at a reasonable hour resolved to hold a similar meeting annually in the Race Week.'

In February 1805, William Whyte, clearly a brave young man, met with three fellow members in Elliot's Rooms and tabled the motion that prices should not be set by the Society. The Society strongly disagreed.

In 1810, he was present when the Edinburgh Booksellers Society decided to invest all of its considerable funds in the Royal Bank of Scotland, now the infamous RBS, and again, in April 1813, when it was decided that, in answer to Mrs Mudie's request for the pension to which she is entitled as the widow of Mr George Mudie, it will be paid – but only on production of a death certificate and after deduction of all the money her late husband owed in dues. At this same meeting, William was elected to the committee of management. It's noted that Mr Creech is two years in arrears with his dues. As may have been obvious from the above, as well as being improvident, Creech was notoriously stingy. I failed to discover if an irregularity in the society's holdings of government stocks was down to Creech.

'Obscure Music Seller'

In 1815, Creech having died, the Society noted to his trustees that the Raeburn portrait they had commissioned was still in his drawing room and they wanted it back, along with his arrears of membership dues. To that end, they enclosed the receipts for the picture and its frame.

William Whyte survived the fray. One wonders what he made of the Society's treatment of widows, given his charitable donations to help poor and destitute women. He would go on to follow Creech onto the Town Council and as president of the Society of Booksellers. The minute of the meeting at which he ascended is not on file, but, on 4 April 1831, the Society met at Gibb's Hotel. Present were William Whyte, President, and ten colleagues. Mr Whyte intimated that since the last meeting, two months before, three members had died. Quite a hit rate. Whyte was then re-elected chairman and remained an active member till the end of his days.

His life in the city had also progressed. On 20 May 1807, Whyte was appointed Edinburgh Burgess and Guildsman. In 1808, he became an Elder of Lady Glenorchy's Church. Elders had many responsibilities, the most arduous of which was the care of members. At first, William had the relatively prosperous Western section. In 1818, however, he was given the lower south division which included some of the worst, most insanitary, poverty-stricken homes from the Lawn Market and the High Street to the closes of the Cowgate. He carried out this work assiduously, running Bible classes for the poorest. Church session minutes are now available online and cast a light on the pre-occupations of the Elders. In 1820, having swithered for a couple of decades about hiring a precentor to lead their singing, the Elders considered whether a band might not be a good idea. A year later, they were condemning Mr John Land for immoral practices unbecoming to a member of their church. He was to be forgiven on evidence of sincere and godly repentance. William was concerned that Lady Glenorchy's original rules for the church should be adhered to, and spoke in favour of their being read out once a year. He also got the doors fixed. In 1823, he was appointed Clerk to the Session. The minutes he wrote look beautiful, with elegant penmanship, and are almost totally illegible. Thankfully, five years later he resumed as Treasurer, and the new Clerk noted sniffily that none of our William's minutes had been authenticated. William's advocacy for a precentor must have succeeded, for, in 1831, at a meeting at 13 George Street, they were commenting that the Precentor's singing was perhaps improving . . . a wee bit. In 1832, backed by Liddle, William requested that the chapel be fumigated with chlorate of lime, a method translated from the French by John Scott, Surgeon. There was cholera again in Edinburgh. The new Clerk recorded that Mr Whyte was concerned that supplies of coal should get through to the poor while he was away for two weeks. Where did he go?

Others of the family attended Lady Glenorchy's. The early communion roll lists his father, his sister Janet, and Margaret Whytt, David's daughter, but towards the end only William remained steadfast.

Alongside his civic and pious good works, William was building his business. In 1808, William Whyte, bookseller, stationer and music-seller, placed a notice in the *Caledonian Mercury*, respectfully informing his friends and the public that he has 'removed from number 1 to a large and elegant SHOP at 17 South St Andrew Street, where he has fitted up a Room for the sale of London-made PIANOFORTES by Broadwood etc.' That year he sold eight square pianos. He then moved his shop, first of all across the road to 16 St Andrew Street, and then to numbers 12 and 14, down a bit towards Princes Street where, until 1821, William Whyte and Company were listed as book and music sellers. Then gradually, his description in the directories highlights the word bookseller.

On 8 July 1813, he petitioned the Dean of Guild Court to make alterations to the shops at numbers 12 and 14. The records of proceedings of the Dean of Guild Court are held in the Edinburgh City Archives. When I first asked to look at William's petition, the public counter was in Cockburn Street, down by Waverley Station; the entrance to the City Chambers is on the High Street, a full twelve storeys above. The bundle of documents handed in by William Whyte, 207 years earlier, was brought to the archives for me. I doubt if, in all those years, anyone else had touched them. They were dusty and speckled with age on the outside, but the script and drawings are pristine.

A frontage sketch shows little alteration to the original façade. Certainly, worse had happened on Princes Street. The next two sketches show the two façades as detached, and then as connected by William's proposed alterations. The sketches are fine-lined in soft black, shaded with grey and pink for the Craigleith stone. They are rather beautiful.

Finally, Whyte presents a plan of the combined shops that will triple his floor space. The façade remains substantially untouched with windows onto the street, but beyond them he has imagined a library, its shelves shaded in grey. It is 23' 9" by 12' 8". There are double windows at the rear and an alcove on the south wall. Two pillars support the roof. Also at the rear, and approached through the library, is the inner sanctum, labelled the writing room, where he would deal with his letters, orders and bills, his instructions to tradesmen and to Mr Broadwood in London. This room has one window and an open wall press. The second room onto the street with its two windows and alcove is also a shop room with two closets. Perhaps the pianos were displayed there. I follow him as he unlocks his door, passes through the pianos and the library to his desk, ready for his day's work, his window open to the trade noises of the little lane at the back, or covered with heavy drapes to conserve what heat the grate offered the room. Or perhaps he had one of those new-fangled stoves imported from Germany.

The plans were accompanied by William's petition, in a clear and controlled hand. I wonder if David wrote it for him. William 'Humbly Sheweth' that he has been in number 12 for some years and now has secured the lease of 14' and wants to make some improvements. His signature, inscribed on 30 June 1813, is angular and elegant, the capital Ws compressed into one single scribble. I cannot find a record as to whether or not he received his permission. I think that he must have, as he did not move again until 1823.

He would most certainly have been aware of the festivities around the performances of the diva, Angelica Catalani, in 1814, and of the arrival of Felix Yaniewicz, in 1815. Yaniewicz, a Lithuanian/Polish violinist found Edinburgh the perfect city for a festival and conceived a hugely popular series of concerts, some of which took place in Corri's rooms. It was a truly international musical festival. Further festivals followed, paving the way for what was to come. Eliza Yaniewicz, his wife, was one of Chambers' Circulating Library's best customers. Her reading included works by Jane Austen and texts in German.

William's father, James, now a bookseller and auctioneer, had joined him in St Andrew Street in 1817, with his saleroom still at 3 Morton Street. In 1824, the year his/my house at 10 Scotland Street was a-building, David, naval adventuring over, went into partnership with William on South St Andrew Street.

Much of their stock was sourced from London and much came by sea. The logistics was surely David's business. It was only in the mid-1750s that a regular overland passenger service between Edinburgh and London had begun, taking ten days in the summer and twelve in winter. By the early 1770s, the journey-time had been halved. A ticket for a fly coach between Edinburgh and Newcastle was issued to a Mrs Inchbald on 2 July 1776, the year of David's birth. This was possibly Elizabeth Inchbald, the actress touring Scotland with the West Digges theatre company. On the back are details and prices for the fast, light fly coaches from Edinburgh to London via Newcastle, York and Grantham, run by James Dun, at the Cowgate Port. The entire journey, which began at 2am from Edinburgh, took four days. On wheels devoid of rubber tyres.

By 1820, powered by war, communication and in particular the Royal Mail had hugely improved. During William's lifetime, war and the steam engine speeded up travel to an extent unimaginable to the previous generation. Ten years before William died, the new train service to London took less than ten hours – not much more than when I first went from Glasgow to London in 1957, on a train packed with soldiers on National Service, and made up of battered pre-war coaches with their deco seat covers and magnificent steam engine. In 1957, I had the advantage of knowing that the times on British Railways' timetable would not vary as we travelled. It was not until 1880, that an act to unify railway time received Royal Assent, and not until four years later, at the International Meridian Conference, was agreement reached that the Greenwich Meridian would be the common zero of longitude and the standard of time-reckoning throughout the world.

There is no firm evidence that William made the same journey to London, nor any that he went to mainland Europe. He would have been a very unusual bookseller had he not. But he *was* unusual and his brother was often in London. Perhaps William felt no need. Or perhaps he had many visits abroad. Or it may be that he was prevented. A large part of William Whyte's life was played out against war. He was three when the American War broke out. France and Spain and then the Dutch joined in against Britain until, in 1781, an exhausted Britain negotiated peace. William was seventeen when the French Revolution took place and twenty-seven when Napoleon staged the coup that led to the war bearing his name, which lasted from 1803 until 1815, with a breather between 1807 and 1809, and the complication of another American War from 1812 to 1815.

When Britain finally appeared to have achieved peace, William was forty-three – but the following years were marked by domestic strife as the British state re-worked the legal definition of treason and nervously suppressed dissent – and by a stream of conflicts, sometimes known as Queen Victoria's little wars, all over the globe, as the British Empire conquered, and plundered. At the far end of William's long life, the last three years were marked by the Crimean War. Only for a few years in the 1800s, was Britain formally at peace. His final days must have been clouded with apprehension about the effect of the 1857 Indian uprising on his friends and family in the Scottish Mission in Calcutta.

In 1824, when David bought 10 Scotland Street, William bought number 12, a far larger affair, and a portion of number 14. He was doing well, and buying carefully. He had spent more than two decades improving his shops in South St Andrew Street and his standing in the city. In 1824, we find him taking in donations for the Edinburgh Society for the 'Mitigation and Eventual Abolition of Negro Slavery'. As an active evangelical Christian, he would have believed that no man could own another. The argument rested on the individual soul – though of course there was no mention of the female soul, even, it would appear, among the many forceful and efficient women who campaigned vigorously against slavery. Their part in eventual abolition was not much discussed until, in 1992,

Clare Midgely wrote *Women against Slavery*. Women were excluded by Wilberforce, who feared they would be more radical. He was right. In 1824, for example, Elizabeth Heyrick published *Immediate Not Gradual Abolition*. There were many women's abolition groups, and the boycott by British women of West Indian sugar may have played a small part in aiding the long and arduous efforts of the enslaved to free themselves. Uprisings and resistance in the West Indies and the fall in commodity prices were fast producing a situation where the economic arguments for ending slavery were compelling. William would find himself considerably better off.

TEN

WHYTE AND COMPANY, GEORGE STREET

William's final move occurred in 1826. Though only a few hundred yards in distance, it was a big step up. He took his business to the spacious house at 13 George Street. Father and brother moved with him. By 1832, William Whyte and Company were *Booksellers to Her Majesty*, in 1839, *Booksellers to the Queen Dowager* and, in 1846, *Booksellers to the late Queen Dowager*, and finally, in 1850, *Late Publishers and Booksellers to Queen Adelaide*.

Here on George Street, quintessential Georgian Edinburgh – though at the slightly less respectable east end – having bought the building, William also set up home.

Number 13 George Street now houses a fairly undistinguished office block. Contemporary etchings, however, show a fine Georgian house. In William's will, he detailed the facilities provided by Thomas Heriot, builder. There was a dining room, a drawing room and eleven smaller rooms; a kitchen, a cellar and a back ground, which he has enclosed and on which he has put 'other conveniences' – one hopes a water closet was among them. William converted the dining room into a large shop with a back shop. He turned the under or sunk rooms, i.e., the basement, into warerooms, accessed from the sunk area at the front, but also from the lane to the side, where one might enter by appointment. From these warerooms an internal stair rose to the shop and the upper part of the house which he used as a dwelling of ten rooms, with a separate entry from George Street. He took time to tell us that there was communication with the common sewers. By now, William, aged fifty-four, was clearly a person to be reckoned with.

He had brought together his home, his partnership with David and James, his shop, his warehouse, premises to conduct his Bible classes, and his circulating library which seems to have been mostly run by his father James. James, according to the Post Office Directory of 1832, was also trading in books behind number 13, in one of the oldest buildings in the area, Rose Court. It dates from 1767, and was the first house built in Edinburgh's New Town. James Craig himself appears to have laid the foundation stone of Rose Court, in what was essentially unbroken ground. Thanks to an alteration plan registered with the Dean of Guild Court in 1819, it is very easy to imagine James entering and leaving this pleasant building, provided for his use by his eldest son. Now called Thistle Court, it is externally very little changed.

The Whytt library was one of many. In the late 1820s there was a circulating library on almost every major street of the New Town and some had several. Prominent among these, was Mr Chambers' Library at 48 Hanover Street. A borrowers register has survived and been georeferenced onto John Ainslie's map of the Old and New Towns of 1804. There, I found that Mr Paterson of 1 Scotland Street was interested in Napoleon, and Mr Singer of 16 Scotland Street, he who read *Flirtation* books 1,2 and 3 by Lady Charlotte Campbell Bury, subscribed for new books at a slightly higher than base rate. At 12 St David Street, John Lewis Balfour was reading *The Children of the Abbey*, a gothic horror by Regina Maria Roche, while, up at the Castle in Fortress House, Mrs General Hay took the *Quarterly Review*. There were as many women subscribers as men, and they read more books. The women with Lady before their names read by far the most, followed by Mrs John Boyce of 41 Queen Street, but she was in the book trade in her own right. These libraries, part of everyday life in their time and setting in Edinburgh's wealthy New Town of the late 1820s, are an index of the Capital's thriving, outward-looking intellectual life.

William's business survived the dip in the fortunes of the book trade in the mid-thirties, presumably because of his diversified income streams. Others were not so fortunate. On 27 January 1833,

William Blackwood, bookseller and publisher of *Blackwood's Magazine*, wrote to his son in Calcutta bemoaning that the Government Ministers were ruining the country with their revolutionary methods. Ten days later he wrote again, saying that booksellers were never worse off in his recollection. William, however, appeared to prosper. There is no detailed record of how he ran his business, one of 105 such businesses in the mid-1830s. Living over the shop, our William no doubt kept long hours.

Municipal reform of 1833, which enfranchised 5000 of Edinburgh's 137000 citizens, changed a Council hitherto dominated by the great and allegedly good. On Wednesday 29 October 1834, a few weeks after his father James' death, *The Scotsman* printed a letter addressed to William Whyte and two others asking them to put themselves forward for election to the Town Council. Eighty men, including D.K. Whytt and Lindsay McKerry of 26 Dundas Street, an address at which we lived for some years in the beautiful, light-filled, top flat, signed the letter. William was 'gratified'. He became a Councillor and added that responsibility to his many others. At the tail end of 1834, the Rev Dr Chalmers, a founding father of the Free Church, in terrible writing, reminded William that he had entrusted to him and Mr Blackwood a proposal to be put to a meeting at the College. Would they please let him know the result? He signs off, 'Ever believe me , my dear Sir, Yours most Truly'.

On George Street, William Whyte and Company continued to publish and print many books for the church and churchmen. Among them, *Sermons by Thomas Snell Jones DD Minister of Lady Glenorchy's Chapel Edinburgh*. It was published on the instruction of the congregation.

Lady Glenorchy was born in 1741 in Galloway. After her husband's death, she devoted the next forty-five years to the evangelical cause. She built chapels in Scotland and England, giving a pulpit to Presbyterian, Episcopal and Methodist clergy alike. In 1772, she founded and paid for Lady Glenorchy's chapel in Edinburgh. Alexander Kincaid, in his *History of Edinburgh from the Earliest Times to the Present Day*, described a plain, lofty, oblong stone building with two galleries round three sides. It held 2000 people, with room in the middle for several hundred of the poor who did not pay. Though founded as part of the established church, it doggedly maintained its independence and in 1843, the congregation aligned with the Evangelicals and left the Church of Scotland.

The basic premise of the Church of Scotland, however it plays out in practice, is equality before God. Congregations decide who to call to the ministry of their church. The governing body was, and is, the annual General Assembly of all the ministers, who elect a Moderator. Adherence to this non-hierarchical arrangement, as various kings and their generals attempted to impose other structures, had caused much death and misery over the years. By the early 1800s, the practice of a landowner or member of the titled classes appointing ministers, known as patronage, had grown, and a section of the Church wanted, at the least, to be able to veto a patron's appointment. In 1842, William printed a long, detailed letter by George Douglas Campbell the 8th Duke of Argyll to his fellow Peers on the urgent need for a consideration of constitutional law with regard to the Church. The 8th Duke was Charlotte Campbell's nephew and a liberal Whig politician who was concerned to hold the church together. He wrote in vain.

Proponents of the veto took to the civil courts who ruled against them. The question was taken to the Church's Assembly, who voted it down. The response of around a third of the ministers, at the General Assembly of 1843, which met in St Andrew's Church, next door to William's shop, was to remove themselves and to form a Free Church. This event had a huge impact on church and civic life – not only in Scotland but for missionaries abroad. For the dissenting ministers, it meant forfeiting homes, stipends and churches. An extraordinary fund-raising effort replaced homes and churches in a relatively short time. A great deal of the money came from plantations in the southern part of the United States, where Presbyterianism was strong. The contributions from these owners of enslaved people led to a campaign whose slogan was 'Send Back the Money'.

Lady Glenorchy's congregation left the site of the future Waverley Station in 1844. Most accounts say that the move was to make way for the North British Railway Company, but, in fact, the Church of Scotland won a dispute over ownership of the building and booted them out. William and his brethren camped in various friendly churches until they settled into new premises funded by William, next door to his property on Greenside Place.

This church had a simple, spacious, classical interior, with a gallery carried on cast iron arcades. The land falls steeply away at the back, from Greenside Place down to Greenside Row, before it rises steeply to the top of Calton Hill. This arrangement gave Lady Glenorchy's church several storeys of basements. The church remained in use – and I remember it well, though I only entered it for up-market jumble sales – until 1978, when the congregation united with a nearby church. The building lay unused until the front façade, which couldn't be tampered with, became part of the Omni Cinema Complex. I pass it almost daily and wonder what William would have made of it. In his will, William directs that the painting of himself gracing his drawing room – which Lady Glenorchy's church commissioned and paid for – should immediately be returned to them. I've been trying for quite some time, without success, to find this portrait which hung in the prayer room. But after William's death, the church combined with another, twice, the latest being the Hillside congregation. The good folk at Hillside have been unendingly helpful, but of the portrait there is as yet no trace. My eternal gratitude would be due to anyone who can identify the hiding place of this portrait. How I would love to see his face.

For now, let's return to the books William Whyte and company published and sold. Above my desk in my office, there's a framed receipt.

On 30 January 1836, Mrs Leckie bought from William Whyte and Company a large scrapbook, and, on 24 February, two copies of *The Peacock at Home*. Mrs Leckie's receipt is signed by William Kennedy, a bookseller in William's employ and a trustee of his will. This is interesting, but what made me part with more than I could afford, to a specialist bookshop in London, was the engraving of William's shop and home. There it sits, east of St Andrew's Church, belching smoke. I am delighted with it.

The Peacock at Home was printed and re-printed throughout the nineteenth century. It was written by Catherine Ann Dorset née Turner, and was a direct sequel to *The Butterfly Ball*. A digitised copy published by Charles Tilt and company in 1831 can be found online. An *At Home* was a feature of British society from the mid-eighteenth century to the late nineteenth, and was a reception for persons to whom the owners of the home had intimated they would be in to receive visitors who would be served refreshments. *The Peacock* is throwing a party.

However pleasing, *The Peacock At Home* was not published by William. His output is made up of sterner stuff. By 1815, music scores had all but disappeared from his repertoire. In 1816, he published *A treatise on celestial and terrestrial globes containing the rise and progress of geography and astronomy – for youth of both sexes*. Both Sexes. For the time, this is unusual, but perhaps not with regards to William.

Books often had multiple publishers and William was part of a network stretching across the land. In 1828, for John Abercombie M.D., he published *The Culture and Discipline of the Mind Addressed to the Young*; for the Reverend Donald Fraser, *Sermons on the Method of Salvation*; for John Alton, *Eight Weeks in Germany: Comprising Narratives, Descriptions and Directions for Economical Tourists*, in which the traveller is cautioned to be neither too suspicious nor too saucy, and is advised to carry solid English gold sovereigns. Whyte also published the heartfelt, but extraordinarily turgid, *A Memoir of Mrs Margaret Wilson of the Scottish Mission, Bombay*, penned by her grieving widower, and *Observations on the prevalence of epidemic fever in Edinburgh and Glasgow*, by Robert Deuchar, which, along with the work of Henry Littlejohn, Edinburgh's first Medical Officer of Health, brought to the fore the connection between poverty and disease. With Longman, William published books about Edinburgh with guides to amusements, curiosities and remarkable objects, and *Modern Athenians. A Series of Original Portraits of Memorable Citizens of Edinburgh* by John Kay.

In the main, he published sermons, sacred texts and exegeses. There was *A Vindication of the Religion of the Land from misrepresentation and an exposure of the absurd pretensions of the Gareloch Enthusiasts*. The Gareloch Enthusiasts was a group based around Helensburgh, near Glasgow. Their critics mentioned speaking in tongues and attempts at raising from the dead, and a good deal of scorn and ire was directed at young women whose minds had clearly been turned by some physical imbalance which needed correction. Whatever the truth of the matter, William was agin' them.

Dr Thomas Chalmers made his home in Edinburgh in 1828. He was a man of reforming social vision who wrote many books, often with very long titles, which William duly published. On 29 February 1828, he published *The Sin and Danger in Circulating the Apocrypha in connection with the Holy Scriptures*, and, thankfully, a *Brief View of Faith*. In 1829, he published *The Doctrine of Universal Pardon Considered and Refuted, in a Series of Sermons* and Andrew Thomson's *Sermons on Various Subjects*, and so on, and on, and on for nearly sixty years.

William was keen on conversion. In 1839 he published *Report to the Society in Scotland for Propagating Christian Knowledge of a Visit to America*, which had been undertaken with the object of converting 'Native Indians'. He also published works by Thomas Smith on theology, mathematics and the Zenana movement for the 'betterment' of women in India.

From 1850 till his death, William's company published for an organisation, founded by schoolmasters, whose aim was to make available a series of books characterised, they said, by simplicity of plan, scientific arrangement, religious tendency, and lowness of price. The authors undertook the work at their own risk and expense.

So far, so expected, but let's consider this: William also published Catherine Sinclair.

At the west end of Queen Street there is a monument, though not a statue, to writer Catherine Sinclair. This fact on its own makes the monument unusual. Apart from the two statues of Queen Victoria in Edinburgh, a city littered with huge statues of sometimes-dubious men in contrived poses and very odd clothes, there are only two statues of women – that of the Woman and Child in Festival Square, a memorial by Anne Davidson to the victims of apartheid, and the well-deserved statue of Helen Crummy, community activist, at Niddrie Mains Road. Neither is wearing outlandish garb and Helen, a small, determined woman, who changed the trajectory of many lives including to a certain extent mine, never struck a pose.

One of thirteen very tall children, Catherine Sinclair was born in Edinburgh in April 1800. Her father was Sir John Sinclair, politician, soldier, owner of a plantation and enslaved people in the West Indies and the instigator of *The Statistical Account of Scotland*. Catherine was his secretary from the age of fourteen. I'm indebted to Dr Diana Leat in the 2021 edition of the journal of the Old Edinburgh Club for an estimate of his character as a self-important bore who collected facts and gave unsolicited advice. Apparently, Sir Walter Scott considered him an unutterable idiot. However turgid his public persona, Sinclair ran a liberal, highly literate and happy household. Catherine's first works were children's books, noted for the absence of overt moralising. She appears to have been a lively young woman with a wide social circle, who was active in philanthropy, improving Edinburgh and the lives of its citizens, setting up kitchens for the poor and installing drinking fountains. Her books were popular, not just in the UK but also in America. William published many, including, in 1836 and 1837, her first novels, *Modern Accomplishments* and *Modern Society* which dealt unfavourably with pretentions of Edinburgh middle-class life and religious and societal constraints on women, and with female education. They quickly sold out and were reprinted several times. Sinclair's most famous work was *Holiday House*, published by William in 1839. It portrays a pair of anarchic children in a realistic light and made a great deal of money. I have a copy. It is a small volume, bound in embossed blue with gold lettering and embellishments, and was given, according to her flyleaf inscription, to Thomas John Dixon by his aunt, Christmas 1843. Catherine was a devout Episcopalian, which did not deter Free Church William. Did he just favour strong women with their own opinions? I like to think of him passing time with Charlotte Campbell and Catherine Sinclair in between his work and his devotions.

One curiosity is *The Bravery and Happy Death of James Covey*, published around 1820. Covey was a seaman much given to sin and blasphemy who, having found God, fought bravely at the battle of Camperdown and remained cheerful when, both his legs having been blown off, he had to undergo further amputation. He died happy some time later, praising God.

I was intrigued when I discovered that William published works of Francois Paul Emile Bois-Normand de Bonnechose of Versailles. De Bonnechose was a poet and historian, author of, *inter alia*, *Reformers before the Sixteenth Century Reformation* and *The Four Conquests of England*. Whyte published the English translation of the former. The answer as to why he published De Bonnechose, lies, as with many other facets of his life, in family. De Bonnechose was the husband of his niece, Charlotte Gourley.

In 1843, William donated seventeen books to the National Library of Scotland. Apart from a *Private Journal of an Expedition Up the Niger*, by Doctor William Simpson, they are all of a religious nature. The library also holds a collection of psalms and hymn tunes set to various airs, published by William Whyte at 1 St Andrew Street. This places the publication date sometime between 1799 and 1807. 'Praise is comely for the upright,' the front cover states. It was presented by Lady Dorothea Ruggles-Brise, in memory of her brother Major Lord George Stewart Murray, Black Watch, killed in action in France on 14 September 1914. Major Murray is commemorated on the La Ferte-sous-Jouarre Memorial, along with 3,379 other British soldiers whose bodies were not recovered. 'Praise is comely for the upright'.

William's devotion to his religion is manifest throughout his life. Apart from supporting his favourite societies and churches, he busied himself with welfare causes, including women who had fallen upon hard times. In 1837, at a meeting of the Society for the Relief of the Destitute Sick, of which James Gibson Thomson was an active member, he was unanimously elected gratuitous Treasurer – in other words, the position did not involve being paid.

In 1843, nearing the end of the 1841–1844 fever epidemics that laid bare the appalling housing and sanitary conditions of Edinburgh's less-fortunate, William gave rather testy evidence to the Poor Law Enquiry Commission for Scotland. It was chaired by Viscount Lord Melville, son of the controversial Henry Dundas whose intervention is held to be partly responsible for the abolition of enslavement being gradual, resulting in many thousands more being taken before the trade, though not ownership, was prohibited in the British Empire. The list of witnesses before his son Viscount

Melville's Poor Law Commission is a roster of the great and the good, with not a woman or a poor person among them. William's answers are short and to the point. Basically, he states his name and number. He wastes not a word and clearly will not speak of anything of which he does not have direct knowledge, or answer questions which require speculation. He must have greatly annoyed the Commission.

So must have Mr Ellice, MP. In February 1843, Hansard reports that: 'He, for his own part, had no belief in the efficacy of the Commission, or in any good that was likely to result from it.' His opinion was that the composition of the Commission was not calculated to produce an impartial enquiry report. Four of the seven commissioners were Scottish Landlords who were known to oppose improvement. The other three were ministers of the established church through whose hands passed all the money provided for the relief of the poor. They were unlikely to give up that power. There was no-one from a large town and no Dissenting Ministers.

The House of Commons heard him out and proceeded to talk about everything except the substance of Ellice's speech. One member blamed the former administration, representatives of whom were outraged and proceeded to blame the clergyman, whose champions blamed . . . and so on. Mr Ellice's objections disappeared in a mess of squabbling. One might have hoped for some improvement in almost two centuries.

In 1843, William, the bookbinder's son from Fife, is listed in a register of the Gentry at Kirkbrae Cottage, Liberton, the home he built for his final years.

On 4 April 1849, William advertised upwards of 1400 volumes of tales, novels and romances, chiefly half-bound in calf, which he was selling as one lot at the very-reduced price of £40 for cash. Catalogues were available at 13 George Street and could be posted to persons at a distance for one penny. Perhaps, some time after his father's death, William was at last disposing of his lending library. Over the years, his name was frequently to be found in the lists published in the *Caledonian Mercury* of benevolent contributions from Edinburgh's worthies. On 20 November 1854, the *Mercury* noted his donation to The Patriotic Fund, along with that of many women and also Hugh

Miller, the geologist who was very active in the early days of the Free Church and must have been well-known to our William. By this time, Britain was deeply involved in the Crimean War and the Patriotic Fund was needed.

In 1856, he lost David, his brother and partner and, in 1857, his widowed sister Grace, who had joined him at Kirkbrae. William died of jaundice on the afternoon of 5 May 1858. On 7 May 1858, the *London Gazette* published a supplement containing despatches received at India House about the Indian uprising and operations at Cawnpore and Delhi, with lists of the 'killed and wounded and persons murdered'. In the bottom right-hand corner of this supplement are death notices, including: 'At Kirkbrae, Liberton near Edinburgh, on the 5th Inst, William Whyte Esq, bookseller, in his 87th year.' As instructed, Alexander buried his uncle William in the Old Calton Burial Ground, in the lair he and David bought together, many years since, so that they might lie side by side.

A lair, I am surprised to hear, is a puzzling term to some. In Scotland, it bears the meaning of a grave or plot. I have the deeds to lair 2938 in Riddrie Park Cemetery, in Glasgow's east end, bought by my maternal grandfather in 1927 to bury his six-year-old daughter, dead of an infection now easily dealt with. 'Betty died in my arms in the Royal Infirmary,' he wrote on the back of her birth certificate. The Glasgow Royal Infirmary is a large east-end teaching hospital, founded in 1794. Through the nineteenth century, new buildings were added, hemmed in by ancient tenements, in which several sets of my ancestors lived cramped and mostly short lives. As a student, I saw the last of these homes with their grubby, resilient children, captured so memorably by the painter Joan Eardley. Over several summers, I was paid to be part of a medical experiment. I found the life of the Victorian hospital fascinating and helped out. Provisions came from the basements in close proximity to the morgue. The corridors were long, echoing and sepulchrally-lit and once, carrying a large tray of eggs, in haste to close the metal concertina doors of the ancient lift, I received a minor electrical shock. So did the eggs. Helping at Emergency on Saturday nights at the Royal in the 1960s, before the area around was cleared, was an education. My grandfather, having survived the walk home to the east end from Clydebank through its blitz, also died at the Glasgow Royal, his lungs destroyed by the poverty of his early life and the minerals he worked with on the Clyde. He, his wife and my mother are now with Betty in lair 2938, a few steps away from my other grandparents, and I am assured I have the right to join them, if I so wish.

In William's will and testament we find the causes and people closest to his heart:

> placing all my trust in the merits and satisfaction of Our Lord and Saviour Jesus Christ for the Pardon of my sins and Eternal Life I desire to devote to God, the God of my Salvation (by whose Care and protection I have been delivered from many Perils and Dangers) a portion of my means and estate to the following religious and charitable objects as a humble acknowledgement to him for the measure of prosperity with which he has been graciously pleased to Bless me . . .

His heart, I do believe, was, with a few salient exceptional moments, a warm and generous one.

His trustees were David, a bank manager, the minister of Lady Glenorchy's church, a bookseller, a merchant, a stationer and his friend and long-time solicitor, Joseph Liddle. His will speaks of a frugal, careful man who has accumulated a fortune. His manner of disposing of it was characteristic: well-thought-out, careful, cannily generous, occasionally tetchy and, for his time, disposition and place, decidedly eccentric. The unmarried eldest son with no issue of his own, he is revealed as central to the family's well-being. He, who in his lifetime may have travelled no further than Fife to Edinburgh, with the odd jaunt to Bo'ness and perhaps to London, had connections in Ireland, India, the US, Paris, Germany and to a sugar plantation on Nevis in the West Indies for which he received compensation for 190 enslaved people.

Yes. He is listed in the database of the Legacies of British Slave-ownership. From what I knew of him after many years worming myself inside his head, this was totally out of character. I had come to know a man, I had decided, who interrogated his every act and thought against a rigorous moral code, a philanthropic music lover and publisher who ran bible-classes, signed anti-slavery petitions, and who published *Slavery Condemned by Christianity*, a tirade from campaigner Andrew Thomson. This man was a beneficiary of the Slave Compensation Act? William's sister, Grace Whytt Gourley, and her daughters hold the key.

Admiral John Gourley's will, written in 1854 from his home in Norfolk Square, Portsmouth, appointed his friend and brother-in-law William Whyte and his beloved wife Grace as executors, and helps clarify William's inclusion in the Slave Compensation database.

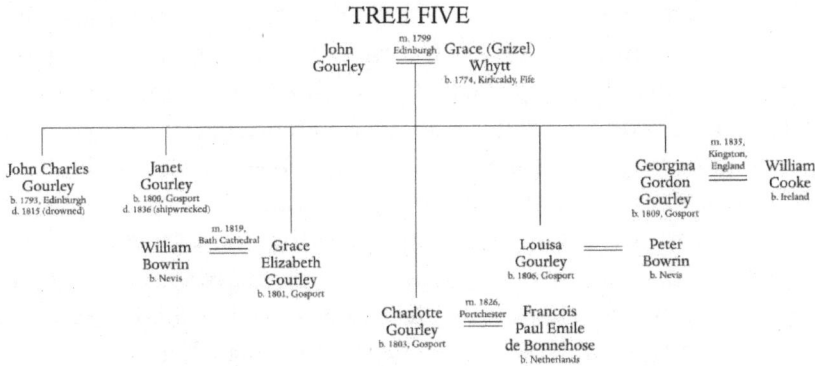

Grace and John had five daughters. The second, Grace Elizabeth, sometimes Eliza, was born in Gosport in 1801. Aged eighteen, in the Cathedral at Bath, she married William Bowrin of Paradise Estate on the island of Nevis. Louisa Gourley, the third daughter, married Peter Bowrin, ditto. They were sons of William Bowrin and Jane Butler, pillars of the economy and society of St Kitts and Nevis. Jane Butler's pedigree is extraordinary and evidences the spiderlike hold of the Butlers on Nevis from the seventeenth century. *Caribbeanna, Miscellaneous Papers on the West Indies* . . . lists Butler wills. Some of the children of the male Butlers and enslaved women are left small portions. One Butler woman casually bequeaths three enslaved persons, one each, to three young men when they attain the age of twenty-one. By the time the Gourley women arrived on the island, the Butlers were in decline, but still owners of many enslaved people.

Charlotte Gourley, the fourth daughter, was born in 1803 in Leith. *Blackwoods Magazine* reports that she was married on 28 May 1826, at Porchester, to M. Francois Paul Emile de Bonnechose, second son of Chevalier de Bonnechose, Secretaire Generale, Versailles. Charlotte's husband was born in Holland in 1801. Perhaps the family had hedged their bets during the 1789 revolution – but they were back in France during the Bourbon Monarchy in 1826, and presumably thriving. Then came the 1830 revolution, and the institution of the republic in 1848. Through all of this, de Bonnechose was a writer – who, as we've seen, was published by our William. He and Charlotte raised three children, one of whom became the Viscomptesse Portalis. Finally, *The Nautical Magazine* notes that the Gourley's youngest daughter, Georgina Gordon, married William Cooke of Ireland on 14 January 1835 at Kingston Church. I wonder where the Gordon came from. In his wanderings across the oceans, did John Gourley meet up with Captain Peter Gordon, or did they meet when Ann Gordon married into the London Whytt family?

Missing from the line-up of daughters is the eldest, Janet Davidson Gourley, born in 1800 and named after her grandmother. John Gourley, as was the convention, listed his surviving children, and so I did not know of Janet's existence until I read her grandfather James' will. Then, by chance, I came across *Clarendon* which left St Kitts and Nevis on 28 August 1836, laden with rum, sugar, molasses, coconut, peppers and cedar. On board were the captain, sixteen crew and ten passengers, including several children and Janet Gourley, returning home through gales in the Atlantic. In the English Channel, storms forced the ship towards Portsmouth. Her weakened hull could not withstand the stress and she appeared to explode, leaving a mass of shattered timber littering the sea and shore. The dead washed up on the Isle of Wight. Though, says Ken Phillips in his 1988 book, *Shipwrecks on the Isle of Wight*, Miss Gourley's body was taken by the sea and washed up at the end of her father's Portsmouth garden.

John Gourley left his household effects to his beloved wife, to be sold on her death, and the proceeds given to the children of Charlotte de Bonnechose and Georgina Cook in Ireland. His bequests to his daughters seem designed to protect them. He had lent money to both Bowrins and wished to ensure his daughters had the benefit, emphasising that everything left to Louisa was for her sole use, independent of the debts or arrangements of her present, or any future, husband. She must have the use of his property in Upper and Lower Canada and of his farmhouse there. Louisa took this offer up, left Nevis, and went with her only child, John Gourley Butler Bowrin, to Richmond, Ottawa, a town founded in 1818 on land taken mainly from Algonquin people. It is not clear if her husband joined her.

John Gourley had a respected and successful career, but losing his only son, whom we are told was a lad of great promise, and then his daughter Janet, and the varying fortunes of his far-flung children, cannot have made for an easy old age. After his death in 1854, his widow moved north to live with William. As William notes in his will, John had left Grace well-provided for. Her estate in Scotland amounted to £173 4/9, half of which was the value of her watches (gold and silver), her plate, body clothes, sundry trinkets and books. In England, she had £18 6/6, courtesy of her Admiral's widow's pension and the Royal Naval Annuitant Fund. There were no household goods. Her elder brother was once again looking after her and, as we see from his will, her children.

It's striking how many of his family and their adherents are indebted to this careful man. The trust estate of the late William Bowrin esq of Paradise on Nevis owes him a large sum but he knows that if he demands, it he will deprive his niece Grace Eliza of her sole means of support. Therefore, he grants her the right to manage the estate and use the profits – that is, as long as it's quite clear that it is his property, and she keeps it in good cultivation, and the works and machinery, the houses and buildings in good repair. She has to present meticulous and true accounts for inspection and must tell his trustees of any money she gets from her husband's settlements. Despite his peevish caveats, he is being magnanimous. Perhaps propelled a little by guilt over the money he received under the Slave Compensation Act, because of the mortgage he held on Paradise? A Mortgage on Paradise.

There's not much to be found out about the life of Grace Eliza on Nevis. A second wife, she was a widow for a long time. She does seem to have spent time in France where one of her daughters was born and also had a home at White Dale, a mansion in Hampshire. When she arrived on Nevis, in the outward part of the Leeward Island chain in the West Indies, presumably just after marriage, she would have found herself mistress of several hundred enslaved people. The island had been a popular stopping off point for ships on the way to America, even before it was claimed for the British crown in the early seventeenth century. It was a source of great wealth to the Empire, due to its place as a focus of trade in enslaved people and the high quality of the sugar. At one point, 20% of all British sugar came from Nevis. The French raided frequently in the first decades of the nineteenth century, and though Napoleon failed in his world domination project, he did fatally injure the sugar plantations. After the successful rebellion in formerly-French Haiti, he offered a huge prize to anyone who could devise a way of crystallising sugar from beets which could be grown in Europe, and, by 1801, an industrial process was extracting sugar from sugar beets in Silesia. In twenty years, it more or less killed the Caribbean trade and the prosperity of the Bowrins.

This prosperity was on the back of one of the most severe Caribbean plantation regimes. In particular, the notorious Huggins family were given to great brutality. In 1835, cholera hit Nevis – apparently arriving with a shipload of immigrants from England – and ravaged the island. A contemporary account regrets the cost of coffins and of burying the dead. The cemeteries were filled, and planter Peter Huggins and his sons buried their dead in Paradise. Grace Bowrin, quarantined in St Kitts, was unaware. When she found out, she was aghast that the Huggins had made of her estate a pestilential graveyard. None of her labourers had died of cholera. She hoped that the Huggins had noted the new sanitary rules and regulations, which required that corpses should be buried at a depth of at least six feet.

In 1833, the enslaved people on Paradise had achieved emancipation and become indentured labourers. That is, they were no longer called 'slaves' but must work, unpaid, for up to eight years, as apprentices to prepare themselves for freedom. To compensate the enslavers for their loss, the British Treasury raised £20m, £15m through a public loan contracted with a syndicate of financiers led by Nathan Mayer Rothschild and Moses Montefiore, and the rest by creating Government stock. A Compensation Commission made up of ten men was appointed and the scheme announced on 18 April 1834 in *The London Gazette*. Claimants had to fill in a form, which many apparently did with ill grace. Agents facilitated the transactions and took their fees. The largest were partners in London banks and merchant firms in the City of London, long involved in the business of enslaving.

In a feat of extraordinarily efficient bureaucracy by the Bank of England, whose Cashiers Department handled the payments, all claims were settled in four years. The Bank Archives hold ledgers listing the payouts in detail. The Legacies of British Slave Ownership project at University College London documents the extent of ownership in Britain and its wide geographical spread and has uncovered a disproportionately high number of recipients in Scotland, many in Edinburgh. While they were predominantly men, there were many women, profiting through inheritance or annuities, and many were absentees, managing Caribbean estates at arm's length through managers. However, a good number, like Grace Eliza, were resident, mostly on smaller estates.

On the island of Nevis, 304 awards, amounting to a total of £149611 13/5, were made to claimants for 8792 enslaved people. On the claim for Bowrin's Estate, recorded on 11 July 1836, there were 190 enslaved people and £3205 11/4 was paid. The award was split between William Whyte of Edinburgh and a member of the Butler/ Bowrin family. Peter Bowrin had tried to claim as tenant-for-life but the counter-claim of William Whyte as the mortgagee, in truth the virtual owner of the estate, prevailed. William received £2759 7/9 and invested most of it in the Glasgow Dumfries and Carlisle Railway. In doing so, he was joining many, many others who invested their compensation in the engines of the industrial revolution. The loan taken out by the state, and given to enslavers, was paid back by British taxpayers, initially, as there was no income tax, through consumption taxes. Like contemporary VAT, these hit the poor hardest. Our final payment was made in 2015.

Two weeks after William's death, the *Caledonian Mercury* published a despatch from Colonel Campbell anent the re-capture of Lucknow with little loss of life – though, disappointingly, he doesn't mention my great-grandfather who got a medal for it. The same edition carried the news that Mr William Whyte, publisher, has dedicated a large portion of his fortune to benevolent purposes connected with the Free Church – including the project of a Cowgatehead church at the Grassmarket end of the Cowgate, a few steps from the first Whytt home in Edinburgh. On 1 October 1860, the *Mercury* observed that the site, once occupied by an inn named for one of the King Georges, was being cleared. The *Mercury* comments: 'This inn sat above shops and mine host's business began on a landing leading to a pretty large house intricate in its arrangements and not all having natural light.' The writer goes on to speculate that,

> 'if the towering, precarious warren, now yielding to pick and shovel had a tongue, it would tell many tales of commerce and of journeyings, of carriers and equestrians and mounted aristocrats, but also of love and hate, of intrigue and gallantry, of deep carousing and mortified penance – nay of bloody frays – and it might be secret deeds of wickedness terrible in conception and results of legal strategy and citizen craft.'

As I write, a developer is busily gutting Cowgatehead church, and erecting around it an hotel which will stretch from India Buildings high up on Victoria Street down to William's church, only the façade of which will remain. The development lies at the back of the Carnegie-funded Central Library, set over many floors that drop from George IV Bridge all the way down to the Cowgate. The library is blessed with wide and tall windows. Carnegie himself laid the foundation stone in 1887.

William was very clear about his wishes. The church was to be plain and substantial with no folderols and dedicated to the needs of the population of one of the poor districts of the city of Edinburgh, in which he resided in early life. One third of the seats should be free, one third reduced and preference given to locals. Finally, I think, we come to the nub of the matter:

'Recommending to the trustees to make the first offer . . . to my nephew the said Reverend Thomas Smith as he has now been many years at Calcutta and the state of his health and other circumstances may render it desirable for him to return and perhaps to remain in his native country.'

Family. Thomas Smith did minister in the Cowgate, being particularly useful when the periodic epidemics of cholera hit the city. He was well-experienced, and worked with Henry Duncan Littlejohn in his efforts to improve sanitation. We will meet them both properly soon.

On 11 April 1862, the *Caledonian Mercury* reports the opening of the church, 'The principal feature . . . is the tower and spire which rises to ninety feet. Square at the base and transforms into an octagon intended as a bell-tower.' The marvel to me is the inserting of this narrow church between a tenement of nine houses and two shops on either side.

To his trustees, William gives care of his properties. First is the house and shop at 13 George Street. Then he lists his acquisitions as a young man. There is a piece of land on Greenside Row; a shop and cellars at 43 Leith Street, which became, not long after William's death, the Black Bull Tavern. This rock music pub, which is mercifully quiet of an afternoon, is on the turn from Leith Street to Low Calton, where a stair, which I use on occasion, running my hand over William's along the ancient handrail, leads down from Leith Street past the Black Bull. Kirkbrae Cottage, his two-storey, nine-room home, became St Hilda's School and is now 81 Kirkbrae. It is an impressive pile. Close by, he owned a stable, washing house and coach house, scattered parcels of land with houses, stables, byres, yards and enclosures, a park, extensive kitchen gardens. In the National Library of Scotland there is an 1855 map by David Chalmers which clearly shows how William Whyte of the Free Church, bought up land encircling Liberton Kirk, and its manse, which had remained with the Church of Scotland in the Disruption of 1843. I wonder how they felt about that.

There is also property on the High Street in Linktown of Abbotshall and the house at 3 Morton Street in Leith, bought at the turn of the nineteenth century by his father James. He notes that, with the house, he also has three cellars and right to the common stair and its pendicles and pertinents. No mention of the ish, however. Next is his share of the property of the late John Padon, distiller at Bo'ness, the land and property he had acquired with his brother David to help out their friend.

Finally, he comes to his Scotland Street properties: number 12, Joseph Liddle's home, 'consisting of a principal or street flat entering by a front door and two ground or sunk flats with the area before the said dwelling house and the four cellars and offices thereto.' He held the land behind the house, on condition that it was not built on. To date, my neighbours have put up only a small shed. At number 14, he owned all the property under the main flat, 'being the sunk and undersunk flats . . . consisting of a shop and dwelling house immediately below the said main flat and two small dwelling houses in the ground or undersunk flat . . .' These undersunk small dwellings are now in great demand as homes, studios and *pieds a terre*. With them came the cellars and rails, and again those privileges and pertinents. This time, he remembered free ish and entry. Then he noted, 'all other lands and heritable estate of every description which shall belong to me at the time of my death.' Where would these be?

I checked the Valuation rolls for 1855–56. In Timberbush, Leith, William owned a vacant courtyard house and washing house; a cellar, washing house and yard, tenanted by John Mason, a spirit dealer; and round the corner at 22 The Shore, overlooking the Water of Leith, the home of his tenant, Mr Mason. Number 21, he rented out to a B. Wood and Co, of Leith, who was an 'Eating House keeper'. He owned jointly, with a Mrs Robertson, the top flat at 2 George Place, the lower parts of which had belonged to his brother David and his kinsman James Aikman.

He had amassed quite an astonishing property empire.

Mrs Robertson is a mystery. In 1855, the house at 3 Morton Street, Leith, was rented by the Misses Robertson, and the millinery business of the Misses Robertson occupied the upper floors of his premises at 13 George Street for a time. I have found no familial, or indeed other, clue – though, given the strictures of his time, and reading between the lines, William valued and respected women. Who knows? Perhaps I wish him to have had lasting female friendships.

All his property at Bo'ness went to David and Ann Whytt, and thence to their heirs. A sum was kept in the hands of the trustees for his namesake, William Whytt, with power to cede control to him when they think best – 'by which arrangement I beg to express my solicitude for his welfare and best interests.' He's even generous to Mr Cooke in Ireland who seems to have been a wastrel. £50 is left to each of the daughters of the Padon family of Bo'ness, as a mark of his regard for their family, and to his niece, Margaret Whytt, his brother's natural child presently residing in Dalkeith, he leaves £50 and an annuity. Alison Kelso, his housekeeper, receives £20, while the shopmen and apprentices are given money for mournings. Thomas Smith gets his library of books and the clothes press in his east bedroom at Kirkbrae Cottage, and sister Grace, the pencil drawings – what were they of? – in his dining room. He wants his servants put into decent mourning, and a plain marble headstone erected in the Calton Old Burial ground. His portrait is to be sent to Lady Glenorchy's and that of his father given to David.

The limited inventory of his personal possessions is striking and brings to mind the phrase *conspicuous parsimony*. I fear I cannot remember its source. It fits William perfectly.

He now turns to using a large part of his fortune for the promotion of his faith and to good works. First, there's money for the education of poor children back in Kirkcaldy and Abbotshall, of any faith and regardless of sex. In Ireland, they must be Presbyterian. He is clearly concerned for the mortal souls of the French, and more widely of Europeans, for he leaves £200 for two colportaurs (i.e. peddlers of religious books) to distribute the holy scriptures on the continent of Europe for a period of two years. Oh, to be a time-travelling fly on the wall to see these itinerant salesmen, travelling through Europe, to persuade the masses that the Free Church of Scotland has the answer.

I remember, to my shame, in my smart-alec first year at university, countering my mother's tentative and deeply-troubled statement that all the other churches must be wrong and the Church of Scotland held the truth. I showed her a map of the world and Scotland's tiny place in it. It didn't convince her and would not have convinced William. He proceeded to leave yet more bounty to the Free Church, especially in the British colonies, and to the Free General Assembly for promoting Christianity among the Jews. They did have a bit of a thing about converting Jews, whom they seem to have regarded as not so much wrong, as strayed.

Turning his eye towards home, William ensures that there is money for the sustenance of ministers, for education and religious instruction in Scottish schools, and for Gaelic schools in the Highlands and Islands. The destitute sick, the poor in need of religion, indigent old women, and the Association in aid of the Moravian Mission were not forgotten.

After all these small bequests, he's digging deep. He has already funded a Native Christian Institute in Calcutta to help spread the Gospel in the East Indies. Now he asks that £3000 be invested in government stock or other security to fund two native youths and educate them to become Christian preachers. Youths studying at New College are also to be supported – but there follows a long list of conditions and rules to be adhered to and, moreover, this list has to be read to the patrons before the nomination of candidates and recorded in the minute books, or nobody gets anything. One feels for his trustees.

They must rent out his building at Greenside and use the proceeds to help deserving persons over fifty years of age of true Christian character who are not on the paupers' roll or receiving aid. A room at Greenside must be kept in good repair for his housekeeper's use, free of rent. More houses and apartments have to be provided at minimal rent to aged persons of true Christian character etc., etc . . . Perhaps he then realises what he's asking of his friends, as he says that if the trustees ever get tired of all this, they can hand over all the management to the Free Church.

We are getting near the end. He wants a neat, plain schoolhouse built to forever bear his name. Ancient and infirm ministers and widows and orphans of such ministers should be looked after; deaf blind and dumb children should be helped in their education. Of course, if the church decides to do all this good work itself, the trustees can wind up the fund and take the money back.

We are at the mopping up stage. All and everything else he dies possessed of has to be split equally between . . . (here he can't decide between 'between' and 'among'. I know his pain) among his nieces, all marital rights specifically excluded. He really had those husbands' numbers. Then, having nit-picked the detail to an excruciating extent, he more or less says his Trustees can use their discretion if circumstances change. After a list of caveats, he signs off.

Only to start up again a few months later. His nephew, William Whyte Cooke, had displeased him by some act or omission, so Cooke's debt is not forgiven, and moreover he must pay interest on the outstanding balance. Georgina had by now decamped to Clapham. Clearly, the Cookes were in a bad way, as William leaves extra sums to their three children, and more if they are in want. None of this help to his nieces, he repeats, is to get anywhere near husbands present or future. Distinctly grumpy. It didn't entirely work. Georgina's husband followed her to London and moved in.

William was eighty-five and watching his affairs like a hawk; the detail is extraordinary. There follow impenetrable provisions, moving small funds from one category to another. He signed the alterations, subscribed by Joseph Liddle, in the presence of two of his clerks.

There's a final, final thought, sent by letter from 13 George Street, to Rev Davidson of Lady Glenorchy's Church, on 14 September 1857, in which Whyte asks his trustees to ensure that when the school is built, finished and opened, his back-up trustees, Mr William Brown esq, Surgeon of Dublin Street and Dr John Coldstream, are given use of it when it is not occupied by masters and scholars. Brown lived out his days at 25 Dublin Street, a rather fine ground floor Georgian home. He died there in 1887 at ninety, having appeared in the record only fleetingly when he was a pall-bearer alongside JG Thomson at the funeral of a Free Church worthy. I wonder if he ever did use that schoolroom.

John Coldstream, William's last doctor, is more interesting. He was born on 19 March 1806, in Leith, and studied medicine at Edinburgh University where he became interested in natural history, and formed a close friendship with the radical materialist, William Alexander Francis Browne, who is celebrated as an asylum reformer, although his devotion to phrenology might give us pause. Browne suggested that insanity was a consequence of the industrial revolution and that the higher incidence in women was a result of inequalities and poor education. I think he may have had a point. He was also an atheist who believed that the mind, far from being a gift from God, was merely a function of brain activity, and advocated the overturn of the church, the monarchy and the aristocracy. Browne was perhaps not the ideal friend for the deeply Christian Coldstream, who was tortured by his failures of character and faith, and who noted in his diaries that he was struggling with corruption, desire and lustful imaginations.

Browne introduced Coldstream to agnostic Charles Darwin which may not have helped. Coldstream proposed Darwin for the Plinean Society, where Darwin announced some of his first scientific discoveries. They became close friends. Together they would trawl the shores of the River Forth in search of marine invertebrates. Coldstream suggested reference books for Darwin's Beagle expedition, and the method of oyster trawl for marine organisms that Darwin took up and used. In his autobiography, Darwin described Coldstream as a prim, formal, highly-religious and most kind-hearted man, who published some good zoological articles. However, though he led a blameless life, his scientific bent and materialist views were deeply troubling to his faith.

Coldstream married Margaret Menzies, with whom he had ten children, while working among the poor of Leith and helping found the Leith Infirmary and the Gayfield Square Home and School for Invalid and Imbecile Children, run by Dr David Brodie, who lived in William Whyte's Kirkbrae Cottage after William's death. Coldstream died on 17 September 1863. All this can be gleaned from a respectful biography, entitled *Dr J Coldstream, the Christian Physician*, by no less a luminary than John Hutton Balfour, Regius Keeper of the Royal Botanic Gardens, Edinburgh.

I'm struck by this instance of William Whyte – the man from an old Edinburgh world, whose particular character I feel I have some handle on – knowing, trusting and appointing as a backup trustee, a much younger, forward-facing, medical man, with very radical modern views and even more radical friends, who was tortured by religious doubt. But then, William did constantly surprise me.

His last recorded thought is for Alison Kelso, his housekeeper. His grammar falls down in this last sentence, but all the indications are that he was hale, hearty and cogent. Five months later he developed jaundice, suffering for only five weeks, and died at Kirkbrae. His death was certified by Coldstream, and by his nephew Alexander Whytt who oversaw his removal to Old Calton Cemetery. Alison Kelso moved into one of his Liberton cottages and was joined there by her niece, Allison Simpson. I was pleased that she would not be alone. Miss Kelso died, aged eighty-five, in 1876. No doubt tutored by William, she made a will, leaving a considerable sum and investments to Allison Simpson – and here is the rub – or Wilson, now residing with her blacksmith husband, at Blueskin, Otago, New Zealand.

The National Registers of Scotland, Scotland's People division, are endlessly helpful. When I first identified William's will, I found myself unable to download it. The explanation was that, since this will was extraordinarily long, it had to be delivered as an email attachment. In my experience of wills, this one is unusual in its length, its scope, and in the way it delineates a life and character. William Whyte emerges, a pious bachelor, connected across the globe by ties of family, benevolence, friendship and belief. He was a complex, exacting, and probably difficult man of energy and courage. I should like to have known him.

Before we leave William, we should pay some attention to his friend Joseph Liddle.

Joseph Liddle lived at 12 Scotland Street, next door to number 10, from soon after they were built until his death. He attended to William and David's legal business, saw the brothers into their graves and administered their wills. On William's death, he listed for sale in the *Edinburgh Evening Courant* William's extensive list of properties. Two months later, he was advertising Kirkbrae, 13 George Street and 12 Scotland Street again, to be sold at auction at Messrs Cay and Black's rooms in George Street at a greatly reduced upset price. Later in the year, Kirkbrae Cottage is re-advertised at a further reduction. I have no idea why these properties did not readily sell. 13 George Street was sold in 1858 to the Clydesdale Banking Company, and smartly sold on to the Royal Insurance Company, who proceeded to embellish the building with ironwork and ornaments in cement. In 1898, the Company replaced number 13 with a six-storey tenement topped with a triangular gable, on which stood a draped female figure flanked by two putti. I fear 1898 must have seen some grave-birling in Old Calton Cemetery . . .

On 15 October 1858, at 13 George Street, William's books were sold. The sale lasted from 11am until 4pm and all stock was disposed of. The *Courant*'s reporter commented that the competition was spirited and good prices obtained from buyers from as far afield as London and Belfast. On 28 June 1861, the sale of William Whyte's interest in the Commercial Bank of Scotland, the Caledonian Fire and Insurance Company and the Edinburgh Gas Company was announced by Joseph Liddle.

Forty-two years previously, young Joseph Liddle, solicitor of Bank Street on the Royal Mile, had married Mary Ann Bogue. Together they would have at least ten children, few of whom reached adulthood. His elder sons became a banker and an accountant, and the next three, clerks. In 1833, his son, William Whyte Liddle, named for his father's great friend, died of influenza, aged seventeen, at 12 Scotland Street. Mary Ann died when her youngest son was three. Joseph had his work cut out. He died in 1864 of hepatitis and diphtheria at 12 Scotland Street. The certificate was signed by his son-in-law. Andrew Howden, who lived in the basement at number 12. Liddle, a man who had spent so much time meticulously sorting out the property and estates of others, died intestate. His meagre belongings were inventoried by his daughter, Margaret, who was about to lose her home. The estate came to just over £500, a great deal of which was sums owed from clients.

After Liddle's death, William Whyte's properties at 12 and 14 Scotland Street were sold off by his remaining trustees to a Miss Agnes Bell of Glasgow. She rented number 12 to a solicitor, and the shop and house at 14a and 14b to a tinsmith, a cooper and a coach hirer. The remaining trustees, and their successors, went on to oversee the elaborating results of William Whyte's will down through the generations.

In 1925, Madame la Comtesse Portalis, born Alice Caroline de Bonnechose, sought the help of an Edinburgh lawyer to establish her as the executrix of her mother, Madame Charlotte Gourley or de Bonnechose. The matter in question was one third of one seventh of the trust estate of William Whyte, registered in the books of council and session in 1858. This included very healthy UK and USA stocks and railway shares. Alexander Henderson Whytt, trustee of last resort, no doubt with the aid of the unfortunate Mr Wark, had proved himself diligent beyond the grave. The last document I found which mentioned William's will is among the paperwork involved in the eventual sale of 10 Scotland Street. Mr William Whyte had a very long arm.

ELEVEN

GRACE AND HER MISSIONARY

Grace Whytt was born at 2 George Place, on 1 April 1815, a few short months before the Battle of Waterloo signalled an end to the wars which had occupied her father for so long. She was ten when – with three older sisters and one younger brother – she exchanged the noisy soundtrack of Leith Walk for the relative peace of 10 Scotland Street. In her short life, she had seen the death of a cousin, two of her infant siblings, her grandmother and her uncle Padon. From Ann and, probably, a Dame School, she would have learned to read and write. Perhaps, like her sister, she had some French. Certainly, she would have been tutored in music and art and needlework. Did her uncle William ensure that she had a ready supply of suitable reading and sheet music? When she was thirteen, Janet, her sister and almost certainly her room- and bed-mate, died. Soon after, her mother Ann gave birth to her last child, William, in the master bedroom, at the north-west corner of 10 Scotland Street. It is a friendly room, if chilly, with a green and quiet aspect: a good place for William to come into the world. At fourteen, Grace would have been expected to help out with him, and with the five-year-old Alexander. When she was nineteen, in 1834, her Aunt Janet and Grandfather James died within months of each other. In her young life, Grace must have spent long periods in black.

In 1835, she was twenty. Time for a woman of her status to marry. Her sisters, Marion and Wilhelmina, aged twenty-six and twenty-two, were presumably taking up whatever matchmaking attention there was going.

Meanwhile, down in Leith, an eighteen-year-old student, was lodging with his sister Mary, wife of John Kay, a schoolmaster in the burgh school, on Leith Links. Thomas Smith was the eighth of ten children of Jean Stodart and John Smith, the minister at Symington, a country parish in South Ayrshire where Thomas, at the centre of a large extended family, attended the parish school. In 1830, aged thirteen – a not uncommon age at the time – he entered the University of Edinburgh to study mathematics and physics, at which he was a bit of a prodigy. The family home was on Vanburgh Place close by William Whyte's adversary, John Thomson. On my way to visit my younger daughter, I pass Vanbrugh Place, a row of Georgian houses, plain-faced and relatively unscarred, whose front windows look over the western end of Leith Links. If I narrow my eyes, I can see him, a year or so older than my granddaughter, his young legs making little of the steep steps to the front door. From the drawing room window, his view would have been much the same as mine, save that my vantage point is a window on the top deck of a Lothian bus. It's a tranquil scene with games being played and dogs walked. From there, he would have set off up the Easter Road, as do I, and over Abbey Mount, down to where there would once again be a parliament a century and a half later, and up Holyrood Road and the Pleasance, or perhaps by the Cowgate to arrive at the University. Edinburgh is a city where, in many places, it is possible to walk with your ghosts.

Five years later, on holiday in Dunglass in East Lothian, Thomas wrote to Mary in Leith. He is very pleased with the 'habiliments', the clothes, she has sent. The two waistcoats are perhaps a little frivolous for one of his years and gravity. He is quarantined at the moment, as there is scarlet fever in the neighbourhood, and several neighbours have died. He writes that he is very impressed with the Bell Rock lighthouse, whose warning light had saved many lives on this terrible coast since it was completed by Mr Robert Stevenson. The lighthouse is the oldest surviving rock lighthouse in the British Isles and is indeed a wonder. Robert Stevenson wrote a detailed diary of its construction which is now available online, and it is a fascinating account of an extraordinary feat of engineering in the most rebarbative of circumstances, with some great drawings.

Stevenson commissioned JMW Turner to paint the lighthouse in a storm, which Turner did, basing his work on Stevenson's description. The National Galleries of Scotland, on occasion, hang the painting alongside those of the Turner Vaughan Bequest, which are shown only in the month of January, when light levels are low and the risk of damage to the delicate watercolours is minimal. Turner's Bell Rock Lighthouse, in its two hundred years, has aged little.

Thomas was intending to return to the west to see his family and was concerned that the recent storms had wrought havoc on the crops. Mary sent this letter on to her mother, Jean Stodart, who had been widowed the year before. It is perhaps no co-incidence that, in that same year, 1834, the bereaved Thomas switched to the study of divinity, under Thomas Chalmers, and met Chalmers' disciple, Alexander Duff, missionary in Calcutta. Both were to have a great influence on him. Thomas left his sister's home and moved to Great King Street, round two corners from Scotland Street, and joined the congregation of St Mary's parish church, just one hundred yards from Grace's front door. Whether they first met in this neo-classical church, with its landmark tall tower, I do not know. I hope they did. The 1824 interior, with its original pulpit and sweeping pews and gallery, is quite beautiful, and now complemented by Ben Tindall's fine modern extension.

In Thomas' long-ago youth, the Church of Scotland was much concerned with spreading the Word, and in 1824 had decided to set up an educational mission in India. Unusually, it was endorsed by both the moderate and evangelical wings of the church, which were normally to be found at war. They did agree that there were problems. There was a danger that recruits might view the mission field in a romantic light, resulting in a high rate of desertion. Also, missionaries were in short supply and many thought that missionary work should concentrate on heathens at home. Midlothian was held to be in great need of conversion. It's not clear what the good people of Midlothian had done to deserve this attention.

The prevailing moral panic over the alliances of East India Company men with Indian women was also felt in the church. Before Alexander Duff sailed to Calcutta in 1830 to set up the Church of Scotland's Institution, he was advised to 'congenialise' with a woman. The resultant union, with Ann Scott Drysdale, lasted forty years until her death. On their initial voyage out, they survived two shipwrecks. Much later, this was attributed by one of Duff's colleagues to the intervention of God, who needed Duff to reach India. He was joined at Calcutta by the Reverends Ewart and McKay, and the three set about converting India, using the innovative technique of teaching only in English. Many languages were considered but English was judged supreme, as was scientific education, which would destroy what they regarded as 'error-ridden' Hinduism. The tendency of scientific education to produce atheism, however, must be countered, they believed, 'by its interpretation through Christianity, as the history of the visible handwork of God'. In all their deliberations, I see an underlying belief that the Scottsh way of life and understanding of the universe, was vastly superior to anything to be found in India, or indeed, it would appear, anywhere else at all.

In Edinburgh in the spring of 1839, two things happened in quick succession. On 7 March, Smith was ordained by Alexander Duff in St Andrew's Church, next door to Uncle William's home and shop. Duff's sermon, published as the *Qualifications, Duties and Trials of an Indian Missionary, being the Substance of Services held at the Ordination of the Rev Thomas Smith*, is held in all the larger libraries still, is available to purchase in paperback, and regarded by those in the know as one of the most significant sermons ever preached in Scotland. According to the *Home and Foreign Missions Record* of February 1839, Smith was amply suited to be a missionary and had been called on, very early in youth, to break the ties of home and country and 'amid perils and privations manifold, to bear the Redeemer's Cross'.

Ten days later, Grace Whytt left 10 Scotland Street, walked through the lane to St Mary's church, and married the newly-minted Reverend Thomas Smith, presumably having taken account of the manifold perils and privations which would be her lot. She was twenty-four and he was twenty-two. This pair, whom we would now regard as barely out of childhood, packed their trunks, fastened them with iron hoops and, as his mother reported in a letter to her daughter Catherine, set out in fine weather, at 4 a.m. on Wednesday 27 March, on their long journey to India.

At first, I assumed they accompanied Dr and Mrs Duff as they braved the relatively new overland route. The Duffs' journey began by mail coach and continued by railway to London. This cost £15 10/-. The crossing to Antwerp cost £4 4/-. Marseilles to Alexandria cost the church a whopping £43 15/1. Unfortunately, the onward travel costs from Alexandria to Bombay is not itemised, but the route is well-documented. From Alexandria, the Duffs travelled by barge down the Mahmoudieh Canal to Enfe, thence up the Nile, first by Nile felucca, then on a small paddle boat, and finally, from Cairo's port to the city itself, by donkey. The journey had been devised as a three-month mail route, from the heart of the Empire to India, by an inventive ex-soldier named Waghorn. He failed rather disastrously but, by 1839, he had provided a decent Cairo rest house for the Duffs before they set off across more than eighty miles of empty desert. If normal practice was followed, Duff travelled by camel, while Anne was consigned to a rickety sand-cart. From Suez, a steamer carried them down the Red Sea to the Indian Ocean. With luck, they arrived there during the few weeks when it was possible, safely, to make the journey across the ocean to Bombay, the modern Mumbai, and then onward to Calcutta.

Dr and Mrs Duff's expenditure, including the sea passage from Bombay to Calcutta, was £374 4/7. The Church of Scotland papers in the National Library tell us that Duff's salary was £300 per annum. From this, he must find the rent for his bungalow, cover domestic expenses and pay a Mrs Campbell for the upkeep of his children in Scotland. The Reverend McLean was remitting £120 to his father for upkeep of his children. Did Ann and David receive a similar stipend for John and Annie at 10 Scotland Street?

Duff's £52 per quarter to Mrs Campbell may have decreased in 1841, when their five-year-old daughter, Anne Jemima, died at 12 Royal Terrace, a grand, four-storey home, part of a long Playfair terrace. Anne Jemima was buried in the South Leith churchyard. The Church of Scotland paid for medicine, for her deathbed and funeral expenses, and Mrs Campbell's mourning and attendance. £14 14/- was paid to a Mrs Trotter for the funeral. Anne Scott Duff was in India when her daughter died, and when she returned to Scotland to visit the grave of her child, she had to enter the graveyard of a Church of Scotland from which she and her husband had alienated themselves.

The Church of Scotland hedged its bets, as far as banking was concerned. The Bank of Scotland, the Royal Bank of Scotland, Coutts, the Commercial Bank, the National Bank, the Edinburgh and Leith Bank, the British Linen Company, of which JG Thomson became a director along with other men of the Free Church, and, on occasions, William Forbes and Company, who could deal in rupees, were all engaged in its service. Teachers were paid quarterly, in arrears. However, in 1840, Thomas Smith was receiving his £300 salary monthly, on account. The couple must have had cashflow problems. The Rev George Smith, at a celebration of Thomas held in 1899, commented that the missionaries, in Thomas' time, received starvation allowances. The salary of £300 does put David's wedding gift to Grace of £200 in a favourable light.

In a letter from Thomas to one of his sisters, I read that he and Grace had taken the long route round the Cape of Good Hope, landing for some time at Mauritius, before sailing on to Calcutta. This lengthy, and reportedly boring, voyage was considerably cheaper than the overland route.

There is a contemporary account by the writer and diarist Emily Eden, who sailed round the Horn with her sister Fanny and brother George, Lord Auckland, the new Governor General of India. Emily was appalled by the incessant loud noises, though she did enjoy watching whales, porpoises and other sea life. She remarked that the midshipmen seemed well-cared for, though one was dying of decline in his hammock, and she enjoyed a performance of Goldsmith's *She Stoops to Conquer*, already sixty years old, and a classic. She was much comforted by her brother. George went on to oversee what is generally regarded as the worst defeat the British Army ever endured, until the fall of Singapore during the Second World War. The rout took place during the first of several Anglo Afghan Wars. George, who appears to have had little interest in Indian history or culture, was blamed for the disaster. He was replaced as Governor General, and returned to England to be rewarded, as is the way of things, with charge of the Admiralty.

In August 1839, the *Calcutta Christian Observer* recorded the arrival, after a journey of around five months, of Thomas and Grace Smith. In his letter of 24 August to his sister Katy, Thomas wrote little of the voyage, but seemed bemused by the fact that, though the weather was so good, Grace, whom he refers to as 'the Goodwife', was continually sick – and particularly had been sick a lot in the morning. She had been well, however, since they landed. In fact, Grace had spent almost all the voyage in the early stages of pregnancy. Clearly there were gaps in Thomas' considerable learning. Towards the end of my research, in the Lithographic Sketches of the Public Characters of Calcutta, I found a delicious sketch by Colesworthey Grant, of Thomas, with his customary elegant signature appended. He was, indubitably, a fine figure of a young man.

The pair lodged, initially, with Dr and Mrs Charles of the Scotch Church. Smith tells us that the climate was not so good as at home, but if one took care and avoided exposure, one might keep healthy, with the blessing of God. He believed they would be happy in Calcutta. He goes on to tell Katy that missionaries in India have very different experiences than elsewhere. 'The natives', he says, 'have so long been accustomed to look up to the Europeans . . . that they pay habitual deference to every person with a white face.' The ones he has 'most immediately to do with are well-educated and accomplished young fellows.' And, 'there is no heathen country in the world where more has been done by means of education in preparing . . . Christianity.' Thomas is so young, and so sure of himself.

But then the mask slips, and he moves on to a constant theme – the lack of letters from home. The couple had been so disappointed not to find letters waiting for them when they arrived. They had expected a packet. I am reminded that he is twenty-two and far from home. He finishes by asking his sister to remember that things that may seem humdrum to her are of particular interest to him at a distance of 15000 miles. Please would she write one or two long letters every month? The boy is homesick.

Grace had other matters to occupy her. On 21 January 1840, ten months after her marriage, she gave birth to her son John, named

Grace and Her Missionary

after Smith's father. She was far from her mother, in a strange land, with a new, young, husband and few familiar faces. It seems she managed well; perhaps better than Ann back in 10 Scotland Street, waiting for news, and unable to be at the birth of her first grandchild. I have been extraordinarily lucky in that.

Meanwhile, her husband, to his immense pleasure, had taken possession of a transit instrument, a small telescope used to observe the movement of stars. Perhaps, as a sleepless new father, he held his son while he scanned the skies above Calcutta. This may be fanciful – but perhaps not. His early letters show an active interest in his children, of whom he speaks lovingly. Not long after he arrived, he started a periodical called *The Telescope*, the fore-runner of the Scots College magazine. I note passing references, in reports, to the energetic Tom Smith – so Tom he was in Calcutta.

On 16 November 1840, Thomas writes to Katy again, scolding her for the irregularity of her correspondence, particularly after the death of their dear mother. He has had nothing since May from any of his sisters. He is only twenty-three, he has lost his mother, and he is hurting.

He ends with yet another plea for more letters. Could they not get together and write? It is so miserable when others talk of the letters they have received, and he and Grace have nothing. His letter is consigned to the post, to travel via Bombay and Falmouth to Libberton, Carnwath NB – North Britain.

In 1840 in the *Calcutta Christian Observer*, Thomas wrote his first article in favour of female education. He believed that teachers must gain access to the Zenana, the female quarters, to which all but the lowest class of women were confined. Biographies of Smith call him the Founder of the Zenana movement but it is more likely that the efforts of many groups, including women themselves, were in play.

Later that year, Thomas was crackling with indignation but clearly trying, if failing, to keep it light. 'My dear Katy, for some time past, to use the flowing language of this country, the rose of desire has been blooming in the garden of expectation to hear from you.' There are under-linings, ink smudges. His nib scores the paper. Did I say his writing is atrocious at the best of times? I have spent many hours on the brown scrawls spidering their way across creases and crumples. Worth every minute, when Thomas bares his soul. The rest of the letter is a bit of a rant. Katy will be surprised to learn he has two women servants, who spend three or four hours a day 'to produce one comparatively good child'. Grace has so much to do looking after the house, what with the 'extreme <u>dishonesty</u> of the servants, the <u>cheating and stealing</u>'. He is incoherent with rage. This is a fragment of a letter, and probably just as well.

In 1841, he became ill, and, on 7 December, he left alone on *Owen Glendower*, for Cape Town. He did not return until December 1842, a full year later. Cape Town was used as a refuge, where Scottish ministers could recover their health. The St Andrews Scotch Church there was the first to admit black South Africans and promoted the St Andrews Mission, to evangelise and educate which, as reported by the Reverend James Adamson, resulted in a 'barrier to the prevalence of Mohammedanism among the emancipated slaves.' Smith filled his time with the preparation of a geometry textbook, which he hoped would fill an obvious gap. The introduction is lucid and engaging, and, with the benefit of my 1950s Glaswegian state school higher maths, some of what follows is even comprehensible.

While at the Cape, Thomas delivered, from the pulpit, *Five Discourses, on the Christian's Patrimony*. I am persuaded by his common-sense and learning therein, then abruptly thrown into confusion by impenetrable Old Testament references, used to underpin his argument. His recourse to the New Testament fares no better. I was introduced forcibly to his conservative biblical faith over seventy years ago, and am grateful for my involuntary knowledge of the King James Bible, but I cannot penetrate Thomas' narrow, late-nineteenth-century mindset. I wonder what it was like to be married to a such man, so sure of himself and his rectitude – or to be his daughter.

Grace was pregnant when Thomas left and, in his absence, gave birth to a girl, named Annie after Grace's mother. Soon after Thomas returned, Grace was pregnant again.

In February 1843, Thomas wrote to ask what his people in Scotland are thinking about the Kirk. In May, the evangelical ministers would walk out of St Andrew's Church to form the Free

Church of Scotland. Ruefully, Thomas supposes that his family will all be on a different side from him. He was right, but would later find that the Whytts were with him. Things were in a bad state. 'What remains of the venerable Kirk of Scotland will soon become a mere tool in the hands of English politicians, who know little and care less about the feelings and principles of Scotsmen.'

His letter home on 9 August is sombre. Grace was expecting a baby in September, her third in four years. She had felt unwell for ten days, but they had thought nothing of it. At midnight on 27 July, Thomas sent for the doctor who gave Grace some opium. About three o'clock, a little baby was born. The child suffered convulsions for a whole day. Thomas wrote, 'It was very painful to watch but I do not suppose he was conscious of much pain.' Really? 'He was soon relieved,' wrote Thomas, 'and just at evening, he died.' The baby lies in the Scots Cemetery and is listed on the records there. His name was David.

Thomas then tried to find a way of reconciling this misery with his belief in a just and benevolent God. It's painful to read. He talks of his grief when his two brothers died. He reflects that he and Grace have much to be thankful for. Grace has been mercifully preserved. 'She has never had the slightest fever in the fever season, and for two or three days she has been sitting up the whole day. She is bearing up wonderfully well under her disappointment.' Disappointment. 'I trust it will prove a blessing to us both by teaching us how completely we are dependent upon the good pleasure of God for all that we enjoy.' And so on. I wonder what Grace thought of God's pleasure and the pain inflicted, not least, on her body. She had been constantly pregnant, or nursing, for four solid years, for one of which her husband was far from home.

However, added Thomas, 'you will be glad to hear that I have got quite well.' The doctor had repeatedly told him he would never be well in Calcutta, and that the rainy season would bring on his disease and kill him. But as healthy people fell, he became quite well.

Did he have malaria?

He switches pace, and writes that from his former letters Katy will not be surprised, 'that we have felt it our duty to join the Free Presbyterian Church. It was a sore struggle ... We shall write by

Express . . . to 10 Scotland Street and ask them to let you know how Grace is going on.' This will be the letter which lets Ann know that her daughter had laboured to deliver a baby which was premature and lived, in distress, only a short time.

A letter, which reached Calcutta on 22 January 1844, told Dr Duff that the Church of Scotland had invoked the law and stripped the Mission of everything. The missionaries had to leave their building, their library, their laboratories – but, unlike ministers back in Scotland, they did not lose their homes, which did not belong to the Church. The missionaries found premises in the homes of supporters, and, in time, built the Free Church Institution. A library was quickly donated and, no doubt to Thomas' relief, a Herschel ten-foot telescope was given to the mission by Mr Stewart of Moulin, Dingwall, Dr Duff's home town. Caroline Herschel was still alive. I wonder if they corresponded.

In April 1844, Thomas reported that Grace had lost all strength. She was pregnant yet again and spending much of her time on the sofa, fearing a repetition of the events of nine months earlier. Thomas says that she is not in bad health but 'only weakly.'

Once again, I reflect on the myth of the fragility of the Victorian wife, who forged her way around the globe, encumbered by clothes and customs, and made homes, babies, and sometimes businesses, for the Empire.

Early in Smith's career in Calcutta, one of his pupils noted that the sahib who taught mathematics never combed his hair and sometimes came to college with a shoe on one foot and a slipper on the other. He once fell into the Hooghly River. News reached the Institution that Tom Smith was drowned. It is recorded that Dr Duff and his staff were in tears, when Tom walked in the door. Unable to swim he had prudently lain on his back until a passing boatmen fished him out. There is no record of Grace's feelings about this scrape.

Tom made journeys to visit other missionaries. Once, returning from Madras and anxious to reach home, he jumped aboard a coasting ship manned by sailors who, as soon as the boat left shore, broke into casks of brandy and became roaring drunk. The boat reached Calcutta after seventy-two days instead of the regular seven to ten. I try to imagine Grace, at home, waiting for a husband who was more than two months overdue. She would have sought information from Madras, and found that he'd set off on a coaster, instead of a regular steamer – and disappeared. She must have assumed him dead and started planning a long widowhood, and return to Scotland.

Tom's love of family is patent. In late 1844, he writes to his sister to say that their eldest son, Johnny, must soon go to Scotland – and he is not happy. He asks Katy to send him a lock of each of her children's hair.

His next letter was sent from Baranagar, ten kilometres north of Calcutta, and the writing is now loose, flattened and very difficult to read. He launches right in with a fierce attack on his sister for not writing to him.

Nowhere in the surviving pages from the 1840s does he mention the births of David Whyte Ewart Smith, born 1847, and William Whyte Smith, Grace's last child, born in 1849. The main thrust is his need for news, and his interest in his nieces and nephews. By now, his handwriting has become jagged and near indecipherable.

Luckily, the writing in his next full letter, sent in 1851, is legible, and his tone is steady. Grace has not been well, but has managed to keep on her legs, and Davie and Willy are in great fettle, unlike so many European children whom their parents must watch, pining away, from day to day. He tells her that he does not want to impose – but will she please write? He sounds calm but weary. It is a long time since they came to Calcutta. 'We are now both getting pretty well up in years. People say that one year in India equals two at home and that would make me forty-five.' He is thirty-four. His hair is quite grey and people often comment on the change in his looks.

He has begun to sound very homesick. A year later, he wrote from Howrah to his niece Jeannie that if ever he came home, it would be his greatest pleasure to become acquainted with her – and with his own children, for Johnny and Annie were now in Scotland, and he was fearful that soon David would have to follow them home. Reading these letters, I am clear he was thinking about making up his mind to come home.

Smith returned to Scotland with Grace and their two younger sons in 1855. Ann and David at 10 Scotland Street were elderly and

David was ill. It was time for Grace to return home to see them, and to take over the care of her two older children. And indeed, to see her Uncle William, the bookseller, whose legacy was to give Grace some degree of comfort, beyond that afforded by Thomas' salary.

While Thomas was home, he arranged for William Whyte to publish *An Elementary Treatise on Plane Geometry, according to the method of Rectilinear Co-ordinates* and before he returned to India, he delivered an essay, *The Future of India*, which was published in *Essays by Ministers of the Free Church of Scotland*. Grace, meanwhile, set up home in Joppa, close by her parents. She was already, at forty-one, beset with the rheumatic gout which would plague her later years. It is a fearsome disease; an extremely painful type of arthritis that affects the toe, the foot and ankle and often, other joints.

After a year in Scotland, Thomas Smith and his son John set off to return to India. Grace would not see her eldest child again.

The pair went first to London, and then by the early train to Southampton, to board the P&O steamer, which would take them via Gibraltar and Malta, to Alexandria. From Alexandria, they took the railway to Cairo. This new railway relieved the 3500 camels that were formerly used to transport coal across the desert to the P&O steamers on the Red Sea. Unknown to Tom and John, their train was carrying upwards of £750000 in specie, that is, in coins. Thomas wrote home explaining that an attempt was made to break the rails, in order to kill them all and steal the money. The plot was detected and foiled, and the passengers knew nothing of it, until they arrived at Cairo. Almost as an afterthought, Thomas wrote, 'I believe one hundred and thirty people were hanged for it.'

Father and son arrived back in Calcutta, just in time for the Indian uprising in 1857. 'We never know what is coming', wrote Thomas, but it is 'a great comfort to know that God's hand will not lose a jot or tittle till all is fulfilled.' I am unable, despite much thought, to parse that last sentence.

The British troops were on their way to reconquer and exact savage punishment. Meanwhile, teenage John spent his nights patrolling the streets. His father called it playing at policemen. 'Johnnie is liking his work', wrote Thomas. What the work was, remained a mystery, until I read in the Register of the Edinburgh

Academy, which John had attended from 1849 until 1854, that he was a 'Merchant in Calcutta'. Thomas ended his letter rather wearily, supposing that everything in Edinburgh was 'going on much as usual with everybody fighting with everybody – well that is better than to have to fight with mutinous sepoys'.

He had not seen the last of the uprising. The Black Watch, the 42nd, arrived in Calcutta, having mislaid their padre. Tom was appointed, and drove down in his buggy to the river, to march out at the head of the regiment. The troops filled his church to the rafters and Tom's first sermon was held to be magnificent. Off they then marched up-country.

According to several accounts, he went up-country with the 42nd to Lucknow, and therefore might have given communion to my great-grandfather, Thomas Carson.

Tom Carson, an orphan weaver from Dunfermline, was with the 79th Foot, all five feet three inches of him. Having relieved the siege of Lucknow, he was lashed for being drunk, imprisoned for three days and reduced to the ranks, a frequent feature of his army career. He was just nineteen years old, having joined the army at seventeen, and I believe Lucknow was his first experience of combat. I'm not surprised he was drunk. In 1871, he was discharged, being unfit for service as a result of secondary syphilis, aggravated by recurrent bouts of malaria due to his long service in India. He had been on the defaulters' roll thirteen times, frequently for drunkenness, and twice court-martialled.

One of the discharge papers documenting his service, which I now own, miraculously survived the depredations of an aunt from Stornoway who had the records of his syphilitic condition destroyed. She hadn't reckoned with the army's record-keeping and the facility now offered by the National Archives which allows me to consult and download the full record whenever I wish.

There was a small pension for his seventeen years' and eighty-nine days' service, from which the three days of his incarceration at Lucknow were docked. Tom reached Britain, was inspected with his regiment by Queen Victoria, and disappeared for ten years. He fetched up sober in Glasgow, got a job labouring on the railways, married a decades' younger woman, lying about his age, and moved into their two rooms with her, her mother, and her grandmother, who was the same age as he, and their sundry and numerous children and grandchildren. He proceeded to father eight healthy children of his own. He died, it is recorded, aged fifty-seven, of pneumonia and heart disease, though I remember being puzzled by adults whispering about 'an Indian fever'. He was much loved and respected by his family and friends. His wife, my great-grandmother, died in the Barnhill Poorhouse in 1943. She had been forty-seven years a widow.

On 5 May 1858, Reverend Thomas Smith wrote a final letter to his sister. The contrast with the letters he wrote as a boy of twenty-two, could not be greater. 'However, the fact is that my health and spirits have not been good for a long time. You will have heard . . . that I had about made up my mind to resign my present appointment and return to Scotland. This I have now done.' In the same mail, he sent his letter of resignation. He so clearly was wanting to be away. Smith was home by early March 1859.

In later years, Thomas Smith spoke little of his twenty years in India and of his mission. I am no graphologist, but I have rarely seen a series of letters where the wildly varying handwriting seem to mirror the writer's state of mind. Thomas was at heart an intellectual and, however much of a devout evangelical Christian, I'm not sure he was convinced that he was in the right place in India. His attitude towards his Indian colleagues and students is of his time. But in his time, he had much influence and control over those he regarded as of inferior race – and gender.

The above quotations from letters are from a collection in the excellent National Library of Scotland. I spent many a day photographing and transcribing them in the airy Special Collections room with its magnificent, distracting views over Edinburgh. Some little time later, I found the letters, beautifully scanned, on the Library's website.

In preparation for Thomas' return, Grace took her family to the south side of the city. Number 4 Keir Street is an eight-roomed, ground floor and basement apartment, much like 10 Scotland Street and built around the same time. The flats are spacious and well-proportioned, and have a magnificent view to Edinburgh Castle.

Grace and Her Missionary

When Grace arrived, there was a cattle market to the west, where the Edinburgh College of Art now stands.

On his return, Thomas was awarded an Honorary MA by the University of Edinburgh and set about readying himself for the Cowgatehead Church. He attended numerous meetings, and gave addresses to a wide variety of august bodies.

In April 1861, Smith is listed in the census at 4 Keir Street with his wife Grace, his daughter Annie, and two sons, David and William. John is in India, and may by this time have moved north to Silchar. The family had a servant, Isabella Miller, aged nineteen from Dunfermline. In August, they will have gone north for the wedding of Grace's brother, Alexander, to Janet Gordon, and, in November, would have mourned her death.

On 11 April 1862, the Cowgatehead Mission Church finally opened. If William sought to give Thomas an easy billet after the rigours of Calcutta, he was perhaps remembering the Cowgate of his childhood. By the time Thomas was installed, it was one of the worst slums in Europe.

Cholera had come to Edinburgh in 1831 and settled down in the Cowgate. Its primary vector is contaminated water or food, but it spreads also by clothing and bedding. Smallpox and typhoid fever shared the route of transmission, were supplemented by tuberculosis, typhus and influenza, and exacerbated by fleas, rats, lice and other vermin. The Cowgate had a large population, packed into one-room dwellings – often several families sharing bedding, and sometimes clothes. There was little access to clean water and less to proper sewage and refuse collection. MiddleMealmarket Stair housed 1530 people in 249 flats with no toilet. The condition of the area and its under-fed and hard-working inhabitants was investigated and described by Edinburgh's first Medical Officer of Health, Dr Henry Duncan Littlejohn. His 1865 Report determined policy internationally until the beginning of the first world war. His method was to investigate and persuade, but the cooperation of those on the ground was crucial. For many, Thomas and his church would be their only place of refuge and source of help.

Henry Littlejohn, speaking at Thomas Smith's Jubilee celebrations in 1899, when both were advanced in years, noted that he was not himself a Free Church Man, but that he would not have missed the gathering, as he was indebted to Smith in his professional life. Littlejohn spoke of Smith not as a missionary, clergyman or professor, but as a citizen. He told of a land of houses – i.e., a high tenement of many small dwellings – next to Thomas' church. It was an overcrowded, insanitary slum, and not long after Thomas arrived, was home to a terrible outbreak of cholera. 'That was my first introduction to Thomas Smith,' said Littlejohn. 'Dr Smith, by his courage and his acquaintance with the disease, pointed out to me the manner in which it should be met, and I have never forgotten the kind encouragement I got from him.' Not only did Smith move amongst the afflicted, he also personally helped with the disposal of the dead. Five years later, there was a smallpox epidemic. Again, Smith arrived to act as Littlejohn's right-hand man.

Thomas may well have had a pressing personal impetus for his altruism. Near the end of 1862, news reached Grace and Thomas that their beloved eldest son, John, had died on 11 August at Silchar, a hillstation in Assam. The tea gardens of Silchar are strikingly beautiful. In John's time they were relatively-recently established and benefiting from the expertise of men and women from China, indentured to build the industry. The town was small and the climate perhaps difficult for John, a novice tea-planter. I cannot discover what took the young man at twenty-two, but it could have been fire, flood or pestilence, in an unquiet part of the world. Silchar now sits in a dangling appendix, surrounded by Bangladesh, Myanmar, Bhutan, and China. From my perspective, it's remote, even with its river port and its airport. Grace would never have seen her boy's grave and I reflect on the blow dealt to his grandmother, Ann, and to his sister, Annie, who surely held his hand for comfort on that long childhood voyage.

John Smith's Edinburgh Academy classmates fought in Afghanistan, China, all over India, and the Crimea. Many died. They were governors of Calcutta, Indian Residents, solicitors in Barbados and Montreal; a Governor of Pentonville Prison, a farmer who joined his brother in Australia and an officer in a Sikh regiment. Then I noticed Robert Leven, who grew up to be a tea planter in Assam. Robert was born in Scotland Street, and as a schoolboy lived nearby at 1 Bellevue Crescent. He passed 10 Scotland Street on his way to and from the Academy. Did John and Robert walk home together and plan their future? Robert lasted longer than John but also died in Assam, aged thirty-nine, of cholera.

By the mid-1860s, Thomas Smith had become very elevated. In my trawl though his life, I found him described several times as one of the ablest scholars and linguists of his time. I can't help feeling he was happiest with a pen in his hand. By 1871, he had acquired a liferent on the eleven rooms of 10 North Mansionhouse Road, which had a long-standing connection with the church. His son David now twenty-four, was farming 410 acres at Coulston Mains Farm in East Lothian.

William, the youngest Smith, at the age of twenty-one was a minister of the Free Church. By the mid-eighties, he was installed at Newington Free Parish Church and living close by in Blacket Place. For some years, the family were gathered together again – all within easy walking distance.

In 1881, Thomas became Professor of Evangelistic Theology at the Free Church College, which was set up at the top of the Mound when the Free Church broke away from the mothership in 1843.

I hope Thomas' new appointment, free of the heavy workload of tending to one of the poorest parishes in Edinburgh, gave him a little more time with Grace, in her last five years. She would have been in considerable pain from rheumatic gout, which was often accompanied by weight gain and permanent damage to the joints and cardiovascular system. Goodness knows what other physical legacies remained of her time and pregnancies in India. Her sister was nearby, her son David was within calling distance, William was around the corner adding to her grandchildren, and Annie was by her side, always. Perhaps she was content.

Annie is an enigma. Her brother's birth appears in the Indian register. Hers does not. But we know from other records that she was born in 1842, and seven years later travelled halfway round the world to 10 Scotland Street. In the census of 1851, Annie was a Scholar. In 1861, she was merely a 'Minister's Daughter'. Her occupation is forever blank. Think, however, what is entailed in being a minister's daughter, in one of the poorest and most disease-ridden areas of the city. Unless she was very unusual, she would have been fully occupied in helping him, running classes and fund-raising, visiting the sick and despairing, and generally being the minister's daughter. In this, she would have been all the more valuable as Grace became ever more ill.

Grace Whytt died intestate at 23 Hatton Place on 3 November 1885. Because she died without a will, her husband had to establish his right as heir, and her son David had to establish his right to the benefit of various Whytt trusts which came to him, rather than Smith. This, they did with the help of Andrew Aikman JP, his late wife's maternal cousin. Grace left almost £2500. She had nearly £500 in the bank and £20 worth of jewellery. In her portfolio, surely put together by Mr Andrew Wark, there were shares in railway companies and in the Edinburgh Gas Company. There were also the receipts from one fifth of her mother's property in Falkirk, of 15 Hart Street, 2 George Place, and finally 10 Scotland Street, at that point occupied by Mr Rodan Hogg, whom we will meet shortly.

Grace's death left Annie with the task of running her father's house and, in 1891, when Thomas became the Moderator of the General Assembly of the Free Church of Scotland, Annie was surely drafted in to fulfil the many functions that normally fell to a Moderator's wife. In 1892, Thomas resigned his academic post and would be permanently under her feet. He was still writing and publishing, and part of the mathematical and scientific world. In 1896, he was one of many distinguished international guests, among whom was Lord Lister, at the Bute Hall, Glasgow University, to celebrate the fiftieth anniversary of Lord Kelvin being promoted to the Chair of Natural Philosophy. In my time as an undergraduate in Glasgow, I sat for a term in Kelvin's tiered lecture theatre on the excruciatingly uncomfortable benches. I have two stools from his lab in my kitchen. I suspect their 1967 replacements have not endured as long.

Kelvin was the pre-eminent mathematical physicist of his time and is recorded as having said that, had Smith devoted himself to mathematical science ... 'he would unquestionably have risen to the very highest eminence in that science, being one of the foremost mathematical scholars of his day'.

Page 103

On Admission
The Left Ankle is swollen & somewhat red. Fluctuation can be felt on the anterior aspect. There was sinus on each side under the malleoli, the probe passed freely through them into the joint, where it was felt to touch diseased bone. Motion almost abolished. Patient complained of pain. Looked anxious, pale & phthisical. Foot dressed with Lac.
Dec 2nd At 10.10 A.M. Pulse 100. Tongue clean.
At noon Mr Lister performed Syme's amputation of the foot in the usual manner. He removed a second sclice from the tibia & fibula on account of tension of flaps. The edges of the sinuses were clipped off & the whole surface of stump was treated with Sol. of Zinci Chlor. & was then dressed with strips of lint dipped in 1 to 10 oil & enveloped in Lac. The arteries were tied with catgut.
Before the operation the foot was cleansed with 1 to 20 Lotion & the sinuses were injected with Zinci Chl.

Page 104

Patient was under Chloroform.
Dec 3rd 1.10 A.M. Pulse 102. Temp 100. Patient has not been sick. Considerable pain in the leg. Had dose of Morphia. Lint changed every 4 hrs. At 5 P.M. an artery was tied.
Noon. Lint changed as before, quite sweet, no suppuration. No pain nor redness. Patient smiling.
Dec 4th 0.30 A.M. Pulse 122. T 99.
11 A.M. P.120. T. 98.6 Patient slept well after 4 A.M. Tongue rather brown in centre. Lint changed twice a day, still perfectly sweet.
10.30 P.M. P 110, T 98.4 Complains of pain at lower part of leg at outer & inner side. Appetite pretty good.
Dec 5 11 A.M. P 110, T 98.8
1 P.M. Mr Lister removed the lint, which was sweet. Washed out the cavity with 1 to 40. Inserted a drain & stitched the flap as usual & dressed stump with Lac. Chloroform. Spray.
Dec 6th 1.15 A.M. P. 114, T 98.4 Had pain during the afternoon. Dose Morph. M XL. Has since slept & is now easy.
10. A.M. P.100. T. 99.5 Tongue clean & moist. Slept pretty well. Pain very slight.
See page 129

Page 132

dressed every day with gauze but still purulent discharge. The Right thigh still discharges a good deal, with purulent odour. A bedsore over sacrum & each trochanter dressed with Protective & Cotton Wool. Stump dressed about every 4 days, entirely healed except a small sinus on each side, a very small quantity of pus can be squeezed out from these sinuses & pressure on heel. discharge quite sweet.
Feb 1st. Patient has been taking sick list upset. Diarrhoea &c. For some hours he had difficulty in swallowing & at 8 o'clock this evening Died.
E.M.

Mr Lister's Case Notes 1, 2 and 3.
A few years ago, The Royal College of Surgeons of Edinburgh digitised Joseph Lister's Patient Casebook 1870-71. I realised that the timescale coincided with the weeks that my great-grandfather had been treated in the Infirmary and started reading. I was amazed to find a complete record of his time there. These are only three of the pages. Thanks to a superb archivist, I have held the book.

Lady Charlotte Campbell. William Whyte (a surname he adopted when he set up his first shop), David's pious bachelor brother, young and energetic, offered Haydn a great deal of money to compose music for a selection of Burns' poems. In doing so, he outbid George Thomson, who had dismissed William as an obscure music seller. The folio of Burns songs which William produced, he then dedicated to widowed beauty Charlotte Campbell, whose Edinburgh literary salons were attended by Walter Scott and his fellows, before she went off to join Shelley's group in Italy.

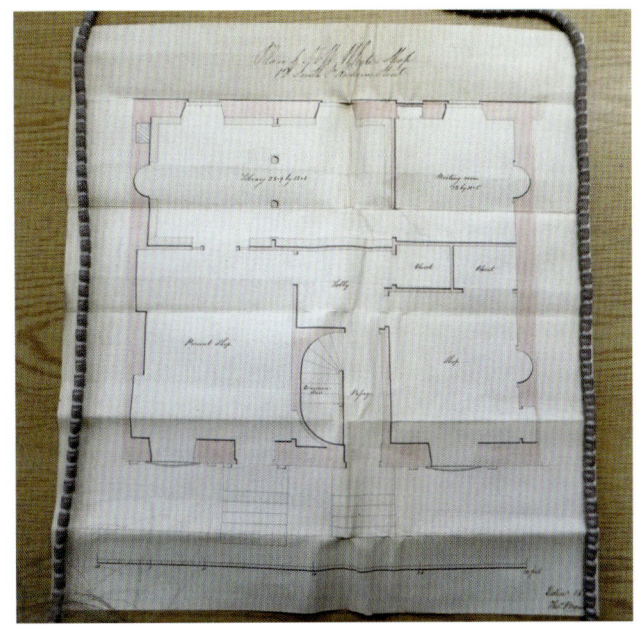

William Whyte's proposed frontage and layout of 14/16 South St Andrew Street. I was handed this little bundle in the Edinburgh City Archives, and I believe no-one else had handled them since they were deposited by William. I'd grown intrigued by this man. He'd penetrated Edinburgh's music and bookselling fraternity and here he was putting down a public marker of his place in the world, and providing premises for his co-partnery with his brother David and their father. I'd very much like to visit these rooms in reality instead of in my mind.

Mrs Leckie's receipt. On 30 January 1836, Mrs Leckie bought books from William Whyte and Company of 13 George Street, Edinburgh. Her receipt is signed by William Kennedy, a bookseller in William's employ and a trustee of his will. This is interesting, but what made me part with more than I could afford to a specialist bookshop in London, was the engraving of William's shop and home. There it sits, east of St Andrews Church, belching smoke. I am delighted with it.

Cowgatehead Church 2021 William Whyte looked after his family, notably the daughters of his sister Grace and Admiral Gourley. He was much concerned with the well-being of his niece's husband, the missionary Thomas Smith. Fearing that Thomas' health was affected by his time in Calcutta, William decreed that a church be built for Thomas in the Cowgate, which was by the 1850s a place of dire deprivation and disease. The church fell into disuse and after I took this image was incorporated into a new hotel.

<u>Thomas Smith in Calcutta</u>. Thomas was twenty-two and Grace twenty-four when they sailed off round the Horn to India. Colesworthey Grant sketched Thomas as a Public Character of Calcutta. Much of his mission consisted of teaching mathematical science, to which he was devoted. During the 1857 Indian uprising, he became for a while chaplain to the 42nd Regiment. According to reports, he went upcountry to Lucknow and so may have given communion to another of my great-grandfathers.

<u>Thomas Smith by John Henry Lorimer</u>. Lorimer was initially unenthusiastic about painting the aged man, but was won over. Thomas is still a fine figure, but the melancholy he spoke of at a valedictory dinner in his honour is, I think, etched in his face. He outlived his wife and all but one of his children. The world changed around him, and perhaps he mourned the certainties of his youth.

<u>Thomas Carson's Discharge Paper</u>. Carson was a very different Thomas. An orphan weaver who signed up at seventeen, the Relief of Lucknow was his first battle – and his first imprisonment for drunkenness. Dismissed after seventeen years in India due to the depredations of syphilis and malaria which the medical officer opined made him unfit for work, he turned up ten years later in Glasgow, married a woman twenty-two years his junior, fathered eight healthy children whom he supported by labouring, and died, respected and loved by his family, aged fifty-seven.

<u>Thomas Carson Paterfamilias</u>

Edwin Eyre Gulland, of 10 Scotland Street, was among the first of the ten men of Scotland Street to be swallowed by the First World War. He left number 10 in 1914 and died in mud near the Somme in May 1915. His widow and children lived on in Scotland Street for some years.

Robert Lawson, of number 25 Scotland Street, joined up in early 1915 and wrote detailed letters to his mother and to his sister until he was killed shortly before the end of the war. My daughter, reading his vivid, heart-rending letters, said she did so hope he would survive. So did I.

Freda White as a Young Woman. Freda, of number 2 Scotland Street, was almost fifty years older than I. She was a lifelong campaigner for peace, working for both the League of Nations and the United Nations, and as a journalist. Latterly she penned iconic guides to areas of France. Freda lived a life I admired, the like of which I hardly knew existed until I met her. She opened my mind to possibilities.

Willie Taylor engineer *extraordinaire* who conducted his machines like a first-class orchestra and fixed all manner of broken things down Scotland Street Lane. A kind and generous man.

Frances Gordon as a Young Woman, Frances, Freda's great friend, was only thirty-five years older than I. Our friendship lasted longer. Like Freda she was a woman with a mind of her own and shared some of her life lessons with me.

Annie died, aged fifty-five, in 1897. The doctor certified that she had suffered dyspepsia and enlargement of the liver and spleen for six days, and congestion of the lungs and pleurisy for four. Horrendous. She died intestate with £17 in the house and personal effects worth £15. But there was money in banks, shares and debentures – Andrew Wark at work again – interest on liferents on railway shares bequeathed by her deceased aunts. She died worth £1272 9/3 with a purchasing power of £166500 in 2020. She had lived for fifty-five years and left almost no trace, which does not mean that she was not an active and valued member of her community. Of Grace's children, only the two youngest, David and William, remained above ground.

Thomas was still studying mathematics and still writing. His output was prodigious and extensive. In 1899, Jubilee Celebrations for his fifty years' ministry were held in his son's church in Newington. The great and the good of the Edinburgh dissenters came together to enjoy encomium after encomium. At the end, Smith spoke. His tone was melancholic. Of his mother's ten children, she herself, one of fourteen, he was the sole survivor. He had over one hundred cousins. Only two were alive and he was the eldest. Most of his colleagues were dead. His tone warmed as he spoke of his time in India and his conception of the Zenana movement. He spoke of his church in the Cowgate and said that no congregation was as attached to their minister as at Cowgatehead. And so on.

His son William, speaking for himself and his brother, said how gratifying the evening had been, etc., etc. In all of the verbose evening's proceedings, there was not one word of Grace, his wife of fifty years, who was by his side throughout his triumphs, nor of Annie, his recently-deceased daughter.

Thomas entered the twentieth century aged eighty-three. At the end of his life, he was eulogised as the last of the Disruption Worthies; a man rich in years and honours. His portrait, painted when he was eighty-six, by John Henry Lorimer RSA, hung in New College in Edinburgh.

In 1999, when the Church Assembly Hall became an interim home for the nascent Scottish Parliament, Smith's portrait was sold by Bonhams and disappeared for twenty years. It was sold on again, and recently I found it. I was welcomed to view the painting. Hanging on a fine staircase, it portrays a very distinguished old man, lined, and white of hair. Quite abundant hair. His posture is erect, he is patently tall of stature, and despite the evidence of the years, he is still a fine-looking man.

On 1 March 1904, Thomas' son, the Reverend William Whyte Smith died of apoplexy. He was fifty-four, and left four children and a widow. This must have been a great sadness to Thomas. Only one child remained to him, David in Tranent.

Then a final blow was sent to try him. In December of 1905, his youngest grandchild, thirteen-year-old William John Whyte Smith, died in the Royal Infirmary, of injuries received by being knocked over by a motor omnibus. On 26 May 1906, the Reverend Thomas Smith died at his home at 23 Hatton Place. His son David signed the death certificate. There were many obituaries.

Thomas' estate, consisting of shares and bank deposits, amounted to £7042 6/10. His trustees were empowered to *sell* to his sons any of his possessions they might want.

The last of Grace's children, David Whyte Ewart Smith, a widowed and retired farmer, died of angina in 1915, leaving a long list of shares in gold mining concerns, spread across the globe.

A gravestone in Newington Cemetery commemorates Grace and Thomas, their son John in Silchar, the infant David, dead in Calcutta some few hours after birth, and their daughter Annie.

TWELVE

10 SCOTLAND STREET AFTER DAVID

The 1855 Valuation Roll, the first of its kind, is particularly poignant. It is yellowed with time. The names of the aged brothers, David and William, are written in ink faded to sepia. William Whyte's old friend and tenant, Charles Liddle, is at 12 Scotland Street. William's flats at number 14, housed a provision dealer, a Mrs Bryce and a gas fitter. Gas had come to Scotland Street, and the evidence, in the form of mounts for gas mantles, remains in several of my rooms. For years, I blithely threw open my bedroom shutters, unaware that the musical bang was produced by wood hitting a gas pipe.

David's last recorded act at Scotland Street was to subscribe one guinea to the Edinburgh Royal Infirmary, which had lately moved from Infirmary Street to the Meadows, where it would remain until the end of the twentieth century. Just to the right of David's name on the subscription list is a report of conditions at Balaklava, as the Crimean War came to its bloody conclusion. By 1854, chloroform, discovered and promoted by the obstetrician, James Simpson of 52 Queen Street, was being used for battlefield surgery. At the Infirmary, Joseph Lister was converting the filthy wards and blood-and-pus-littered operating theatres into clean and aseptic places, where the diseases of the hospital: pyaemia, gangrene, erysipelas, would not thrive. Although Ignaz Semmelweis had made the connection between filthy surgeons and death – and latterly Lister was in touch with Semmelweis and Pasteur – it was Lister who worked out how to use the knowledge. He tested his ideas rigorously, and kept case-notes on all patients – among whom was one of my great-grandfathers. Only one of Lister's Patient Casebooks, found in the 1880s in a dustbin, survives. At the Royal College of Surgeons of Edinburgh, a superb archivist let me hold and breathe the book. Thanks to Mr Lister's meticulous records, I know that, at half-past midnight on the day he died, my great-grandfather's pulse was 122 and his temperature was 99; and that, at noon the previous day, he was smiling. His name was Neil. Jumping from a cart, he injured his ankle which became infected. Somehow, he made the 100 plus mile journey south from Doune. Mr Lister successfully amputated his foot, but there was undiscovered infection elsewhere. On 1 February 1871, at 8pm, Neil died.

He was thirty-one. There was no money and no pension, and so he was buried, courtesy of the city, in the unmarked common ground of Warriston Cemetery. I contacted the City's burial record department, not really believing I would get a result, and was supplied with a sketch, coordinates and a description of nearby stones. My French grandson and I visited his great-great-great-grandfather, and found a grassy mound, ringed with fallen stones and shaded by ancient trees. The Water of Leith runs close by. It is a peaceful, green place. Neil's wife, Jane, and five children, one a month old, were destitute. Jane set up as a seamstress in Perth and made a living, with all of her children taking part in the process of garment making. Her fourth child was my grandfather who grew up to marry a woman called Whitson, a name which we'll meet later in this story.

Neither David nor William would have contemplated entering the Infirmary. Hospitals were for those whose homes, if they had them, were unfit for the sick. Nevertheless, the Whytts and many of their peers made substantial contributions to their upkeep. The Royal Infirmary as I write, is coming to terms with the fact that from 1750 until 1892, it owned and profited from the work of enslaved people, and later indentured labourers on the Red Pen estate in Jamaica, left to the Infirmary by an Edinburgh surgeon.

By August 1856, as David was spending his last days in Portobello, Mr Robert Crawford had taken up residence in 10 Scotland Street. Between David Kedie Whytt's death, in 1856 and 1924, when the last of his grandchildren sold it, 10 Scotland Street was rented out. It's not so easy to unravel tenants' lives, but dogged investigation over a couple of decades has yielded some good stories.

Robert Crawford was the eldest child and only son of Mary Wylie and James Crawford, a bank agent in Old Cumnock Village, Ayrshire. In the 1841 census, Robert was twenty. He had three sisters, one named Marion. By 1851, Robert, now a practising solicitor, was living on the Square in Old Cumnock with his new Greenock-born wife, Marion King. On 10 July 1853, The *Glasgow Herald* announced her death. They had been married less than three years.

Robert left for Edinburgh and became a Solicitor of the Supreme Court. From 10 Scotland Street, he wrote in support of *The Scotsman* newspaper's role in ensuring freedom of speech. I have not been able to discover who, on that occasion, was out to get *The Scotsman*.

His sister Marion was in the West Indies. On 19 November 1847, on the Plantation of *Lusignan*, in Demerara, British Guiana, she married Alexander Stewart, a sugar planter. British Guiana, now Guyana, was officially incorporated into the British Empire only forty years before Marion arrived, and slavery had been abolished only thirteen years previously. *Lusignan* was an eighteenth-century cotton plantation which had switched to sugar and, at the turn of the nineteenth century, it was a prosperous enterprise which rewarded its European owners well. The conditions of the enslaved workers were brutal and sexual abuse endemic.

The 1823 uprising of 13,000 enslaved people began at plantation Success, owned by John Gladstone, father of the future Prime Minister. During the uprising, the military arrived at *Lusignan* and were faced by a group of around 200, armed with cutlasses. Joshua Bryant in *An Account of an Insurrection of the Negro Slaves in the Colony of Demerara* writes that, after discussion, arms were laid down and the manager, Mr Murray, and four overseers were released from the stocks behind the sugar works. The casual mention of these stocks is chilling. Very few white people died, as most were treated like Mr Murray and merely locked up. Brutal punishments were handed out and many rebels hanged, decapitated and whipped or burned to death. Alexander and Cudjoe, enslaved men from *Lusignan*, received relatively light sentences: Alexander was sent up the coast, Cudjoe was flogged and then sent to the workhouse for life. I'm perhaps wrong to consider these lighter sentences, since being 'sent up the coast' might well have been a fearsome punishment, and life in a workhouse was frequently short. The people of Liverpool presented John Gladstone with a silver plate in recognition of his service.

Ten years later, there were 480 enslaved on *Lusignan*. Compensation of £12392 15/6 was paid to two owners. Lying on the east coast, it was said to be one of the finest in the British West Indies, with an ornamental garden. Nevertheless, Marion would have been dealing with incessant rain, swamps just beyond the plantation boundary, clothes rotting in wardrobes and rattlesnakes, even in ornamental gardens.

In 1852, a notice of sale listed indentured labourers from India and China on the estate, some of the thousands brought by the British to replace enslaved labour. They may not have been classed as enslaved, but they were certainly unfree and, for many, their conditions were little better than their predecessors'. In 1854, the minutes of the Ladies Emancipation Society recommended a tract entitled *Journal of a Voyage with Coolie Emigrants from Calcutta to Trinidad*, by Captain and Mrs Swinton, which contained an account of mortality on emigrant voyages. In the Ladies' view, the contracting partners – that is the estate managers and the labourers – are, on the one hand, clever, scheming businessmen bent on oppression and profit, and, on the other, 'ignorant heathen', who don't understand the agreement they sign, and find themselves on a long miserable crossing to a land where they will experience extreme hardship.

John Brummell's *Demerara after Fifteen Years of Freedom*, published in 1853, gives a fascinating, thorough, contemporary and firmly biased and racist account of the colony. Alexander Stewart, blessed with free accommodation, servants, horses etc., would have been paid an excellent salary and bonuses to put into a pot to take home.

In 1850, on the *Lusignan* plantation, Marion gave birth to Mary Antoinette. Perhaps the birth was hard, for she made the long voyage home for the birth of her second child, Anne Marion. In her absence, her husband was appointed Justice of the Peace. Marion sailed back to *Lusignan* and, in 1854, gave birth to Jessie Elizabeth.

Finally, she travelled back across the Atlantic, presumably carrying her children with her, all the way to 10 Scotland Street, where on 17 March 1858, Marion gave birth to a son, Alexander Robertson Stewart. By the time the 1861 census was taken, her brother Robert Crawford, had left for Queen Street and Marion to South Edinburgh. Within two years, Alexander Stewart retired and Marion's last child, George Patrick, was born. Marie Antoinette left home to marry; her sister died of tuberculosis, followed soon after by their father. He left a healthy estate, most of it in railway stock and bank shares in British Guiana, and an uncomfortably large insurance policy on the life of his wife who was twelve years younger than he. His will is an exercise in control. His widow cannot change their joint will and, in law, must be regarded as 'naturally 'dead. Because he is. If she re-marries, she loses everything. Stewart wrote his unsatisfactory son Alexander, born in Scotland Street, out of the will. A small amount was to be doled out if it was thought good for him. Understandably, he disappeared. I unearthed the wills of two Alexander Robertson Stewarts in Tasmania and Melbourne. Perhaps one of these is he. I hope not the latter, as the poor man died in 1913 in an insane asylum, where he signed over all his worldly goods to his attendants. George Patrick, the youngest, had moved to the west of Scotland. Marion, after giving birth to all those children and doing all that travelling, appears to have spent her long, last years alone and in relative poverty. She died in 1892, aged sixty-eight. George died only seven years later, at *Villa Lusignan*, in Paisley.

I looked a little further into this family's ties to *Lusignan* and Demerara. In the index of eighteenth and nineteenth-century Guiana residents, compiled and maintained by Tikwis Begbie, there are nineteen Crawfords, including our Marion. It seems Marion had family in Demerara. Four Crawfords received compensation for enslaved people. Again, I'm taken aback at how one nineteenth-century New Town house, through family, marriage, inheritance and mortgage had intimate relations with slavery.

At the 1861 census, only a young domestic servant, Margaret Cranston, was registered at 10 Scotland Street. Joseph Liddle was still at number 12 and advising the younger Whytts. At 16, in one of the three flats on the stair, were Elizabeth Grant, and her niece

Mary Lithgow, a governess, both from Ireland. Elizabeth Grant was the daughter of a Lieutenant in the 5th Domingo Hospital Corps which, I believe, was American, and Mary Lithgow was a doctor's daughter. They had young boarders: two Thomson sisters from Leith, two Aitchison sisters from Coldstream, and three very young Grant sisters, Georgina, Edith and Evelyn, whose parents were William and Jane, of the Agrawattee tea estate in Ceylon, where the two elder sisters were born. In the *Indian News* of 15 November 1856, there is noted the birth of a daughter to the wife of Wm Grant Esquire at Agrawattee. The child was Georgina. Her birth is sandwiched among reports of a steamer sailing from Singapore with treasure retrieved from a wreck; a notice that the Reverend GAF Watson has been told to proceed as Chaplain with the Persian expedition; the murder of a Sergeant Major in Calcutta by a Private in revenge for ten days extra drill; and the erection of a Free Church of Scotland Mission Station at Nagpore by Miss Mary Barclay at her own expense. Evelyn, William and Jane's youngest, was born in Rothiemurcus, presumably when their mother had brought the older girls to Scotland to be boarded at Elizabeth Grant's school.

When we moved into 10 Scotland Street, there were bars at the back windows. I had them removed when my children were grown, and then regretted it, as they, in turn, produced children. I didn't much consider why they had been installed or by whom. I now believe it was Mrs Grant: within a month of the census, she and her niece had moved a few yards up the hill to 10 Scotland Street. On 15 May 1861 *The Scotsman* announced that Miss Lithgow, having removed to a commodious main door house, could now offer board and education for additional young Ladies, and Day Scholars could now be enrolled.

On 22 October 1862, Miss Lithgow was supporting a bazaar, held on behalf of the building fund for the Gayfield Square institute for educating imbecile youth, a cause favoured by both William Whyte and Dr Coldstream. Two years later, on 13 May, at 11am, Miss Lithgow hosted a sale of useful household furniture, the property of the late Misses Catherine and Elizabeth Bruce, of 16 Scotland Street, aged seventy-nine and seventy-eight, respectively, who had died within eight days of each other, a few weeks previously. Among the items being sold, were a square piano, an eight-day clock with chimes, and mixed napery. Catherine and Elizabeth's nephew, John Bruce of the Reform Club, Pall Mall, London, notified both deaths, and left the clearing up to his late aunts' friends.

In the late spring of 1863, the three Grant girls, the youngest only four, received the news that their mother had died and been buried in the Old British Garrison Cemetery at Kandy. The inscription on her stone records that she was Jane Fraser, wife of William Grant of the Templestowe Estate, where she died suddenly aged thirty-one. Her husband mourns an affectionate wife and exemplary mother. Her contemporary, Hugh Blacklaw, wrote of starting his career as a planter on the Templestowe Estate, a coffee plantation of 400 acres. There was one road from Kandy. You had to hire a horse at one shilling a mile, and ride from breakfast till evening, a long and tiring journey of thirty-three miles. He wrote that his reader would understand how isolated and helpless he and his fellows were, as there was no doctor nearer than Gampola, twenty-seven miles away. It is likely that the Grant sisters had little memory of their mother.

In 1865, Miss Lithgow posted a notice in *The Scotsman*, at once desperate and fierce:

Strayed last Sunday morning a small SKYE TERRIER BITCH, nine months old, Dark fawn, with Black Points. Last seen near to the Royal Circus. The Finder will be Rewarded on returning it to 10 Scotland Street. Any person found keeping it after this notice will be prosecuted.

Next to it – and nothing at all to do with Scotland Street, yet unforgettable – is: 'Found an unfinished vest. Apply 33 Elder st'. That vest has haunted me for years.

Miss Lithgow and her young ladies may have enjoyed an innovation at the bottom of Scotland Street. Next to the station, on the site of the former Canonmills Loch, Mr John Cox had built an open-air gymnasium. John Cox was part of J&G Cox Ltd, Gelatine and Glue manufacturers of Gorgie Road, a landmark in Edinburgh for many years, supplying their glue to outlets world-wide. Their gelatine was also used to produce plates for the new-fangled photographic craze. My children's great-great grandmother worked there in the late 1870s, before embarking, at seventeen, on a disastrous marriage which was, according to her granddaughter, the death of her.

John Cox's big idea was a gymnasium where patrons could exercise in the bracing fresh air. At sixpence per day for an adult and three pence for a child, it was an immensely popular attraction. Illustrations show a huge circular affair. This puzzled me, until I read that it was a 600-person rowing machine, known as the Great Sea Serpent. In July of 1865, the Edinburgh Rifle Volunteer Band played the Grand March of the Great Sea Serpent for the first time. It was composed for the occasion by its bandmaster, Mr Laubach, who lived nearby at 7 Broughton Place. The band also serenaded people on a giant seesaw, an apparatus devised to imitate the sensation of escaping from a sinking ship. One could also take a turn on stilts, a springboard, and, in winter, go ice-skating. I do hope that the Lithgow and Grant boarders took advantage of this facility, so close to their school.

I mentioned Mr Laubach's address. For almost twenty years, I owned a beautiful, much-missed flat, at 7 Broughton Place, which housed my student children, various adherents and assorted waifs and strays. The rooms of my flat were beautifully proportioned and blessed with five astragalled windows to the floor and little balconies and lots and lots of light. When I bought it in the mid-eighties for a small sum, it was in a very bad way. I was told it was at the wrong end of the New Town and on the wrong side of the street. Broughton Place, with Scotland Street, has now moved considerably upmarket. Times change.

Downstairs from Miss Lithgow's establishment, Mr Scott, the baker, was using his good offices, and *The Scotsman*'s personals, to find employment for a young woman from the country as a wet nurse. He also had to announce the death of Mary Jane, his youngest daughter. The Scotts were charitable people. In 1862, George Scott subscribed a guinea for the unemployed operatives in Lancashire and other cotton–manufacturing areas of England. His son Alex subscribed to a Wizard of the North benefit concert for the Destitute Sick. Tickets for benefits could be had from Mr Scott at 10A, alongside William Whyte, other prominent booksellers, tea and china merchants and apothecaries. Scott also rented out rooms to workers and artisans.

On 12 July 1866, two Polish men, Albert Smitzntz and Stanesway Mico, of 10 Scotland Street, were in court answering the charge that, in the Machinery Department of the International Exhibition of Industry Science and Art on the Meadows, they attempted to pick the pocket of Miss Ada Johan Harmayer Fothergill, of the Imperial Hotel. The evidence of Miss Fothergill and her mother, that one of the men had put his hand in her pocket, was judged insufficient and the case adjourned. On the following day, a witness told the court that the accused had lived in his house for several years and had been no trouble. The foreman at the Sugar Works in Bangor Road said that both had worked there, and were well-behaved. The judge gave his opinion that men whose hands were hard with toil were not inclined to pick pockets, and sent them home to 10 Scotland Street.

In 1866, Miss Lithgow wrote to the Domestic Service section of *The Scotsman,* on behalf of an ayah, who was seeking an engagement to accompany a family to Ceylon, Bombay or Calcutta. She was well-recommended and her terms were moderate. Apply, 10 Scotland Street. Did this unnamed ayah accompany the Grant sisters to Scotland and now, a decade later, was no longer needed? If so, the youngest lost the only mother she had known. Throughout the nineteenth century, the press carried many advertisements on behalf of ayahs looking for posts which would enable them to travel home. I failed to unearth more about the Grants' ayah. Ayahs were never given their names nor listed in the census return, as far as I can discover, and the voices of those who lived in Scotland from 1802 are utterly silent. Advertisements are, almost without exception, written by employers in racialised language. Yet there were many ayahs in Edinburgh, breaking conventions of gender, race and class, ferrying their charges across the Empire, and caring for them until they settled into boarding schools scattered across the New Town. In 1851, at 39 Drummond Place, where Miss Lithgow was then employed as a governess, out of ten pupils, seven were born in India, two in the East Indies and one in England. For a young person alive in the twenty-first century, it is difficult fully to comprehend how the Empire was everywhere in British life.

Miss Lithgow continued to advertise her establishment until 1868, when Alexander Henderson Whytt returned to claim his parents' house. Mrs Grant and Miss Lithgow moved to Glasgow.

Writing the above, I realise that I have now reached a time in this tale which, for me – in a way – is in memory. My grandmother was born on Duke Street, Glasgow, in 1865, and my grandfather, in 1867. Despite a starkly poverty-stricken childhood after his father died in Joseph Lister's care, he lived long enough for me to meet and remember him.

In 1871, when my grandfather was four, Scotland Street was home to grocers and dressmakers, mantle makers and engine turners, a coachman, a smith, a hosier and glover, and a nurseryman. The street continued very cosmopolitan. If we look a little deeper into the censuses of the latter part of the nineteenth century, we find, with notable exceptions, a shifting population ranging widely across class and professions, and rarely made up of a majority of people born in Edinburgh. Then, as now in the third decade of the twenty-first century, the area which is now North Edinburgh and Leith constituency benefits from a well-above-average proportion of inhabitants from across Europe and the rest of the world.

10 Scotland Street was being run as a lodging house by Laura Small, a widow from Ireland. She had two daughters, Laura, sixteen, and Mary, seven, who were born in New York and Newport, respectively, and a three-year-old son, Robert, born in Broughty Ferry, by Dundee.

Laura Ann Gosson had married Henry Watt Small, a linen merchant, in New York, on 9 November 1853. They returned to Scotland and had at least six children, one of whom, his father's namesake, died at three months in Broughty Ferry, followed in short order, by his father of heart disease. Laura's youngest child was only three. In need of an income, she moved her family south and set up as a landlady in number 10. In the 1871 census, Laura's boarders are listed as George R. Merry, a classical master from Kilmarnock, and the wonderfully-named Woodruffe and Maximilian Peacock, twelve and eleven, from Brigg, Lincolnshire. The boys attended Edinburgh

Academy and became farmers and horse breeders, Woodruff in Lincolnshire and Maximilian in the USA. Looking after the household were Jessie Kinnes, a house-tablemaid from Fife, and Anne Reilly, a cook from Ireland. On the night of the census, Ann Gregory and Jane Keating were visiting. None of these eleven people hailed from Edinburgh.

On 10 May 1873, Laura Small advertised for a clean, active girl to take charge of children and assist with housework. A week later, she sold off a 'Carpet (tapestry) of 18 ¾ yds, with rug to match, nearly new and very pretty' for eight guineas. On the same page is an advertisement offering a reward for the return of yet another dog – a black and tan terrier bitch – English, lost in Scotland Street Lane. English terriers are now extinct.

And then Henry Small's estate was at last settled, leaving his widow comfortably off. The Inventory lists three insurance policies, one in New York, and a large sum on the books of Small and Boase, Manufacturers and Merchants, Spinners of Hemp in three works in Leven and Dundee, which was founded in 1868, a year before Henry's death. In total, there was £6844 7/3, which would be around £752840 today. Unfortunately, the will is missing, which is very unusual. It might have shed light on why Laura had to take in boarders. In any event the cash on the books of Small and Boase, a new firm which had invested in three mills, would have taken some time to extract. The company also had to fight, through the Edinburgh Courts, a case brought by a fourteen-year-old boy, whose arm was taken by the cogs of a warping machine. They lost, and from the gruesome details provided, they should have.

A clue as to why Laura moved to Scotland Street may lie with Charles Boase, her husband's partner's father, a banker and philanthropist and a pillar of Angus society. After leading a blameless and profitable life, he became enmeshed in the Catholic Apostolic Church, an institution which pops up with some frequency in this story. To pursue his calling, he moved to 25 Drummond Place, round the corner from number 10.

Back in Scotland Street, in 1871, Mr Scott the baker had retired and there had been a development: the baker's home and premises fronting onto Scotland Street are now labelled 10A. When I first arrived on

Scotland Street, there were two small, derelict flats towards the back of the building, which one entered by the lane. These basement rooms, in 1871, held Alexander Gordon, a Chelsea Pensioner, his wife and two small children, and seventy-year-old Euphemia Ferguson with her daughter Elizabeth, a dressmaker, who had moved downhill from 3 Broughton Street when Mr Ferguson died.

Broughton Street numbers now commence at 19. 3 Broughton Street was on the southern side of the triangle of houses and shops opposite St Mary's Roman Catholic Cathedral. I just remember this triangle. It was an island of little, busy shops under crammed tenements that were full of life and noise. It was knocked down in the 1960s to make way for an ill-fated roundabout, crowned by a kinetic light sculpture that didn't move and rarely lit. The community disappeared, dispersed to the outskirts of Edinburgh.

Further down our stable lane, now named West Scotland Street Lane, lived thirty-two people in eight rooms over five dwellings. Two dressmakers and a daughter of one of them; a gatekeeper at a brewery with two children, plus his sister and a visitor; and Sarah Lumsden, sixty, an unmarried washerwoman, occupied three one-room homes. A coachman, his wife and five children, plus a boarder, had two rooms; as did Donal McDougal, a cab proprietor, his wife, his six children and his father-in-law, a farm servant. In two rooms lived James Crease, a last maker, with his wife and four children, including a son who was a piano tuner, and daughter Margaret, who was a relief stamper. My mind took me to a glorious image of women stamping (holding high their petticoats), with, in the background, relief stampers, standing by so a break might be taken and feet rested. Unfortunately, relief stampers, a trade which flourished in the second half of the nineteenth century, were persons employed in stamping engraved or embossed designs, especially on stationery. Unbelievably, the Oxford English Dictionary which I consulted spelt stationery with an 'a'. Stationary. Stamping stationary. Stationary stamping . . .

Of course, most of the lane buildings, were occupied in relative luxury by horses.

In William Whyte's 12 Scotland Street, long inhabited by his friend Charles Liddle, were the German-born Austrian Consul,

C.O. Nanmany, his Swiss-born wife Anna, and their servant Elizabeth Hohmann. One of my old friends was for many years, the Honorary Austrian Consul and flew the Austrian flag from his home a few paces from the final home of Ann Henderson Whytt. There were many good dinners in the Austrian Consul's welcoming kitchen, from where I might take in Ann's view over the Water of Leith.

Laura Small was followed at number 10 by William Denoon Young, who was an engineer and wire fence manufacturer, close by, at Beaver Bank. Although Glasgow vastly out-paced Edinburgh, which lacked a ready source of raw materials for heavy industries, by this time, there were brass and iron founders scattered over the city, and one, which lasted till a few years ago, at Beaverhall. I had David's door-scraper mended there. Mr Denoon didn't last long. His business failed in February 1876.

I am depressing myself with this catalogue of woes of number 10's tenants.

And then – I am sure to the great relief to the landlord Whytts – along came the persistent Archibald Rodan Hogg, who was still in place in 1883. He was a solicitor, mainly selling houses through *The Scotsman*'s columns. In 1877, he advertised for a Clerk with a knowledge of bookkeeping. Salary moderate: apply, 10 Scotland Street. On 1 May 1878, his housekeeper, Mrs Moodie, wanted a girl who could do plain cooking and wash. A year later, a woman from the country, both respectable and young, sought a situation. Alongside these 10 Scotland Street advertisements, someone was looking for a 'Party to adopt a boy, aged seventeen months, left friendless through the death of his mother'. No premium would be charged. And again, another Party was looking for a boy of six or seven to adopt. He must be healthy and good-looking. Informal adoptions continued until 1930 in Scotland.

Interspersed with notices for sales and trips and employment are many seeking Governesses with good French and German. The middle classes of Edinburgh knew that knowledge of several languages was of immense benefit in many ways and contexts. *Monolingualism Is Curable* should be inscribed over the door of every department of education.

10 Scotland Street

On 9 August 1879, Margaret, Archibald Roden's wife, gave birth to a son, David. Mrs Moodie immediately advertised for a Girl (strong, active) wanted for the nursery, to assist with housework. Which room, I wonder, was their nursery? In 1881, a daughter appeared. At the census, Margaret's sister-in-law was present and, of course, the three servants in the basement, Grace Comb, Mary Fraser, and Anne Houston.

In the 1881 census, the Hoggs were from home. Downstairs, at 10A, there were the Moodies and seven children. At 12 Scotland Street lived the widow Marianne Hay, born in Edinburgh, her eldest daughter, and her three younger children, all born in the Cape Colony. The Empire strikes again.

On 19 January 1886, Mr Roden Hogg brokered a sale of household furniture for the venerable auction house of Lyon and Turnbull. When we moved to Edinburgh in 1966, we haunted Lyon and Turnbull's Lane Sales on Thistle Street Lane. Many of our acquisitions from that time are still with me. No-one wanted the old furniture, boxes of cutlery, or heaps of tarnished brass which turned out to be Georgian lamps. To this day, I use a pair of hand-crafted scissors bought in a shilling box, a hospital lamp, wheeled down the hill by my elder daughter when she was five, countless chairs, and several cupboards. Behind me, full of the tapes, discs, and drives of my trade, is a tall, multi-drawered mahogany chemist's armoire, bought at a Saturday morning sale and somehow brought home by my husband and his father. My father-in-law was a docker and could move anything with a pair of gloves and a reasonably long batten. In 1973, a Martin Brothers vase, described as 'rather fine,' financed a trip to Portugal in our 1937 Lagonda, our family car for many years. The contemporary Lyon and Turnbull, a successor company only in name, is now housed in some splendour nearby, and, on occasion, I buy and sell there. The staff are knowledgeable and welcoming and the goods far superior to our battered finds.

The last we see of Mr Roden Hogg – whose collaboration with Lyon and Turnbull 150 years ago sparked this aside – is his appeal for his 'Collie (black and tan pup) dog lost on Thurs night at Silvermills. Reward Hogg 10 Scotland Street, 10 April 1886.'

10 Scotland Street After David

In 1891, number 10 was up for rent for 50/-. Poor Mr Hogg had moved to Newington, and, on 18 October 1892, died after suffering a fearsome-sounding cerebral congestion for six days. Number 12 was also uninhabited. The street, sliding down the social scale, was now home to shop assistants, schoolteachers, bookkeepers, a police sergeant, and a lot of children.

In the stable at number 8 Scotland Street Lane, presently my garage/workshop, Mr Adam Dickson had been a horse-dealer for some ten years, when in January 1894, he was brought before Sheriff Orphoot of the Edinburgh Bankruptcy court. The *Edinburgh Evening News* reported him as stating that he had no horses at present, but that, during the last year, had four or five horses at a time. The problem was that during his entire dealership he had kept no accounts, resulting in a Micawberish deficit of more than £30 – around £2500 in today's money. I was glad to read that Mr Dickson was not imprisoned. A month after Mr Dickson's trial, my friend Freda White was born at 3 Drummond Place.

10 Scotland Street was not empty for long. In June 1892, an advertisement in *The Scotsman* had promised that, 'Girls coming to Edinburgh will find a comfortable home at The Golden Eagle Institute, 10 Scotland Street.' I'm afraid I thought the worst. It took a bit of digging to find that the Institute was part of the Golden Eagle Friendly Society. In the Glasgow *Post Office Annual Directory* for 1899–1900, we find that the society provided marriage portions and an income during sickness for young people, both male and female; free medical attendance and medicine; and life insurance, endowment and pensions from the age of sixty-five. Shop and warehouse girls and domestic servants out of situations were boarded at a very cheap rate. The Institute is there in the advertisements and in the street indexes, but internet searches throw up only birds. Was there a brass plate with a soaring eagle on my door? I can find no trace, except for a recently opened educational institute in India.

Perhaps one of these boarders in the Golden Eagle Institute, is responsible for the 1895 advertisement of the loss, from 10 Scotland Street, of a 'Dark Brindled Irish terrier with a white metal collar.'

By 18 October 1895, the Institute had removed to Frederick Street, and Adamina Chisholm, wife of the architect Henry Francis Kerr, was installed in 10 Scotland Street. Here she gave birth to a son. With them the couple brought along their boarder, Adamina's sister, Anne Geoghan, a music teacher, and their servant, Anne Cummings Simpson. At 10A, three bakers are on the voters' roll. The women who worked and lived with them, are, of course, not on the roll.

The Kerrs moved on very quickly, and were replaced by Charles David Murray, a man who really caught my interest. Charles was the grandson of Charles Hope Murray, who lived on Calton Hill where his father was Governor – and his mother, according to *Pigot's Directory* of 1825, was Governess – of the Bridewell prison. By all accounts, they were well-liked, although, by the end of his tenure, the Bridewell was known among the criminal classes as 'Murray's Academy'. A place to perfect your skills. Charles's elder brother, David Murray, was accountant to the prison, which paid for itself by the sale of the convicts' work. This David is credited with virtually creating the principles of Scottish accountancy, and therefore the world, if not the universe.

The Bridewell was built between 1791 and 1796 by the architect, Robert Adam. It was the first to incorporate the invisible supervision of prisoners proposed by Jeremy Bentham, and named by him a panopticon. The design ensured that warders could see each prisoner without being seen, and no prisoner could see another. The Bridewell and its neighbour, Calton Jail, were used, on occasion, to house prisoners sentenced to transportation. A number of the 1820 Radicals, among them my great-great-great-uncle, Alexander Hart, were taken by steamboat to Newhaven from Stirling, where they were condemned to death, and thence to Calton Hill by coach, for interrogation.

Prison reformer, Elizabeth Fry, judged the prison kitchen too small but the food excellent. The infirmary she found commodious, with a small room for infectious diseases, but she was concerned about accommodation for prisoners awaiting the gallows. In Scotland, six weeks intervened between sentencing and death, whereas, in England, the sentence was carried out immediately. A small notice from 1864 caught my eye. A prisoner from the jail, handcuffed and secured, escaped while being escorted through Scotland Street Tunnel. I know the tunnel. The man was a genius.

Reading of the Bridewell, I realised that for some years in the late 1960s, I knew a man who had been incarcerated there. Arthur Woodburn was an early member of the Independent Labour Party, of which my grandparents were early Glasgow supporters. Arthur was a First World War conscientious objector, outraged by the profits accrued by armament-makers. He was held in the Bridewell, which he described as, 'the poorhouse of all prisons with the cold chill of a cold fortress.' By all accounts, it was either famously cold, or stinking on the rare hot day. Willie Gallacher, a fellow prisoner, said, 'it was the worst prison in Scotland; cold, silent and repellent. Its discipline was extremely harsh, and the diet atrocious.' I remember Woodburn and his wife Barbara, who represented Leith Central Ward for thirty-two years, when they were in their late seventies and eighties, still vital, engaged and very genial. Arthur left the prison in 1919 and returned to the site in 1947, as Secretary of State for Scotland. His walnut-panelled offices in New St Andrews House were built on the ruins of his former prison. Of the original 1815 complex, only the Governor's house, where Charles Hope Murray lived as a youngster, remains on the hill.

Charles Hope Murray set up as an accountant and joined the Excise. He married, was posted to Glasgow and had two sons, David William Murray and Charles Hope Murray (the second). These two set up as silk merchants, Charles in Glasgow, and David in London. David married, had two children and died of alcoholism. His wife, Rachel Gavin, brought her children back to Edinburgh and sent her son, Charles David Murray, later of number 10, to school and on to Edinburgh University, where he graduated in law. He was admitted as an advocate in 1889. In the mid-1890s, he moved into Scotland Street.

Meanwhile, in Glasgow, his uncle, Charles Hope Murray (the second) had had a son, Charles Hope Murray (the third), Charles David Murray's cousin.

Bear with me.

On 1 August 1896, Charles David Murray announced his marriage to Annie Florence Nicholson. The extravagantly-bearded the Very Reverend Dr James Cameron Lees DD, minister of St Giles High Kirk congregation, officiated. Dr Lees, lately of Paisley Abbey, held the elevated position of Dean of the Chapel Royal and Thistle until he died in 1913. The poor man lost his wife in 1887, his daughter in 1894, and his son in 1905. I suspect the flummery of being Queen Victoria's, Edward VI's and George V's Chaplain in Ordinary, even with all the ermine-trimmed robes and gee-gaws to which his titles entitled him, was little consolation.

No doubt, the groom's cousin, Charles Hope Murray (the third), now a stockbroker in Glasgow, travelled to Edinburgh for the wedding. Eight years later, in 1904, Charles Hope Murray (the third), married Maud Whitson, the daughter of Alexander Whitson, an iron merchant.

And here's a thing: Maud Whitson was the great-grandchild of Joseph Whitson and Elizabeth Hart. And so was my grandmother, Ann Whitson, who had a few months before given birth to my father.

In a convoluted and very extended way, I am related to Charles David Murray, who lived in my house at the turn of the last century and became the Lord Advocate. And this Lord Advocate was therefore connected to my transported convict great-great-great-uncle, the Radical, Alexander Hart, who was Elizabeth Hart Whitson's uncle. I should explain that the two branches of the Whitson family diverged, and my line mainly lived in two-roomed tenements in the east end of Glasgow and worked in the mills.

Having settled her son, Rachel Gavin Murray retired to a small house by the Royal Botanic Gardens in Inverleith Row. She did not enjoy it for long. She died intestate, barely three years later, leaving a tangle of liferents on numerous shares inherited from her husband. These included shares in linotype machines, insurance, Glenlivet whisky, the Professional and Civil Service Supply Association – a department store on the Strand in London – JP Coats, the Paisley thread manufacturers, various bank accounts, and interest on the trust estate of her grandmother, Ann Liston, of Leith Mount. In England, Rachel had shares in the Nobel Dynamite company. The contrast between her portfolio and the Whytt's empire-based shares, of half a century before, is striking. Charles David Murray, of 10 Scotland Street, sorted it all out, signed the declaration, answered to God for his signature, and paid duty of £90 5/6.

10 Scotland Street After David

Newlywed Annie Nicholson and Charles David Murray announced that they would be 'At Home' at 10 Scotland Street to receive visitors on 12–15 October, and requested no cards. Annie Nicholson would have five sons, burying one of them ten days after giving birth to the third; would watch another, having survived a devastating accident, leave Scotland forever and – having outlived her husband by thirty-two years – would die, aged ninety-four, in 1968, a few hundred yards from the beautiful, cold-water, shared-toilet attic in Dean Village, Water of Leith, for which we were, in 1968, paying a rent of £10 a month.

Back in 1901 in the census, Annie was alone at 10 Scotland Street, with two children, David Charles Graeme Murray, three, and Crichton Gavin, eleven months. And, of course, Jessie Sutherland and Elizabeth Broom in the basement, to look after them. The birth of her third son, Anderson Hope, also at 10 Scotland Street, was announced in *The Scotsman* on 28 July 1903. The register entry was corrected on 19 October to Keith Anderson Hope Murray.

In 1906, Annie was at Fernie Castle, Monimail. On 22 August 1906, while there, she gave birth to Charles Dean Leslie Nicholson, her fourth son in nine years. Five days later, six-year-old Crichton died of a perforated appendicitis. He must have been in agony.

Annie may have been at Fernie Castle for some time. In April 1906, the Council inspected 10 Scotland Street. The drains report was damning. It described a dirty pan, an unventilated apartment, and choked and blocked drains.

Under my house is the junction where the ordure of thirty-one households, including several on Drummond Place, meets up to be carried away in original Georgian drains down to the Water of Leith. Back in 1864 it had been clear to the Council that dump-everything-in-the-Water-of-Leith-and-hope-for-the-best was not working. An old plan of the Police Commissioners to build an interceptor alongside the Water of Leith was revived and over five miles of brick-built sewers were constructed. They were egg-shaped for better flow. For the most part they still work well. But the drain beneath my house dates from 1824 and is weary. When it blocks, my kitchen sink is the first place where the thick black muck emerges, blinking into the light. One New Year's Eve, I found a tide advancing malevolently across my kitchen floor. Since then, we, myself and my excellent neighbours, have been blasting and repairing regularly. In an age of disposable nappies, wipes and liberal use of cooking oil, these drains struggle to cope.

Back in 1906, the Council official flushed out the pan and cistern and recommended a new pan. He summarily disconnected the bath and wash hand basin. Understandably, by 1908, the Murray family had exchanged 10 Scotland Street for a five-storey, eighteen-roomed townhouse at 62 Great King Street. There, Annie gave birth to her fifth son and last child, Frederick Hope Murray.

In 1909, Charles David Murray was appointed King's Counsel. In the census of 1911, Annie was counted with her two sons and servants at 62 Great King Street. Her husband was in Leuchars at Craigsanquhar, a pile of twenty-nine rooms, with his two younger sons, aged two and three, and several servants, one of whom, thankfully, was a nurse/domestic. Were they taking a break?

During the 1914–18 war, Charles Murray worked for the War Office and was appointed Director of National Service for Scotland. Post-war, he became Sheriff of Renfrewshire and Buteshire, MP for Edinburgh South and the Dean of the Faculty of Advocates. He must have been working long hours and often away from home. His eldest son, David Charles Graeme Murray, who was seventeen when the First World War began, seems to have received only home postings. On 5 August 1916, he was driving his motorcycle along the Bouprie Road near Aberdour. In the sidecar was sixteen-year-old Mary Isabelle Williamson, daughter of bookseller Robert Milne Williamson of Leopold Place, Edinburgh, and his wife Isabelle Mary Vanhear. The bike collided with a van. Mary Isabelle suffered fractured ribs, lacerated lungs and shock, and died at the scene. David Murray was badly injured. The procurator fiscal recorded Mary's death as the result of a collision between a motor van and a motorcycle. I see this formulation often and wonder if the writers believe that these vehicles propel themselves. David Murray had switched to the wrong side of the road to avoid a van which was approaching on his side. Whereupon, the van switched to its correct side and the two collided head on. David's father Charles, a King's Counsel and Lieutenant Colonel etc., demanded compensation from the driver's employers. He wanted £1000, an enormous sum, and for the firm to be prohibited from trading. There's no sign that any compensation was demanded for the death of the sixteen-year-old girl.

In 1921, David Murray was listed as a Lieutenant in the Lights Corps of the City of Edinburgh Fortress Volunteers. He applied to join the British army as a mechanical engineer/draughtsman and was found to be six feet tall, Presbyterian, with fair hair and blue eyes. He was certified fit on 16 April 1921, and appointed acting sergeant at 26 York Place, Edinburgh. Two months later, he was discharged under para 392(11): 'Discarded as having been irregularly listed,' which sounds like a euphemism for 'we can't use him'. He took himself off to France.

His father Charles was now Solicitor General for Scotland and sworn into the Privy Council. He was promoted to Lord Advocate in 1922, and quickly elevated to the Bench as Lord Murray, a post he held until his death, aged sixty-nine, on 9 June 1936. He was the Right Honourable Charles David Murray, Lord Murray, Companion of the Order of St Michael and St George, Privy Council of the United Kingdom, King's Council, Deputy Lieutenant, Fellow of the Royal Society of Edinburgh. His son Keith came north from London to sign the death certificate. Lord Murray is buried on the central roundel in Warriston Cemetery. His headstone commemorates himself with a list of his honours, his second son Crichton Gavin, his beloved wife Annie – and Comtesse Elena Maia Sollohub. I did not expect that.

At the Town Hall in Cannes, on 6 November 1922, with the British Vice-Consul officiating, in the presence of the bride's father, Vladimir Sollohub, Count, and the groom's father, Charles Murray, Lord Advocate, David Charles Graeme Murray married Countess Helen Maia Sollohub of Les Cabriers, Mougins. The Sollohubs, I surmise, were Russians on the run from the Revolution. There are photographs of the wedding on the web. Count Vladimir sits covered in medals and ribbons, relics of his glorious past. The bride's mother, Princess Elena Shervashidze, gazes bleakly out from between the low brow of a hat and the furred bodies of small animals, arranged round her neck. Perhaps she is mourning the fall from grace of her daughter. Princess Elena was of the ruling family of Georgia-Abkhazia, which had been recognised as one of the princely families of the Russian Empire by the Treaty of Georgievsk. But Helen, dressed in fashionable 1920s gear, looks to be a cheery soul, as does her husband, David, who, in his natty suit, has an air of James Stewart about him. Helen, Comtesse Sollahub, died in July 1945. David died thirty years later, aged seventy-nine, at 81 Avenue Les Ternes in the 17th arrondisement of Paris. Probate of his estate in England was granted at £41820 on 26 June 1978. There's no indication that he ever returned to Scotland.

Annie and Charles' third son, Keith, also born at 10 Scotland Street, was a man of numerous accomplishments and international honours. He became an academic, an agricultural economist by trade, the Chair of the University Grants Committee, the begetter of UCCA (the forerunner of UCAS), a moderniser, defender and expander of universities, and a power in the land. He was instrumental in the reform of Australian higher education and spent much time there. He became a life peer in 1964, taking the title of Baron Murray of Newhaven, in the County and City of Edinburgh. This event took place three months short of a century after his grandfather, the bibulous silk merchant, had married his grandmother, Rachel Gavin, daughter of of William, General Merchant, of Williamfield, Newhaven. Newhaven must have been a refuge for Rachel's uprooted children, and perhaps also her grandson Keith.

After retiring, Keith Murray served as a trustee on the Leverhulme and Wellcome Trusts. He never married. He died on 10 October 1993, in Putney, leaving an estate valued at £1173780. A click of the mouse brings up portraits of the velvet- and ermine-clad elderly man who was born in my house in 1903. My first click and sight of his portrait convinced me that, somewhere and at some point in the nineteen-sixties or -seventies, I had met Keith Murray. His obituarist, sent by the *The Independent* newspaper to interview him, concludes a friendly portrait of a clever, powerful man with the remark that he found Keith Murray, in his 80s, in his Westminster flat, engaged in embroidery.

After Annie and Charles moved to Great King Street, 10 Scotland Street entered an odd period of several years, when nothing much

10 Scotland Street After David

seems to have happened – though of course there were always the lost dogs. On 19 August 1904, *The Scotsman* advertised a 'Lost Airedale (smooth haired) address on collar; reward 10 Scotland St.' Tenants of 10 Scotland Street appear to have been distinctly careless of the whereabouts of their dogs.

According to the 1904–1905 Register of Electors for the Council, a greater proportion of the inhabitants of Scotland Street are tenants. The economic class of residents is not so much going down as on the slide. There are vanmen, labourers and dressmakers in addresses formerly occupied by their presumed betters. However, at number 8, there is a David Keith Balfour Whyte – an evocative name – who has the somewhat alarming profession of Assistant Extractor at the Court of Session. At number 22 is a welcome breath of things to come, with Ms Cairns, a single woman, living alone and giving her occupation as journalist. Was she a member of a suffrage society? Very few records survive. Voting in Parliamentary elections would not be open to all women aged twenty-one and over until 1928. I was brought up short when I first realised that my financially-poor but energetic, politically-aware and intelligent grandmother could not vote until she was forty-one. I'm indebted to my friend Dr Esther Breitenbach, who has made a study of women's political history, for the information that in the Women's Library at LSE, in the forty-fifth annual report of the Edinburgh Society for Women's Suffrage of 1913, she found the names of four women of Scotland Street. Subscribing 1/- each were Miss E Kinnear Wilson at number 2; Miss J Inglis Walkinshaw, a retired teacher who, until her death in 1936, lived at number 11; and Miss Annabelle Clark, a School Board teacher, at number 31. Her sister Elizabeth, who was not a subscriber, gave 5/-. Elizabeth was a Mistress of Method, which rang a very faint bell until I realised that, in 1965, I had attended the Methods Department of Jordanhill Teacher Training College under the tutelage of a Mistress of Method. I believe 1965 saw the last of them.

In 1904, there was no voter at number 10, but from 1906 until 1909, Thomas Nightingale Broughton, a brewer, was registered at the address. When he moved into Scotland Street from lodgings in Albany Street, he had recently married Sophia Binnie Drybrough, the daughter of a fellow brewer, of Gogar Park, the home of the Drybrough brewing dynasty. I do hope the bathroom had been fixed. They were both twenty-seven and were married in Corstorphine, by no less a person than the minister of Glasgow Cathedral. They left Scotland Street in 1910 for larger premises on Edinburgh's south side.

Oddly, in 1907, while Mr Broughton and his heiress wife lived at number 10, they hosted a sale of the property of the deceased Miss Potts, which included a lady's bicycle. Miss Alice Potts was a single woman of thirty-four, the daughter of a miner and a deceased mother. Alice died of acute pneumonia at 1b Scotland Street on 24 January 1907. Her death was registered by her friend Henrietta Elder, of 9B, directly opposite number 10. Henrietta was the wife of Thomas Elder the grocer, and the mother of six daughters, ranging in age from sixteen to six. I'm told that they all worked in the shop and have an image of them, behind the counter, ranged by height, ready to serve.

On 13 February 1908, a Mr R. B. Drybrough of 10 Scotland Street, presumably a relative of Mrs Broughton, attended a ball in the Assembly Rooms dressed as a 'French Pierrot. white with black pompoms, character makeup, etc.' Later that year, the Whytt trust sold the baker's equipment at 10A and the baker's shop was no more. The only remnant now of that premises, over one hundred years later, is a dip in the carriageway of the lane where the road – despite my intermittent appeals to the Council – is, I believe, subsiding gently into the ovens. For the next few years, the tenant of 10A was a confectioner, Mrs Wilhelmina Eliza Smith, who was succeeded by a roadman and a charwoman. The fabric of the basement deteriorated further.

On 14 June 1909, Charles Ernest Alison, a master printer, was pleased to announce that his wife, Emily Edith Mills, of Birmingham, had given birth, at 10 Scotland Street, to a son, Thomas. On 8 February 1910, Mr Alison wrote in disgust to *The Scotsman*, to add his voice to that of others who had protested the treatment meted out by the Treasury to Dr William Spiers Bruce and the Scottish National Antarctic Expedition. To paraphrase a rather verbose letter: Dr Bruce, had made many Antarctic expeditions, and Sir

Ernest Shackleton himself had said that Dr Bruce made much more of a contribution to science than his own expeditions ever could. Moreover, the great value of Dr Bruce's research had been amply proved and acknowledged by all the scientific societies, Universities and Museums, at home and abroad, and the Admiralty had used his work. Yet, while Captain Scott and Shackleton received grants, when Dr Bruce asked for support for his new Scottish National Expedition, he was met by a blunt refusal from the Imperial Treasury. Mr Alison, his outrage palpable, called on his fellow-countrymen to agitate to ensure that Dr Bruce was supported in his great work.

I wrote that last paragraph on a train from Aberdeen to Edinburgh, and returned to my office to open my computer. On it I found a message from a member of the then-current Scottish Government to the effect that the said Government was working to rehabilitate the said Dr Bruce. A memorial to Bruce has been placed on Signy Island in the Southern Antarctic Ocean. There is also one at Surgeon's Hall in Edinburgh, near to where Bruce set up his Scottish Oceanographical Laboratory. He and his findings are now acknowledged as crucial to our understanding of the Antarctic, and his careful methods and conclusions are contrasted, by many, with the aims of his rivals who were concerned with increasing imperial prestige. But he was apparently described, by those inclined to kindness, as uncharismatic, and more accurately, it seems, as being as prickly as a Scottish thistle. Perhaps that explains the neglect.

The outraged Mr Alison and his wife and children were counted in the 1911 census in Scotland Street, and then they moved on. Yule and Co, house and estate agents, advertised: '10 Scotland Street, 2 public, 6 beds bath etc at 47/- per year.'

Down the road at Scotland Yard, the Gymnasium was no more and was replaced by a football ground, the home of St Bernard's FC until the Second World War. During the 1930s, a greyhound track surrounded the pitch. St Bernard's were popular locally but hit their biggest ticket sales when, in 1932, they lost to Hibernian FC, but only by 1–0.

On 26 April 1912, there was a sale at 10 Scotland Street of 'the property of a Lady Going Abroad'. The catalogue gives a snapshot of the contents of my house at the time. There was household furniture, including a mahogany sideboard, a mahogany wardrobe, an oak cabinet, an harmonium with eight stops, chests of drawers, washstands, mirrors, six walnut chairs, easy and occasional chairs, bedsteads, a clock, curtains, dining and occasional tables, carpets, linoleum, kitchen dresser, a mangle, a wringer, a pedestal, a meat safe etc . . . Oh, for a wormhole in time. Actually, Aphra Walker Deans, our Lady Going Abroad, might well feel entirely at home in most of my rooms. Who was she?

Aphra Walker married John Deans, a farmer, in Glasgow, on 18 December 1893. She was eighteen and he, thirty-eight. Her first child, Aphra Colclough, was born four months later at Fenton Barns Farm, Dirleton, just south of Edinburgh. Contemporary farm records show a large and prosperous undertaking. But Mr Deans was a peripatetic farmer; their next child was born in Ayrshire, and their third, in Aberdeenshire. Then, John Deans came to rest in Portobello, just outside Edinburgh. His widow gave his profession as retired farmer. With three children under five, Aphra Deans must have weighed up her options and decided that boldness was her friend. She moved into Edinburgh, renting 10 Scotland Street from 1911 to 1912, and selling all her worldly goods, before travelling to Liverpool to embark on an assisted passage for Australia. I wonder if her daughter Aphra, who had been a student at the Art College, became an artist. She married a man named John Paterson, from Kilmarnock, had two children, and died on 23 May 1950, in Chatsworth, NSW. And that is all I could find.

10 Scotland Street was next briefly occupied by a Mr Edward Smith and his lodger, Alexander Crofton Sleigh. In the former bakery below them lived Miss Emily Vidler, an art student. This is the second example of a woman with a profession living alone. The rest of the lower area had been designated a store, and was vacant. Its descent into the abandoned shell I found in 1974 was almost complete.

THIRTEEN

TEN IN FORTY-ONE

The next family to live in my house were the Gullands. Edwin Eyre Gulland was born on 12 September 1876 at 8 Register Place, a few steps from the building which houses the record of his birth, marriage and death. He was thirty-nine when he died in the mud near the Somme. He had attended George Heriot's School in Edinburgh from 1887–91, and played for the first rugby fifteen. On the school's roll of honour, Edwin's photograph portrays a good-looking man, with a magnificent moustache and a twinkle in his eye.

He was employed by Messrs J. Montgomerie and Company in Haddington, and was already in service with the Royal Scots part-time before the war. The school announced his death along with the information that he had left a widow and a family of four living at 10 Scotland Street.

Edwin was a sergeant in the 8th battalion of the Royal Scots, territorials from East Lothian. The battalion crossed to France early in November 1914 and were sent immediately to the front line. In March 1915, they withdrew to prepare for a major set-piece battle under the oversight of Field Marshal Earl Haig. It was a disaster and they lost many men. Edwin Gulland was killed on Sunday, 16 May, the first day of the battle at Festubert, a debacle. He was buried in the Guards Cemetery, Windy Corner, Cuinchy, in the Pas de Calais. On the Commonwealth War Graves Commission website, it's clear that his body has been exhumed and reburied in the cemetery. On the same page there is a Sergeant W.B. Clark and fifteen others, each referred to only as 'Unknown British Soldier.' From this, we can deduce that some scrap of identification must have remained on both Edwin and Sergeant Clark's bodies, and nothing on the others.

Over the years, the identities of the men who died in the 1914–18 war have been painstakingly researched and collated. Those of the women, not so much. Over 1400 women of the British Empire have been commemorated on panels in York Minster. There will be many missing. They were drivers, pilots, foragers, members of each of the forces, doctors, nurses and orderlies. At home, they died working on munitions and explosives. I have not been able to connect any of the names at York Minster or on the Roll of Honour in Edinburgh Castle to Scotland Street. Very few women were commemorated on local memorials. I spent eleven years working with various organisations to put the name of a woman, which is on the York Minster panels and on the Roll of Honour in Edinburgh Castle, on her local war memorial, which listed only men, including her brother who died of a fever in training in Canada.

The first Scotland Street resident to die was Glen Moncrieff Laing, of number 33. Glen was the son of William, a copper engraver, and Christina Henderson, and the third of ten sons who might be taken by the war. In 1901, Glen was nineteen, and a tailor, and, by 1911, a private serving in India with the 2nd Battalion of the Queen's Own Cameron Highlanders. He died around 14 September 1914, three weeks after the British force landed in France, and five days after his regiment arrived at the front to advance on the Aisne. My uncle was in the forward guard with the North Irish Horse. He survived, though his horse did not. So many horses were killed in the war, that many men of the regiment ended it on bicycles. Glen Moncrieff Laing was 'presumed dead', which means that his remains could not be identified. Six hundred men of the Cameronians were lost on 14 September, many of them killed by rifle fire from the British lines behind them. In all, 3,500 men of the first division were casualties that day. The British commander, Sir John French, deplored the heavy toll, but said it was absolutely necessary to defend the River Aisne. Four other Laing sons fought and survived. Given the perilous nature of their exploits, Christina and William may have felt relieved to have lost only one.

Next to be swallowed by the war was John Victor Irvine, a private in the Royal Scots, at number 31, Glen Moncrieff Laing's neighbour. John Victor was the youngest of eight children of John Bruce, a stationer, and Jemima Irving. He joined the Royal Scots and was with the 4th Battalion when they landed at Gallipoli. On the day he died, his battalion was sent forward to secure a trench. The intelligence was faulty. Chaos reigned. Major D Yuille of the 4th Battalion is quoted in R R Thomson's *The Fifty Second Division 1914–1918*:

> Unless one has seen it there is no imagination that can picture a belt of land some 400 yards wide converted into a seething hell of destruction ... The noise is an indescribable, nerve-racking, continuous, deafening roar, while drifting clouds of smoke only allow an intermittent view of the damnable inferno.

John Irvine, aged twenty-seven, died on 12 July 1915, in one of the most futile attacks of the war – and that is saying something. Along with 20958 others, he is commemorated at the Helles Memorial. Of this number, 1506 were Indian, and 249 were Australian. Fifty-three bodies, including John's, could not be identified. The Helles Memorial is a few miles down the coast from the Lone Pine Memorial, where is commemorated Lance Corporal Richmond Whytt, who came all the way from Australia to die of dysentery just three months after John Victor Irvine.

On the same day, 12 July 1915, James Sanderson aged 31, of 10B Scotland Street, a Private in the Kings Own Scottish Borderers, died in the same attack on the Turkish trenches at Achi Baba Nullah. He was born in Galashiels, worked as a Law Clerk and moved to Scotland Street with his wife, Margaret, and two small children. On the official page recording his name, there are eleven men, of whom one was killed in action, one died of wounds, and the others are presumed dead. That is, their bodies were not recovered nor identified. The official War Diary for the day records that on 12 July, the Battalion, having been repelled by the Turks, had to retreat through fire of their own artillery, and also fire from enemy artillery, machine guns and rifles, causing heavy losses. Three days later, casualties were listed: Officers Killed five, Wounded six, Missing seven. Total eighteen. Other ranks Killed fifty-seven, Wounded 203, Missing 275. Total 535. James Sanderson, whose final resting place is unknown, joined John Victor Irvine and Richmond Whytt on the Helles Memorial. Nearby is Edwin Eyre Gulland's cousin, William Gulland, a Leith bookbinder.

On the Gallipoli list of dead, a few names above James Sanderson's and John Victor's, is John Sprott Sinclair of 41 Scotland Street, the last house before the corner, who died on 21 July 1915. These three young neighbours were from the same regiment and the same battalion. John Sinclair, however, was not blown to bits, but was transported to a hospital at Alexandria where he died of his wounds. He was buried in the Chatby cemetery.

Private John Arthur Maguire of 13 Scotland Street died on 17 April 1917. His mother, Ellen Murray, and his father, John, a bookbinder, had married in 1895 at St Patrick's Catholic Church in the Cowgate. John Arthur was born on 29 June 1896. 13 Scotland Street is almost directly opposite number 10 and very similar. I can see it as I write. I searched a long time for John Arthur Maguire's death – then I found him. He died in France in April 1917, fighting alongside Edwin Gulland's nephew, Frank, who died a few months later. They were privates in the 2nd Battalion Canadian Mounted Rifles. This was unexpected, but also welcome, information. Many British records were lost during the WW2 bombing of London. The Canadians kept meticulous records and have digitised and made them available. In search of John Maguire, I found two documents. One was two pages long and the other was an extraordinary thirty-eight. He had joined up in Vancouver in May 1915 as Arthur Murray – his second name and his mother's maiden surname. As the documents piled up, his name was corrected with, 'Also Known As John Arthur Maguire.' John gave his age as twenty years, eleven months. In fact, he was barely nineteen. My friend Charlotte in Toronto pointed out what I had missed – that his use of an alias could be to cover the fact that he was underage. Before he landed in France in December 1916, he made his will, leaving everything to his mother, Mrs Ellen Maguire of 13 Scotland Street. Ten weeks later, in early April, the Canadians suffered 3598 deaths, and 7004 men wounded during the Battle of Vimy Ridge. One of these was John Arthur, who was recorded as 'non-effective' through death, 'DofW.' Died of Wounds. He had named as his next of kin, his mother, Mrs Ellen Maguire, of 29 Gillespie Crescent, Edinburgh. His father was still at 13 Scotland Street. For a Catholic marriage at this time, this is very unusual. What did Ellen's husband – or indeed Ellen – do that caused the end of their marriage, with Ellen leaving the family home never to return? A medal, scroll and plaque were sent to Mr and Mrs Maguire at 13 Scotland Street. Mr Maguire wrote to the Canadian authorities and a firm black line was drawn through Mrs Maguire's name, which John Arthur had given as next of kin. His father's is substituted. However, his will was verified. His mother received $483.90 for the life of her son.

John Arthur was buried in the Pas de Calais in Wimereux Communal Cemetery, in Plot 2, Row H, Grave 7. There is a small flat stone for each grave. Some are inscribed. His is not. And that appears to have been that. There is no way of discovering what made Ellen Murray leave 13 Scotland Street to board in Gillespie Crescent, or why her son nominated her, rather than his father, as next of kin. It's disturbing that the dead son's wishes could be overridden by his father, who emigrated to Canada soon after. Three remaining sons stayed in Scotland long enough to see their sister marry a poultry farmer and then left for Canada in quick succession. The third son sailed from Glasgow on the Canadian Pacific Steamship, *Metagama*, on which my own father, aged twenty-one, made the same voyage eighteen months later. Ellen is listed in 1932–33 as living in London and as the owner of not 13, but 11 Scotland Street. Number 13, then, and for some years, was owned by a Mrs Rose LE Maguire 1054 Spadina Crescent, East Saskatoon, Canada. Surely, the widow of one of Ellen's sons. I surmise that Ellen followed her married daughter to London. I have imagined for her a happy, busy old age in Crouch Hill with her daughter and grandchildren, and occasional visits from her three boys, as the Atlantic crossing became quicker and cheaper.

The Canada/Scotland relationship is sewn through with such stories. I might well have – or someone bearing a passing resemblance to me, might well have – been writing this in Canada. My father, who sailed home for a wee visit to Scotland on *Metagama*, found a return to Canada impossible, as the crash of the late 1920s wiped out his chance of work in his trade – though he sent his excellent references across the globe. He'd had a fine life near Timmins, in northern Ontario, working at the McIntyre gold mine, boarding in South Porcupine, with the wilderness all around. It was only by chance that he did not live out his days in Canada. There was a woman he loved waiting for him. Some twenty years ago, I travelled by tiny propeller plane to Timmins. As I remember, I flew for three hours, stretched out on a divan back seat, by night, slowly, over rough, corrugated country, lit brightly by moonlight. My dominant thought, looking down, was, who were these people who had built roads and railways over this impossible terrain? The stewardess brought me more than my fair share of wine.

Timmins, in my father's and the Maguire's time in the mid-1920s, was a booming mining town, lately reached by the railway line – the same line by which I returned to Toronto. The town I visited two decades ago was a ghost of what it had been. I found a Days Inn where the public rooms were in the window-less interior, and the food problematic for someone who does not eat meat. I also found an excellent library where the language slipped back and forth in English and French, and a helpful librarian. I discovered a 1920s busy, young, mining community that explained my father's excellent ballroom dancing (he taught me and I'm not bad), his silver cup for curling, his football referee certificate, and his beautiful, old, unusually brown, bellows camera and boxes of negatives. It also offered an explanation for the tiny bit of gold pyrite in his bureau drawer, and the oilcloth-wrapped, disabled handgun, which was not-well-enough hidden in our shed in a suburb of Glasgow. I don't know what happened to that gun. If I know my engineer father, it's in numerous bits strewn across some moor somewhere.

I rested by the lake in Schumacher, where he sat in the late 1920s in his mid-twenties to eat his lunchtime sandwiches, and looked over to the iconic McIntyre headframe. It's the last remaining symbol of the Porcupine Gold Rush and has come to represent it. The drawing office – my father, who left school at thirteen, had started work in a garage, and through dogged night-school attendance had turned himself into an engineer/draughtsman – is long gone. But I'd seen the plans, and knew what parcel of air to the right of the headframe had housed his drawing board, and thus him. His best friend, a young Greek, with whom he canoed the lakes and hitched to New York, stayed in Canada and thrived, as did several of my other relatives and many, many other Scots.

The Maguire's story is reflected in multiple, if not most, Scottish and Irish families. It started in earnest with the Clearances and the famines and peaked in the Depression, but from a grey and tired 1950s and early 60s Britain, many were still taking that boat trip. And so, though it seems harsh that her remaining three sons all left Ellen for Canada, it was a common experience.

The next young man to be killed, on 18 July 1917, was the splendidly named Victor Charles Augustus Macleod, of 19 Scotland Street, a Second Lieutenant in the Cameronian Scottish Rifles. He was the son of Robert Crawford Macleod and Jane Fairley, who married by declaration at the Edinburgh Sheriff Court on 24 April 1882. Jane had been boarding, next door to Thomas and Grace Smith's former home, in Keir Street, since she was fifteen. Robert had been left at fifteen, after the deaths of his parents, to bring up five younger siblings. Robert and Jane were very young and, as far as I can see, totally alone, but they made a go of it. Robert became a lithographer and printer, and together they had nine children, giving them names such as Leo, Claud, Cornelius and Cecil. By 1911, the family were installed in 19 Scotland Street, a house of ten rooms spread over two floors. Robert now had his own paper and stationery business and his children were banking and insurance clerks. At forty-six, Jane Fairley had lost three infants, had four sons of military age, and her husband was an officer – but it was her youngest for whom she should have feared.

Victor Charles Augustus joined up at nineteen, almost as soon as the war started. His regiment was the local Queen's Own Cameron Highlanders, aka 79th regiment of Foot – the regiment my great-grandfather joined in 1855. I doubt if he and Victor would have had much in common. Victor's photograph in the Heriot's School Roll of Honour shows a rather grim, determined-looking young man. He was made second ieutenant in 1915, proceeded to Egypt in

January 1916, and was wounded in April 1917, before being killed fighting Turkish soldiers in the desert south-east of Gaza, Palestine, on 18 July 1917. He was buried in the Gaza Cemetery. He was twenty-two.

Wallace Williamson McFarlane, of 41 Scotland Street, was a Quartermaster Sergeant in the Royal Army Medical Corps. He died on 9 January 1918, also aged twenty-two. He was born in Glenfarg, a neat little village in Perthshire, where his family ran the bakery. Until the 1970s it was on the Great North Road to Perth, and I have memories of the glen itself, and the narrow green windings of the road, overhung with trees and often treacherous with leaves. Today, the M9 has elbowed the glen aside. The family moved to Edinburgh and Wallace became an engineer/fitter apprentice with Bertrams. He was almost eighteen when he joined the Territorial Force in March 1913. His enlistment papers tell us that he was most unusual, in that he was 5'10 ½" tall. On the day after war was declared, he was drafted into the Royal Army Medical Corps, inoculated, medically examined, and like many others, was found to have terrible teeth. He had twelve fillings and five extractions before being assigned to the Mediterranean Expeditionary force. He wrote his will, leaving everything to his youngest brother, Charles, of 41 Scotland Street, and embarked for Alexandria, thence to Abbassia just outside Cairo, where, at the Canadian hospital, he had more dental treatment. Abbassia was fiercely fought over by British and Turkish soldiers trying to secure the Suez Canal. I read that Walter was in transport and, assumed, as an engineer – until I realised he was attached to the Camel Transport Corps. There are many brown images online of the British army with their camels and their rows of bell-tents in the desert. When I was a girl, the tents we used were all ex-army, and most were regulation, heavy, canvas, bell-tents. With four other wee girls, I once won a bell-tent-erecting competition. We did it in eleven minutes – including rolling and tying off the skirts. They were excellent airy habitations for up to eight people, their design ensuring a small amount of personal space at the periphery and a jumble of feet at the pole.

Wallace was promoted to Quartermaster Sergeant and regularly sent on courses, one of which, at Tel El Kebir, was for treating gas casualties. He died, after surviving four years of war, of an abscess on a tonsil, in hospital at Kantara. Wallace is buried in Kantara Cemetery, surrounded by many Australians, Indians and Scots, and is remembered on the War Memorial that sits in the middle of Glenfarg village.

The last man from the street to lose his life to the war was Robert Loudon. Robert was brought up in the four-storey, sixteen-room house at number 12 Broughton Place, almost directly opposite the Padon home. In 1905–06 the rateable value of the house was £50. It sold on 19 July 2019 for £1300000. The family moved to 20 Scotland Street and, from there, Robert enlisted, aged eighteen, in the 13th Battalion, Royal Scots.

The 13th became part of the British Expeditionary Force, moved to France in July 1915, and remained there throughout the war, fighting in some of the fiercest battles and suffering over 50% casualties. Robert survived the Battles of the Somme, Loos, the Marne, and the first battle at Passchendaele. It is a litany of the worst places to be. As the final weeks of the war played out, his battalion was tasked with attacking, taking, and then defending, a place called The Quarries. The records say that the German defence was fierce and unrelenting. Second Lieutenant Robert Loudon, twenty-two, was killed in action on 13 September 1918. The Battalion was relieved three days later, and the war itself ended two months later. Robert lies in the Noeux-les-Mines Communal Cemetery Extension in the Pas de Calais, along with 313 others, in a relatively small burial ground. Among this number are seventy-one Canadians, one South African, 230 United Kingdom soldiers, one airman and eleven Germans. His parents provided an inscription, 'NOT GONE FROM MEMORY NOR FROM LOVE BUT TO THE FATHER'S HOME ABOVE.'

Having researched these young men as well as I might, I decided to run their names through the National Archives website. In all nine cases there was nothing. However, the search did throw up Robert Kirkwood Lawson of 25 Scotland Street. Against Robert's name was noted: 1915–1918 letters rel(ative) to his service with the Argyll and Sutherland Highlanders, held in the Imperial War Museum in Lambeth. I calculated, nearing the end of the 2021 pandemic travel restrictions, when I might be able to get myself there, and contacted the archivist to book an appointment. None was available. Then she emailed me news of a cancellation. The Museum is housed round a large central hall hung with fighter planes. Pausing only to buy a spitfire baseball cap and take photos for my armament-obsessed grandson (who is the nicest, kindest, wee soul on the planet), I found myself hefting a fat file onto my allotted desk. Robert Lawson wrote at length and often to his mother in Scotland Street and to his sister Bessie, who was clearly a modern woman, supporting herself as a clerkess in a bank in London. In Robert's letters, I found a detailed description of his training, the variable quality of the food, his hut accommodation, and how heavy and unwieldy was the pack he must carry to prepare himself for the battlefield. It is a terrible thing, hung about with belts, bags and straps. In it, he carries a greatcoat, boots, shoes, socks, mess-tins, and strapped on it, a blanket. In the front bag, he has his grub, knife, fork, spoon, and his shaving and washing equipment. In the pouches on the side, he carries his ammunition. In addition he carries his rifle, bayonet and entrenching tools, which consist of a pick and a shovel. I have one of these entrenching shovels, bought at a rural jumble sale, and it is not light. He tells Bessie that he is now good at packing it all but cannot say that he can carry it as well. After initial training and before he is shipped out, he is allowed a day's leave. Without telephones, mobile or otherwise, arrangements go wrong and he travels, with difficulty, to Bessie's digs in Barnes and then to the bank, but can find her nowhere and returns to St Pancras discouraged and having spent all his money. After he lands in France, his letters become more guarded as, of course, they are censored. In July 1916, he is back on the front line after a short break and glad that things are relatively quiet as compared to their last billet where they had no peace, day or night, 'and the wind was always up'. The chaps they relieved have 'had a bad cutting up'. He finishes this letter by saying it is very hot and he must go, 'as the sweat is pouring off me and I am fedup writing and I think that Allemand is going to let us know he is not yet gone home, so I'll close with Best Love, Bob.' His cheerful, friendly character shines through, though he is clearly discouraged by living in a trench with his feet in six inches of mud and rats who steal his biscuits. In the autumn of 1916, he has his boots off five times in fifty-one days and sleeps where he stands, wrapped in his greatcoat. After a gruelling patrol, he becomes ill and is sent to a Clearing Station where he is delighted to have a bed and as many blankets as he likes. However, he is then sent on a sixteen-hour journey by Red Cross Train, no faster, he says, than an Edinburgh car (tram), to a tented General Hospital. Back at the line he is pleased with a new kilt and warm shirts as his have been destroyed by hugging the barbed wire and the filthy trenches. He ends this letter by saying his sister is a lucky girl to be going home next week. How he longs to go with her. But he must bide his time. He encloses a photo labelled: *After two years in France*. His image speaks more of his experiences than his words.

Through 1917, he speaks of hoping to find something really French for Bessie. I am put in mind of a delicate silk handkerchief in a turned wooden box with a faded rose painted on the lid, sent from France in 1916 to my grandmother, by her brother-in-law, and now on the chest beside my bed. The accompanying letter survives. He had chosen the wee silk handerchief because it seemed, to him, really French. He asks after my mother, his three-year-old niece. His name was William Alexander Carson. He joined the Royal Engineers in September 1914 and was demobbed in October 1918 after four solid years in France. Unable to settle down, he worked on ships and travelled the world, settling shortly in Canada and then the US, drink and unwarranted bursts of optimism clouding his judgment. He was found dead on a pavement in Edinburgh after a life blighted by those four horrific years.

By the end of 1917, Robert Lawson has buried several friends and put heather on their graves. Bread is short and parcels are not getting through. As 1918 draws near, he writes of the armaments left lying around which will blow up unwitting future tourists. He becomes more resigned. After a big push, he reports that he is unharmed but has lost everything and has only the tattered clothes on his back. He is most annoyed about losing his shaving kit and his Balmoral – his hat. He asks Bessie if she has his Glengarry, yet another hat. He will need it when he gets home. He is struggling to control the lice on his body and clothes. Then, at last, he has some leave and, on 9 December 1917, he writes to Bessie from 25 Scotland Street. I look at the worn steps of number 25 and see him take them two, at a time, in his tattered, filthy kilt, to where his mother waits at the open door. By 21 December, he is back in the land of shell-holes and sandbags. The mud is so bad that he and his fellows discard their kilts in favour of long rubber boots and trousers which are several sizes too big. In the early spring, he is in hospital for a while but soon returns to the line, worrying about aerial activity both in France and over London. He tells Bessie that he is sure this is the finish and he will be home by summer. In the mean time, he is looking forward to new adventures before his longed-for return takes place. During the spring he is on loan to the Gordon Highlanders and talks of cooking bacon and bread so that no smoke gives away his position. But he is hoping soon to be back with the Signals. The last letter in the bundle is dated 16 June 1918. It took some time for news to filter back to Scotland Street. His remains were found at Pierrefonds, marked by a wooden cross. The date was given as 24 July 1918. No effects were by him. Later, his remains, like many others, were exhumed and re-interred and marked with a cross, on which his mother requested the words, 'In Proud and Loving Memory.' She was not informed officially of his death until November 1918.

Robert's mother was still at number 25 in 1921, living with her daughter and sister-in-law but also with her other son, Thomas, and his wife Mary, and their son Robert Kirkwood Lawson, born eighteen months or so after his uncle's death.

These ten deaths of men of Scotland Street are those I can find. There may well be more. There are forty-one addresses in Scotland Street. It is quite a tally. Last to die, Robert Loudon of 20 Scotland Street, lies in a burial ground that is just fifteen minutes from the resting place of the first to die, Edwin Gulland of number 10. In 1915, their Royal Scots Battalions were fighting in the same sector. Perhaps they met in the mud. John Sinclair and Wallace McFarlane shared the same address at 41 Scotland Street. Four doors along lived Glen Moncrieff Laing and directly next door, John Victor Irvine. Five doors away was Robert Lawson; another five to John

Maguire and three doors from him, Victor McLeod. Number 20, the home of Robert Loudon is opposite the McLeods and five doors down from number 10 which housed both Edwin Gulland and James Sanderson. As I said, it's a short street – and by 1919 a street full of grieving families and women whose lives were changed beyond repair.

FOURTEEN

DECLINE AND RESURRECTION

In April 1917, 10 Scotland Street was advertised for rent, at an annual rate of 45/-. Number 4, with whom I share a wall, was 50/- shillings, but it had electric light. I should think electricity was not installed in my house until after it was sold by the Whytts. And I believe that nothing else was done on that score, for fifty years, until we first rewired the house in 1974. The original fuse boxes were not replaced until well into the twenty-first century. I still hoard fuse wire. You never know.

The house entered multiple occupancy. The widow Gulland, still only thirty-nine, stayed on. The proprietor of 20 Scotland Street morphed, in the 1930s, into R.C. Loudon Limited, a property company, and Isabella, Robert's sister, lived on at number 20 until at least 1940. The family bought 4A when the basement rooms were detached from number 4. There are very few houses in the street which still have their original basements.

In the 1921 census, the five Gullands had three of number 10's nine rooms. Two Gulland boys were now working, one as an apprentice turner at Bruce Peebles, a company founded in 1866, which, through many changes of name and ownership was still offering coveted apprenticeships to the fifteen-year-old boys I taught in the sixties. By 1940, the widow Gulland and three of her children had moved across the road to 9b Scotland Street. She ended her days, as far as I can make out, living with family on the Southside until she died, aged eighty-four, in 1966, fifty years after her husband, Edwin.

Decline and Resurrection

In 1921, two of the nine rooms at number 10 were occupied by James Dryburgh, an Inland Revenue Officer, and his wife Catherine, and in another four rooms, lived Mary Kirk and her two sons, an insurance collector and a mason's labourer, and their sister, a draper's shop assistant. The servants' basement was now a home.

Six people were packed into three rooms at 10A. Head of the household was Susan Gibbons, a widow. She had three grown children living with her. Her eldest son was an out-of-work wireless operator. Her daughter and second son worked in a law firm. She also had two boarders, Hugh McCutcheon, an out-of-work salesman, and Audrey Dickson, a waitress at Patrick Thomson, a large department store on North Bridge with a palm court on top. There, one could partake of tea and fancies to the subdued strains of an orchestra, while admiring panoramic views of Edinburgh. PTs, which once operated in the Luckenbooths, was opened on the bridge in 1886 and lasted till the mid-1970s. On the one occasion, I entered the portals, I asked for coffee and got Nescafe, served by a waitress in a white lace pinny and cap. I felt like a bad actor in one of the church hall amateur dramatics of my youth.

At 10B, Annabella Reid, a widow, who worked in a baker's shop, had two whole rooms to herself. She shared the basement, however, with George Bevan, a plasterer's labourer, his wife and two stepchildren.

Down West Scotland Street Lane, numbers had fallen. In the two rooms at 2a were John Finlay, a saddler, and his wife Lily, who, like Margaret Crease fifty years before, was a paper stamper. John Finlay was probably the last worker associated with horses down the lane. There was a chauffeur, the first of his kind, in two rooms at number 4. Jane Steel from Kirkwall, with her daughter and grandson, had the other two rooms. Numbers 6 and 8 were uninhabited, while, in 7, were James and Mary Duncan, fish merchants. Finally, in the two rooms at number 20, down the little side lane, lived Helen Smith, who appears to have been divorced. A first. Only the eldest of her six children, Thomas, aged fifteen, was not a scholar. He was an apprentice woodcarver. I wonder how long his skills were marketable.

The 1921 census was planned for Sunday 24 April. Post-war depression had produced industrial unrest which led to a series of strikes. The census was moved to June. This resulted in some skewing of results, as the month of June, in some parts, was a popular holiday time. The change of date does not seem to have affected Scotland Street, perhaps because the Edinburgh Trades Holiday was in July.

Many changes had taken place since the first census in 1841, eighty years previously. On the night of that census, more than one hundred distinct families were counted. There were 425 people living in 540 rooms in 110 households. Eight houses were uninhabited. In 1921, 395 people lived in 540 rooms in 100 households. The ratio of male to female remained fairly constant, though the totals had dropped. There were fewer large families, so fewer children. In 1841, there were solicitors, bookbinders, a gardener, a music teacher, a physician-surgeon, several school teachers and preachers of the gospel, booksellers, a newspaper editor, masons, bakers, coachmakers, an engraver, a carpet weaver, a meal dealer, a dressmaker, advocates, accountants, bankers, an artist's colourman, a mathematician, a genealogist and publishers, along with the housekeepers and many servants. The contrast between 1841 and 1921, in the way that the people of Scotland Street earned a living, is striking. In 1921, there are many more office workers: twenty-seven clerks and clerkesses, three bookkeepers, and ten typists. There is one advocate and one solicitor and I can find no booksellers. At number 15, is Egypt-born Mohamed Wafik Yakan, a medical student who subsequently spent his days in Chester. There are only eleven servants, all female, and only a handful in manual employment, of whom most are unemployed. Two women are cashiers at the Picture Palace and one is a professional pianist. There are two artists, several men and women in the printing trade and four medical students, two of whom are women. Many are involved in shopkeeping, from grocers to clothiers, and one man is a representative of the Shell Spirit Company and another of Cerebos Salt. One man labours at the Royal Botanic Gardens, as did a recent tenant in West Scotland Street Lane, and one is a chargehand of riveters at the Admiralty in Leith. Two shipwrights have come from the south coast of England to work in the government yards at Rosyth and five men work in various roles on the railways. There are several civil servants and bank workers and two work for the New Zealand and Australia Company. As always, the majority were born elsewhere and the count provides a snapshot of society. The numbers born in the Empire were much reduced: one in the Cape Colony, three in the Penang Straits Settlement, two in British Guiana, three in the USA and one in Canada, seven in Ireland and only one in India. I noted the egg merchant and his son, whose premises were still signed in ghostly fashion when I first walked down the lane.

In 1921, the Whytts were moving towards selling up. Most of the houses in the street were rented out, with proprietors living elsewhere. There was still a home and workshop at 1A, and shops at 3A, 2A and 9B. Number 14B, which had housed a furnaceman at the Waverley Glass Company and his family, had been condemned as unfit for human habitation by the city authorities.

At number 10 was Ethel Mary Kate Muil. Ethel was born in Newington, in 1882, to Robert, a law agent, and Christina Aitken. When Ethel was six, Christina died of peritonitis and Ethel went to live with her grandparents in Elgin. In 1901, when she was nineteen, her father died of injuries received from falling from a window. One of the other two entries on this page is the death of John Ferguson, a shoemaker, who two days earlier had also died after falling from a window. They fell from different windows, but the doctor certifying both was the same Henry D. Littlejohn.

This was Sir Henry Duncan Littlejohn, Police Surgeon, forensic expert, and admirer of Thomas Smith. The son of a baker of 33 Leith Street, he was a remarkable man. After education in Edinburgh, Paris, Vienna and Berlin, he returned to Edinburgh to pursue a highly regarded career in public health and legal medicine. Littlejohn's cases included deaths by firearms, poisoning, stabbing, strangling. He was an expert in all the many ways a person may be done to death, and used fingerprints, bite marks, and photography as evidence in court, where he appeared as an expert witness in more than one hundred capital charges.

He was deeply involved in a number of notorious cases and seems to have considered himself a bit of a detective. While he did this more newsworthy work, he was also quietly beavering away in the field of public health to improve the lot of the citizens of Edinburgh and beyond. In 1865, he produced a report on sanitary conditions in Edinburgh which made the crucial links among poverty, employment and public health. In his time, the death rate per thousand was reduced from twenty-four to fourteen. As we've seen, he was a friend and colleague of Thomas Smith at the sharp end, in the Cowgate. He did much charitable work, and incurred the fury of his fellow doctors by promoting the act which made compulsory the notification of all cases of infectious diseases. Finally, this busy man was a founding member of the Scottish Burial Reform and Cremation Society, created in 1888. He died in his bed in Arrochar, north of Glasgow, at an advanced age, after courting death numerous times by jumping, in his long frock coat, on and off moving tram cars, and having seen into their graves three medical practitioners who had refused to certify him as being fit to have life insurance. He was, of course, cremated.

So Ethel Muil's father was well looked after, as was Mr John Ferguson, the other defenestration on the record page – though, at forty feet, his fall was less spectacular than Mr Muil's at fifty-five.

Ethel was left an orphan. A few months after her father's death, she joined the post office as a telephone operator, and in 1920, when she was thirty-seven, she was listed as a post office supervisor, living at 10 Scotland Street, when she married James Petrie at the Palace Hotel on Castle Street. Petrie was a Surveyor of Posts and Telegraphs in the Colonial Service, on leave from his labours on the Gold Coast, now Ghana. Having survived yellow fever and mosquito-borne diseases during his stint working for the Colonial Office, he died in 1935, aged fifty-five.

Ethel was replaced as tenant by Mary Pirrit, who, with her husband Charles, a railway clerk of the London and North East Railway company, and her sister, Jessie Brown, had been registered to vote in 1920 at 12a Scotland Street. By 1923, Charles and Mary were separated, and Mary had reverted to her birth name, the first in this narrative to do so. Times changing.

Mary and Jessie moved to number 10 and made improvements. I have endeavoured to make as few improvements as possible. Behind me as I write, in Ann Whytt's dining room, is her black marble fireplace with early-twentieth-century red tiles and brass canopy, which I polish when I notice it's become too mucky. I know Mary and Jessie put it in, because, on 20 May 1923, they advertised for sale, 'a Grate (dining room) with fender to match. Very handsome £4 10/-.' This would have been the original Georgian grate, a number of which we found in New Town cellars in the late 1960s. When you touched them, they crumbled to little piles of rust.

A year later, the house was sold. I have written before of the deeds of my house, the first dated 1822. From 1856 to 1924 a series of notarial instruments conferred their one-fifth rights to 10 Scotland Street, from his sisters and brother and their heirs, to Alexander Henderson Whytt and his trust, and thence to his children. When the house was sold, the only trustees left standing were Alexander's sons, David Whytt, living in Yass, Australia, and Doctor Alexander Whytt, in Surrey. The sale was not without its problems, as evidenced by a case brought by David Whytt's Australian heirs – and the 1925 eik on both Marion and Wilhelmina's wills, the last transaction to be recorded on the vellum.

An eik – pronounced 'eek' – in Scots law of succession, is a document, that allows an executor to administer a part of an estate that had been overlooked, or has just materialised, after the original confirmation of the will has been obtained. In this case, the eik was granted forty years after the sisters' deaths. The sale to Mary Simpson Bremner Pirrit and Jessie Raitt Brown was concluded on 22 August 1924.

In order to buy 10 Scotland Street, Mary and Jessie granted a bond for £400 to Dorothy Palmer, of 3 Swan Walk, Chelsea, London. Despite the fact that both Jessie and Mary were nurses, there would be few avenues, other than through personal friendship, for two women on their own to raise such a sum. This state of affairs did not change for a long time. I was refused a mortgage for a tiny Colonies house in 1968, despite the fact that I was a wage earner in a secure job. Clearly, as I was twenty-three and married, I would become pregnant and have to resign my post, as was the case at the time. Once again, female friendship came to the rescue. We were lent the necessary sum by a woman who has remained a good friend to this day. The Employment Protection Act would not come into force for another ten years – which, incidentally, accounts for the gap of five years between my daughters. I remember clearly, at my friend's Aberdeenshire home, trying to explain this to a farmer, as we drank his whisky. Stan wanted to know why I only had one child, and that, a daughter. Obviously, I should provide an heir. Avoiding the primary problem with that statement, I explained, to his utter incomprehension, that I was waiting for the passing of the Employment Protection Act, which would protect my job while I had a child. 'Forget the Government and breed the loon,' he cried. He could not conceive of a woman whose salary was crucial. Now most families cannot subsist without two wages. Stan's wife, Elspeth, gave me a fine houseplant. She died over thirty years ago but her plant still flourishes on my window sill.

Installed at 10 Scotland Street thanks to Dorothy Palmer's loan, Mary and Jessie would have been able to avail themselves of a grocer at number 9 and a dairy at number 2a, which was still operating rather intermittently and dismally when I came to the street. Motor cars were quite rare, and horses still in use. In 1930, there was advertised for sale, the property of a gentleman, 'a six-year-old brown horse of 16 hands and all harnesses and warranted sound.' This horse could be seen at 10 Scotland Street Lane. In 1931, Mary assigned her half of the house to Jessie and left.

In the following year, *The Scotsman* published a judgment in an action brought by Mr William Stevenson, joiner and furniture dealer of 9A Scotland Street, against Miss Jessie Raitt Brown of 10 Scotland Street and PC George Wishart of Gayfield Square Police Station and the Corporation of Edinburgh: 'That Peculiar Edinburgh Accident, Guarding the Gap.' The action was raised on behalf of Mr Stevenson's son, claiming £1000 in compensation for injuries to the boy. On 21 October 1932, around 4pm, a motor vehicle left unattended in Scotland Street set itself in motion, mounted the pavement and carried away about six feet of railing, leaving a large and dangerous gap, into which the boy fell, sustaining serious injuries. The argument hinged on the proprietor's duty to keep the railing in a safe condition. The judge dismissed the charge, stating that the boy had been warned and had disregarded the warning. It's not unknown for cars to fall into basements. I've seen it happen twice in the time I have lived in the New Town, and indeed, in the days of fly-off handbrakes, I'm surprised there were not more incidents.

Perhaps unnerved by this experience, Jessie moved in with Mary on the Southside and advertised the house for rent at 47/- a year. Possibly, there were no takers. In 1933, Miss Raitt's solicitors advertised for sale, as a property investment, numbers 10, 10A and 10B Scotland Street along with two stores – the back lower rooms, now of 10B – which could be expected to yield an annual rental of £42 6/-.

Number 10 was bought by John Daniel Stewart, and his three sisters, Barbara, Jane, and Agnes. Like his father before him, John Daniel Stewart was a minister of the Catholic Apostolic Church, founded by the London Whytt's pastor, Edward Irving, whom we met before in correspondence with Thomas Carlyle. Irving was an obscure teacher before being ordained and taken under the wing of Reverend Thomas Chalmers, who was working in one of the poorest areas of Glasgow. Irving's preaching was theatrical, apocalyptic and very, very long-winded. His exhausted Glasgow congregation, attending on their one day off from work, were not impressed.

In 1822, he was sent to London, to the Caledonian Chapel. We find him writing to a patron about the qualities needed for an elder of his church. Such a man, he says, must have piety, integrity, soundness in the faith and good report in the church. He then lists five suitable candidates, one of whom is our Ebenezer Alexander Whytt, whose personal qualities must have outweighed his lack of business acumen. Irving also solicited help from his patron, Henry Drummond, for Ann and Ebenezer's eighteen-year-old son, whose promise he thought was being frustrated by his father's latest business failure, which had forced the family to move in with the widowed matriarch, Ann Gordon, in Barnsbury. Drummond secured help from the Caledonian Society.

The Caledonian Chapel congregation grew too large for the Hatton Gardens establishment and in 1823 it was decided to build a new National Scotch Church. Ebenezer Alexander Whytt and Ann contributed a small amount.

George Canning, a future Prime Minister, spoke in the House of Commons of Irving's commanding stature, the symmetry of his form, the dark and melancholy beauty of his countenance. Fellow Members of Parliament, the aristocracy, the learned and the intellectual, anyone who was anyone, crammed into his chapel. Tickets were printed to control the crowds. If the ticket was numbered, you got a seat. If not, you stood for up to three hours to be lectured on the imminent end of the world. The congregation moved to the vast, new Regent Square Church, and Irving's preaching grew increasingly long-winded and hysterical. I hope that the Whytt's contribution ensured they had a seat.

The London Missionary Society, which trained and sent men and some women to 'convert heathens', invited him to preach. For three-and-a-half hours, he spoke of the inferiority of missionary societies as compared with the individually-inspired missionary. Outraged, the London Missionary Society disowned his sermon. There were reports of hysteria and of persons speaking in tongues in his church. This was too much for the National Scotch Church worthies and Irving was ejected. Even Thomas Carlyle was having doubts. But Henry Drummond, a hugely wealthy politician, banker and acolyte of Irving's, was unwavering. Together, they founded the Catholic Apostolic Church. Instead of a pulpit, there were seven seats for Angels, flanked on each side by three Elders. On the row below were the Prophets, and below them the Deacons. There seem also to have been a lower rank of the Gifted, which contained women. Drummond became an Angel and the massed ranks of the saved took over from Irving and demoted him, to a Deacon.

In the winter of 1834, Irving travelled by horseback to Glasgow to establish an Apostolic church there. He died on arrival and was buried in the crypt of Glasgow Cathedral. The scandal rumbled on. The Church of Scotland was most exercised about Irving's ascribing original sin to Jesus Christ, and the debate was long and intricately detailed, requiring the publication of many commentaries on the Old Testament. I sometimes wonder what could have been achieved in the fields, say, of medicine and engineering, if half of the brightest and best men of Scotland, had not been obsessed with arguing

Decline and Resurrection

about the number of angels on the head of a pin. And if women had had access to education.

The Scotch Church in Regent Square got themselves a good Presbyterian Minister. The Apostolic Church which Irving founded marched on, still believing in the imminent apocalypse – as far as I understand it – and, in 1936, the minister of my local Apostolic Church and his three sisters bought 10 Scotland Street. I wonder if they spoke in tongues in their dining room, where I write. If so, no echoes remain.

The structure of the church had little changed, with its angels and prophets. Women's position was still inferior. But in the church of John Daniel Stewart on Mansfield Place, a few hundred yards from 10 Scotland Street, worship took place beneath the sublime paintings and decoration of Phoebe Traquair. These have been restored and, though the church was deconsecrated after Stewart's death, and is now used for functions, her work can still be seen.

John and his three sisters moved into my house in 1933, whereupon the sisters proceeded to die in an orderly fashion: Barbara in 1936, Jane in 1937, and, finally, Agnes in 1943.

The siblings owned the house jointly and had mutual wills, so that, when one died, their share went to the others. By 1943, the whole property belonged to John. He rented the basement to Henry Dryden, motor driver, and his wife Jessie and engaged a housekeeper, Miss Catherine Barclay. At 10B, now owned by the Allison family, there were four separate one-room homes. Three were inhabited by an engineer, a scavenger and a garage attendant. One was vacant.

John Daniel Stewart died aged eighty-nine on 16 April 1958 of senile heart disease and pneumonia. His death was certified by his housekeeper, Miss Barclay. Three years earlier, John had sold the basement rooms of 10 Scotland Street to Jessie and Henry Dryden, and the stair door to the basement was bricked up. Little else was done beyond re-designating the basement 8A. When I switched off Jessie Dryden's water in 1974, she came into my kitchen and, pointing at the butchered fireplace now filled with a cracked and disreputable 1950s effort, she told me that Miss Barclay would sit by it to take tea and would sometimes invite Mrs Dryden to join her. Another image behind my eyes.

The couple who bought the basement from the Drydens undertook a big restructuring of the flat, despite the fact that the woman was nine months pregnant. As it happened, one of my daughters was also nine months pregnant. Their very young, but immensely accomplished plumber, working against due dates, decided he had to cut off their and my gas to remove a pipe which appeared in their ceiling, ran the length of one of their bedrooms, and disappeared into the ceiling again. That is how we discovered that, when gas had been installed, the solution to supplying it to my kitchen had been to run it through a servant's bedroom in the basement. The plumber worked till after 11pm and returned the next morning very early, to instal a pipe in a most imaginative fashion to my kitchen, where my daughter, now in full-blown labour, was holding hands with her sister and breathing determinedly. I did think both children should have been named after him.

The other wee problem, which did not arise until the elder Drydens departed, was the wording on the deeds when the basement was sold to them. With reference to the garden, the ownership was decreed to be divided by 'a fence erected or about to be erected'. This is what's known in the trade as (insert expletive) sloppy drafting. That took a bit of sorting out.

In 1958, John Daniel Stewart's trustees sold number 10 to a man who died in 1960, leaving the house to his wife. In 1973, A young couple acquired the property, and, early in 1974, they sold the house to me and Pip. We made it our home for nearly thirty of the forty years we spent together, recreating at number 10, for the first time since the Whytts, I think, the kind of home and long marriage which they achieved – one which built lives, nurtured children, saw the older generation, and some souls far too soon, through their last days, and was frequently filled with friends, excellent dispute, laughter – and meetings, launches, funerals and weddings. Not much has changed, apart from the marriage bit which ended, when it should have, amicably.

Many years earlier, when our first daughter was born, we lived in a beautiful top floor flat in Dundas Street. It had a stone-flagged kitchen, a cupola over the internal hallway, glorious decorated fireplaces, and the windows in its two drawing rooms were floor-to-ceiling. These high windows rattled, banged and shuddered. The plaster on the ceiling of the vestibule was doubtful. We heated the bathroom with a greenhouse heater, which ran on paraffin from the grocer on the corner. We cooked on two old gas stoves, bought from Lyon and Turnbull's auction and inserted into the huge fireplace in the kitchen. The stairs up and down the communal close were long and steep. But the view was glorious. At twenty-seven, I acquired my first washing machine, plumbed in by one of my pupils, just in time for the birth of our child. When, unusually for the time, I returned almost immediately to work, we had the great good fortune to engage a lovely woman, the wife of a retired miner, to look after the child. After two years, she could no longer manage the stairs. To keep her, we had to move to a ground floor flat. I saw the for-sale notice, and one dark evening, on my hurried way to chair a meeting, spent five minutes looking round a grubby, ill-lit, not-been-decorated–for-decades, ramshackle flat, with a truly terrible bathroom, and a kitchen consisting of a broken Belfast sink lying on the floor. The electrical sockets, pitifully few in number, were small and antique. It had been unoccupied for years. I wanted it immediately. Pip agreed. And that is how, after five moves in eight years, we came to a stop in 10 Scotland Street.

I'm going no further into the lives of those who may still walk the planet, and I apologise if I have mistaken or misinterpreted anyone, or any event recognised by a descendant of a person mentioned above. To re-iterate, I have used many primary sources – but also memory. In places, I have interpreted and occasionally speculated. When I have done so, I have said so.

It has occurred to me to wonder if 10 Scotland Street is exceptional in the histories that came together here and radiated far and wide. I think not, and suspect that, in its long existence, most of the houses of the New Town of Edinburgh would have tales to tell.

Coincidence and long relational lines have run through this story. If the original deeds of the house had not been preserved and I had not been captivated all those years ago by David's signature, who knows how I would have spent the many hours researching and getting to know him, until he became My Davy and a permanent resident, as long as I am here, of this house. I made a film once about a wonderful artist who, late one night, in the restoration room high above the National Gallery on Trafalgar Square, looked long at a painting she loves. It was painted by Zurbaran around 1635 and is of St Francis in meditation. 'I have become slightly confused,' she said, 'with whether or not I have fallen in love with the man . . . or the painting . . .' I think I know how she feels. The story or the man.

I can't leave number 10. What would become of Davy Whytt and Ann Henderson? Or of the ghost of Milo, the cat who hated everyone except me, and didn't much like me. He rests under a stone from Dalnamain, a place he loved, in the garden where Davy's maidservants hung out his sheets and shirts. There would be resistance from a host of people across the globe, who visit, sit round my kitchen table to update their stories and, standing in my lobby, reminisce and refer to the middle bedroom as my younger daughter's room. She has not lived here for nearly thirty years. Davy and the house are stuck with me.

FIFTEEN

EPILOGUE

Walking with Ghosts

Knowing so much – and imagining so much – about the people who lived in my house before me, makes them an occasional presence as the days pass in 10 Scotland Street. My dead, some of whom I have loved dearly, are the ghosts I walk with. Does everyone do this? Perhaps only those who have lived long. It's sometimes a bit crowded.

My friend Val McDermid, who wrote such a fine and generous foreword to this book, suggested the epilogue might be something along the lines of: the history of the house through the time and space of my stewardship; the people who have eaten and slept beneath my roof, from the street to the wide world; and the many conversations, the politics, the artistic and filmic projects hammered out round the kitchen and lobby tables. I decided to honour some of my ghosts and not to list the many people who still live, and make my time in this house so interesting, fulfilling and sometimes positively joyful. They know who they are. I hope this final chapter meets with Val's expectations.

In the early decades at 10 Scotland Street, we were hospitable in a way that was common at the time. I would open the door to find a beaming friend bearing flowers, a painting, a gift for a new baby . . . advancing into the lobby, palpably ready to make the occasion enjoyable and memorable. Up for a really good time. Our home was the birthplace of many an enterprise which drew in people who were decades older, and who were happy to lend an ear, influence and experience. In that, I think, we were singularly fortunate. The downside, of course, is that I have accumulated many ghosts.

For a short time, in my twenties, I had two great female friends who lived close by; Frances Gordon in her fifties and Freda White in her seventies. I had recently graduated from Glasgow University and was accumulating educational qualifications; Frances had a degree from the London School of Economics, gained in the 1930s, and was a linchpin in the political and cultural life of Edinburgh; Freda was one of the first graduates from Somerville College, Oxford, an author, journalist, campaigner and lecturer of international renown.

It was obvious to the predominantly male St Andrew's Ward Labour Party that we three, being women, should organise the jumble sales. In spite of my nascent feminism – it was 1966 – I agreed to be sent jumble-selling and thus to spend time with these women in Freda's flat at 2 Scotland Street.

Freda White was born in 1894, at 3 Drummond Place, a hundred yards from 10 Scotland Street. Her father, Thomas, a solicitor, died when she was seven, leaving seven children aged one to eighteen. According to Freda, her mother, Ada Watson, was a forceful and intelligent woman who gave her brood a happy childhood. She sent Freda to St Leonard's, and then to Geneva to study Geology and perfect her French. In 1913, aged nineteen, she went to Somerville College, studied Modern History, and left in 1916 without the BA she had earned but would not receive until 1921, when degrees for women were first awarded. But, by then, everything had changed. On 9 September 1915, her beloved brother, Major Alexander White, was killed in the Dardanelles by Turkish shells made by a British firm. Freda became a lifelong campaigner in the cause of peace.

She went to Corsica, courtesy of Elsie Inglis, to find the Serbian Relief Fund working under very difficult conditions – including, she said, the interventions of Henry Dundas, the British Consul in Ajaccio – with survivors of the journey through Montenegro and Albania. Most of the women workers were nurses with the Scottish Women's Hospitals. Freda was no nurse, but she was a born organiser. In late 1918, she returned to Edinburgh, and as soon as

Epilogue

the League of Nations was underway, she left and worked for the League between Geneva and London until 1939. Freda was the League's expert on mandates, the arms trade, Abyssinia and Palestine. She wrote League pamphlets and lectured in the cause of peace wherever she found a platform. In 1934, the *Kent and Sussex Courier* records that, at a meeting of the Women's International League, Miss Freda White, a member of the Executive, denounced the subterfuges of armament manufacturers. 'War brings misery and ruin to everyone concerned but is pure gain for arms manufacturers. They must oppose every move towards peace.' In 1935 in Motherwell, at the autumn meeting of the Wishaw branch of the League of Nations Union, the hall was packed to hear Miss Freda White BA, author of *The Abyssinian Dispute*. 'Abyssinia being uppermost in everybody's mind just now, an expression of opinion on the present critical situation coming from such an authoritative source is sure to make a profound impression,' said the *Motherwell Times*. A week later, *Notes and Comments* reported that, 'Miss Freda White has a poor opinion of the English. She says if you wish them to assimilate a fact you must first of all boil it.' The language and tone are to the life but she did not have a low opinion of the English or any other nation – rather, sharp and analytical above everything, she was visibly exasperated by wilful blindness and obfuscation. In 1936, she addressed a conference on World Cooperation. In 1937, recently returned from Spain, she presciently pointed out the danger of sporadic fires which sometimes spread until they devour entire civilisations. Longman Green published her *Short Account of War in Spain*. On 11 February 1939, as Secretary of the Mandates and Minorities Committee, she stated that what has been wrong with British policy in the last seven years is a 'lack of settled principle'. A very characteristic phrase. She tried to convey how British foreign policy was understood abroad, and commented on the difficulty of an attempt to dissociate legal from moral and ethical rights. We could do with her like today.

On the outbreak of war, Freda felt the failure of the League personally but believed that though such an organisation might fail and fail again, it was our only hope.

In 1940, she became assistant editor of the *New Statesman* under the editorship of Kingsley Martin and, in 1943, moved to the left-leaning *Daily Herald*. At the centre of wartime intellectual life, with many friends about her, her international work continued. In 1944, speaking at a conference on the Danubian Satellites, she voiced her concerns about the industrial stripping of the territories taken by the Russians.

She published her account of the first Assembly of the United Nations and a pamphlet, *Conflict Over Palestine* in 1946. In 1947, she returned to Scotland as Scottish Officer of the United Nations Association. In 1951, she published her first travel book – the extraordinary and still-in-print classic of travel writing, *Three Rivers of France*. In 1954, she left the UN to concentrate on travelling in, and writing about, France, publishing *West of the Rhone: Languedoc, Roussillon, the Massif Central* in 1964, and *Ways of Aquitaine* in 1968.

The research for these books was carried out in her Morris Minor, often with a white-knuckled but resigned Frances Gordon in the passenger seat. Freda was an impatient and terrible driver. By the time I knew her, she was a white-haired, determined figure in trademark tweeds and lacy jumper, with an incisive, sometimes sharp tongue, counterbalanced by a keen intelligence and deep concern for family and friends.

On occasion, she would startle with moments from her past. Freda remembered going to the High Street where, from cramped little shops, the successors of the luckenbooths, she would buy Georgian glass for her mother with pennies doled out by her nursemaid. The house on Drummond Place had fifteen rooms, the top floor being the domain of nursemaids and children. From the highest landing, they would watch Ada's soirée guests arriving on the drawing room floor. These sights, transmitted straight from her memory into mine, are vividly with me still. Behind her home was a drying green; Drummond Place Garden, her playground, and, when girls were banned from climbing trees, Freda organised squads to climb them all. Some years later Lord Rutherford walked with her in the Garden and explained to her the splitting of the atom and its potential power. When she asked if it might be used as a weapon, he replied that no-one could possibly be so stupid.

Epilogue

I asked her once if at Somerville she'd known Vera Brittain whose *Testament of Youth* had much impressed me when, probably too young, I'd read it. Freda thought for a minute and said, 'That woman used her intellect as a stiletto for her passions.' And that was all.

She travelled light, but in her flat, high on the corner of Scotland Street, were many books and objects of curious provenance, some from China, allegedly from Soon Mei-Ling, the wife of Chiang Kai-Shek. She is remembered with affection by her neighbour who lived above her in the sixties, and by my friends from that time. But her busy, effective life – save for her travel writing – seems to have disappeared from the record. I think of her trying to study for final exams while mourning her brother, travelling in dangerous waters to Corsica, penning her winning essay on peace in her lodgings at Great Ormond Street, biting her lip, mostly in vain, in what was still very much a man's world. She insisted that it was important to teach people to think. And then one must fight to control the urge to tell them what to think. She knew her own mind and she had a tongue on her.

Freda White lived a life I admired, the like of which, until I met her, I hardly knew existed. She opened my mind to possibilities. At North Edinburgh's raucous Burns Supper, she silenced the room with a rendition of *Bonnie Leslie*. In early 1971, she came for tea and ate a little ginger bun. And then she didn't eat anything anymore. Eventually she moved into a nursing home on the southside. We went to see her there en route to a party. It was mid-May and a fine sunny evening. She was dozing, a novel by Walter Scott, open in her hand. She had herself lifted, settled, brushed off and turned to us, 'Right my dears. About the Common Market . . .' In a few days, she was gone. The funeral was quickly over and we repaired in sombre mood to our flat where another dear ghost-to-be, historian George Hammersley, balding, bespectacled, stooped and heavily German-accented, fell through the doorway, whooping with laughter till he had to be calmed with water. He'd arrived late at the crematorium and slipped in at the back. Startled by the religious tone, he realised he was at the wrong funeral. He left at the end, commiserating gutturally with the deceased's lined-up relatives who seemed equally bewildered at his presence and outraged by his very bright red tie, worn in Freda's honour.

Frances Gordon, at her home at 10 London Street just round the corner from Scotland Street, gave me her friendship and that of many others, notably, Ritchie Calder, journalist, peace activist and proponent of the Open University, and Giles Robertson, Professor of Fine Art and inaugurator of the Talbot Rice Gallery. The gallery's opening party was memorable. He and his wife Eleanor lived in an extraordinary house on Saxe Coburg Place where impromptu dinners often followed openings.

Frances operated a calling system around Drummond Place. Anyone who was unwell, having a hard time or had just moved in, was visited. In spring, she bore snowdrops. At our home, she would make her last stop for gin and discussion on whatever cultural phenomenon currently gripped Edinburgh. She missed Freda but, like her, did not live in the past. Over the years, I gleaned a little. Frances Jack was born into a prosperous Scottish carpet-manufacturing family but failed miserably to measure up to its idea of a young lady. After various escapades, which she related briskly – being sacked from school for blasphemy, riding her brother's motor bicycle into the dining-room windows because, though he had shown her how to start it, he had failed to indicate how she might turn it off – it was decided that a social work course at the London School of Economics would be appropriate. Why her parents thought that the LSE in the thirties, seething with left-wing politics, was a good idea, I cannot imagine. It was an excellent move for Frances, who found her tribe, discovered left-wing politics and married Cecil Gordon, a South African of Russian/Jewish origin. Frances worked in a lab throughout the war until a bomb destroyed it, showering her with glass. But Cecil was elsewhere. He joined first the Operational Research Section of Coastal Command, and then the Air Ministry. There he worked on mathematical models which proved that the criterion being used to optimise the efficiency of available aircraft and personnel was in fact adding to inefficiency. With colleagues, he devised procedures which resulted in a significant increase in flying hours. For this work, he received an OBE – not something

Epilogue

Frances ever mentioned. After the war, he moved to an operational research unit at the Board of Trade. It seemed he and Frances were firmly at the heart of the post-war Labour establishment. But the Board was not sympathetic to Cecil's ideas. It is possible that what was referred to by colleagues as his highly polemic style of argument, had something to do with it. Cecil returned to academia, specialising in Social Medicine at Edinburgh University. Frances followed with their daughter. Cecil died suddenly, aged only fifty-three in 1960. Frances, dealing also with the needs of aged parents, was bereft. She won through, making a life for herself at the heart of intellectual Edinburgh. Like Freda, she spoke little of the personal, with a couple of salient exceptions which I found to be true. 'One learns something from each lover,' she told me, re-filling my glass in her beautiful drawing room overlooking East Scotland Street Lane, with its tennis courts and allotments. And, 'death and sex go together,' she said. She gave me a cameo brooch which I passed to my daughter Frances, whose name is no accident. Frances Gordon died in February 1989, and there is a part of me that is relieved that this fiercely-political woman did not live to see the results of the events later that year. I miss her still.

The third of a trio of neighbour-ghosts lived on Drummond Place, in a busy five-storey house. Elizabeth Aytoun, born in 1913, was a child when her father died. Edward Cadbury, with whom her father had set up the Woodbrooke Quaker College, became her guardian. She, too, went to St Leonard's, and then to Oxford where she found communism, and began a life of activism and peace campaigning, working for the League of Nations Association and the Transport and General Workers Union. She met Frank Girling when both were volunteers in the Pyrenees during the Spanish Civil War. They returned, having narrowly escaped death, and married in 1939. With her sisters, Elizabeth inherited a castle near Glenshee. During the war, it housed refugees, soldiers on leave, and the exhausted. Frank was posted to India where, I was told, he defected from his unit to join the Indian Army. After the war, he became an anthropologist. His doctoral research in Uganda was cut short when he was declared persona non grata and ejected. He and Elizabeth left the communist party along with many others in 1956, when the Soviets invaded Hungary and the facts of Stalin's regime began to be known. In the early sixties, Elizabeth opened Edinburgh's Partisan Coffee House, which became a hub of radical politics, leavened by music. Frank returned to academia in Sheffield, cycling back and forth each term and making many forays abroad. He retired in the 1980s and could be found handing out pamphlets in the Kirkgate in Leith, until ill-health stopped him. Elizabeth, I knew through Frances and politics and various campaigns, but Frank, I got to know during the Anti-Poll-Tax movement, where he was always in the middle of the fray as we blocked streets to bailiffs. Elizabeth died in 2005. I'm glad to say I count her granddaughter as a friend.

I'd come to Edinburgh in 1966, and spent weeks trying to join the Labour party. The one phone in Ruskin House, North Edinburgh's HQ, rang out. Then one day, the young Chris Harvie, future Professor at Tubingen and MSP, called at the door of our wee flat under the eaves in staunchly not-Labour Well Court, Dean Village, and was moved almost to tears by a friendly welcome. We turned up at the next meeting of the local Labour party in their dingy, under-heated HQ, and were ushered into a small room. There we found Martin O'Neill, who was later an MP – I chaired his adoption meeting – and Freda White, Frances Gordon and Robin Cook, who was much later to intrigue Scotland Street when his security parked up and my assistant came to tell me that the Foreign Secretary was in the lobby. Robin was a close friend till he died. His powerful, principled resignation statement in the House of Commons, when British troops were sent to invade Iraq, is the finest parliamentary speech of my lifetime. He is a very present ghost in these political days.

Then there are the ghosts of Bertold and Hana Hornung, survivors of the Holocaust and the Soviets, who fled Prague in 1968. Frances befriended them and gave me access to a whole world of European culture. When Berty spoke of Empire, he meant the Austro-Hungarian. Both Berty and Hana had numerous languages and Hana was expert in modern art. Berty was an architect/planner and was justly celebrated when finally he returned to Prague. In the early 1990s, I was given a fellowship in Berlin and started a long love affair with the city and the lands further east. Berty spent many hours discussing them and his his beloved German culture with me. His health was wrecked by the forced labour he endured during the war and he became housebound. We spent evenings together in their modernist flat, releasing Hana for a few hours, and talking, talking. She was abroad when he died and I held his hand and bade him farewell in German poetry. He laughed a lot, did Berty, and so does his ghost.

Across my kitchen table, I see Professor Anne Ferguson. We first met as undergraduates at Glasgow University. She loved the Scottish mountains and climbed them with her first husband. Anne became a highly-respected and influential teacher, clinician and researcher and one of Britain's most distinguished gastroenterologists, with an international reputation. She was particularly concerned with encouraging women in medicine and spoke to me of the barriers even she had had to overcome, the parts of her life she had not had time for, the cultural exploration she looked forward to. Her bolthole was her cottage at Benderloch where my children went often with their father. Her second husband was a fellow doctor with whom she had some very happy years until she died, aged only fifty-seven. The Anne Ferguson Building at the Western General Hospital is named for her. I remember her laughter and her enormous care for her patients.

Until surgery put an end to it, I too climbed, and latterly when my climbing partner re-located south, I took to the hills with Malcolm Slesser, explorer, scientist, polymath and bon vivant. I helped him to find a publisher for *With Friends in High Places,* which is worth a read. We celebrated his eightieth birthday early one fine autumn morning, on the summit of Ben Nevis. His ghost sits patiently belaying me in driving snow near the top of the said Ben while I refuse to give up on a stuck piton; howls with laughter as he realises he has locked his bike, not to my railings in Scotland Street, but to itself, and stirs my heart with a pibroch on his boat, somewhere in the Minch, after an excellent dinner.

From my bed, I look towards the window and see, outlined against the light, John Mackintosh, Professor of Politics, and MP for

Berwick and East Lothian, a close friend. I remember him in his element on the House of Commons Terrace, at home in Nether Liberton, hosting dinners for assorted friends and politicians of all persuasions, holding forth in miners' clubs across East Lothian, in my kitchen with John Smith, as they took a break from canvassing. But most often John's ghost stands at my bedroom window, where I came upon him finding peace from a party to welcome my younger daughter to the world. He is holding the tiny baby in his arms and he is weeping. When my daughter was barely eight weeks old, I left her, for the first time, for an hour on his bed while I watched him being lowered into the earth. He had told no-one of his illness. Dr Una Maclean, his wife, remained my friend till her death, decades later, joining the group of women who financed the start of Engender, the campaigning and research organisation, and signing off always, 'Yours in Sisterhood, Una'. At my invitation, she spoke to the early 1970's consciousness-raising group, hosted by another ghost, Mitzi Maitland, in her New Town flat. Una told of her early life on a now-deserted Scottish island, of being a female medical student in the 1940s and her subsequent work in Aden, where she treated the wives in the harems. From there, she went to Nigeria where she worked with traditional Yoruba witch-doctors, persuading them to use western medicine, when useful, and was involved in the Ibadan smallpox epidemic of 1957. She worked in cancer research and blood transfusion, and became an academic while raising her five children and coping with being the wife of a charismatic politician. My most potent memory of her is in my green room at an all-female birthday party I had when I was stretched fragile with chemotherapy. I seem to remember dancing in the lobby, after which we sat down, and for some reason, sang songs of our youth, several passed down by grandmothers and, in one case, a lost lover. Una's song, in a high, sweet voice, came from Africa.

I'm wary of turning this into a tedious list, but have to mention feminist writer Susie Innes, holding forth as we met to plot Engender; Bernard Crick, Professor of Politics, who hosted so many fine suppers and was an excellent friend and frequent guest; Sandy Neilson, whose influential Fifth Estate Theatre Company,

Epilogue

devised in my lobby with no little amount of whisky, I chaired; Ninian Johnson, architect/planner, great friend from university days who died young of leukaemia – he sits in our old velvet cane chair, drinking Christmas port and toasting life's absurdities; and Janey Buchan, indefatigable activist and MEP, who bought her clothes by grabbing off a rail a handful of dresses, of the right size more or less, regardless of style. I remember Ritchie Calder's eyebrows as she hoisted her skirt to grasp the hot handle of the coffee pot on my green room stove, while talking animatedly, and without cease, on our tactics for taking over the Scottish ITV franchise. That was a great deal of fun and, thank goodness, unsuccessful. Here, where I write in my office, there was a mattress which sat on the floor until we acquired a bed frame. And here I brought morning coffee to Sylvia and Doug Gilmour because their boy David's band was playing in Edinburgh. I met them through our late ex-common-law brother-in-law, a genial geneticist, whose ghost stretches his long legs in his ragged US flag trousers as he tells stories of his long and varied life in Cambridge, Papua New Guinea and Vanuatu. And then there was David Daiches, used to being recognised for his scholarship and writing, who was delighted when we first met, in the spring of 1978, and I identified him as Jenni Calder's father and wanted to talk to him about her book *There Must be a Lone Ranger*; Hamish Henderson, marching into the kitchen, plonking himself down to declaim his latest poem; poet, New Yorker essayist and translator, Alastair Reid, who went chuckling along my bookshelves, so pleased with the number of volumes we had in common – these shelves contain his works, some given by him, but the biggest gift he gave me was the friendship of his wife, Leslie; Dr Ian Duffield, historian and host. On the day I started as a very young teacher at the school just through the lane from Scotland Street, I met Jill, his wife. She invited me to a party. We turned up at their ground floor flat in Dublin Street to be greeted by Ian, long red hair wild about his hugely smiling face, dressed in what looked very like the garb of the Moderator of the Church of Scotland. I had to persuade my husband to come in with me. He was glad I did. Two years later, after Ian returned from researching in Nigeria, he would, on occasion, exit his flat, now a high attic in Dublin Street, wearing complete flowing Nigerian robes, to pick up his children from London Street Primary. We had a friendship which lasted for more than fifty years. He was an enthusiast about my work for this book, and a mine of information. And then there is Pat, whom I met in a hospital corridor over a quarter of a century ago. We laughed our way through surgery, chemotherapy and radiotherapy, emerging battered but determined. And then I got better and she did not. On one last trip north together, she bought me a root of wee flowers which now turn several yards of my garden blue each spring. I knew her for less than three years and will never forget. And down Scotland Street Lane, there is the ghost of Willie Taylor, engineer *extraordinaire* who performed miracles on tired old Indian motor bikes, with their distinctive guttural notes, latterly in my garage when the bike shop moved out. He conducted his machines like a first-class orchestra and fixed all manner of broken things. He was a kind man. He phoned me on the morning of the day he died to say that there might be a wee cat stuck in my garage. There was.

Some of my ghosts manifest themselves internationally. Jim Haynes, he of the Paperback Bookshop and the rhinoceros head, who hosted for decades Sunday dinners in his Paris *atelier*, sits at my lobby table with John Calder, publisher, opera enthusiast, Beckett expert and exponent, and possessor of the most extraordinary basement library in Montreuil, just outside the boulevard peripherique. John's ghost drives me, braced, through Paris traffic to wordy dinners with the aforementioned Jim. In Café Einstein, on a leafy Berlin street, I remember one last lunch with playwright John McGrath. When John leaves, his place is taken by Bakhtiyar Khudojnazarov, born Tajikistan, alumnus of the Soviet Moscow VGIK State Film School, who made his home in Berlin to conjure up his unique and beautiful films.

Then, always just out of reach, there is Uta Ganschow, my sister/friend. Her shade stands with me as the sun goes down by Mont Ventoux, trembles in the air beside me in the Outer Hebrides and atop Calton Hill, with Edinburgh spread before us. She walks with me the streets of St Petersburg, Bucharest, Belgrade, Zagreb, Prague . . . and all the other cities where we worked together, out

Epilogue

of our base in Berlin. At her hospitable table in her beautiful Wilmersdorf attic, my second home, we talk through the night of David and Ann and 10 Scotland Street and my latest find in the archives.

'One last glass?' she says. 'Riesling or champagne?'

SELECT BIBLIOGRAPHY

This list is very select. Since I first picked up Tom Johnston's *History of the Working Classes in Scotland* Forward Press 1920, from my grandfather's box, a significant proportion of my reading has contributed to this book. I have grouped roughly into blocks which seem to cohere, for me at least.

These are the books I like and seem most pertinent: Numerous and various by Rosalind Mitchison, Leah Leneman, TM Devine, Esther Breitenbach, Stana Nenadic, Richard Rodger, Richard B Sher, David Daiches and, for archaeology, Anna Ritchie – although as I write this, I realise how invidious such a list must be with its many omissions. *No Gods and Precious few Heroes,* Christopher Harvie, Edinburgh University Press 1998; *Scotland in the Age of Improvement,* Ed NT Phillipson and Rosalind Mitchison, EUP 1970; *The Biographical Dictionary of Scottish Women,* Edited Elizabeth Ewan, Sue Innes and Sian Reynolds, EUP 2006; *Order and Space in Society,* ed Thomas A Markus, Mainstream 1982; *Power over Peoples: Technology, Environments, and Western Imperialism, 1400 to the Present,* H L Hoskins in *History,* New Series, Vol. 9, No. 36 1925; *Gender in Scottish History,* ed Lynn Abrams, Eleanor Gordon, Deborah Simonton, Eileen James Yeo, EUP 2006; *The Inner Life of Empires,* Emma Rothschild, Princeton University Press 2011; *India in Edinburgh,* ed Roger Jeffrey, Social Science Press 2019; *The Life of Robert Louis Stevenson,* Rosalind Masson, W &R Chambers 1923; *Mary Fairfax Somerville,* Martha Charters Somerville, Elibron

Classics 2005; *Peter's Letters to his Kinfolk,* John Gibson Lockhart ed Walter Ruddick, Scottish Academic Press 1977

Feeding Nelson's Navy Janet Mac Donald, Chatham Publishing 2004; *Sustaining the Fleet 1793–1815; War, the British Navy and the Contractor State,* Knight, R., and Wilcox, M, The Boydell Press, 2010; *A Social History of the Navy 1793 -1815,* Michael Lewis, Allan and Unwin 1960; *The Wooden World an Anatomy of the Georgian Navy,* NAM Rodger, WW Norton 1996; *Shipboard life and organisation 1731–1815,* B Lavery, Routledge 1999; *The Prize Game,* Donald A Petrie, Berkley Books; *Great Evils of Impressment,* Captain John Gourley RN, Longman 1838; *Britain Against Napoleon,* RJB Knight, Allen Lane 2013; *Physical and Social Profiles of Early American Seafarers 1812–1815,* IRA Dyer in *Jack Tar in History,* Howell and R Twomey, Fredericton: Acadiensis Press 1991

Unpublished Theses: *The Victualling Board 1793–1815, A study of Management Competence,* Macdonald J, King's College London, 2009; *War, Naval Logistics and the British State – Supplying the Baltic Fleet 1808–1812,* Davey, J., University of Greenwich, 2009; *The Administration of the Transport Service during the War against Revolutionary France 1793–1802,* Condon, M., University College London 1968; *Concert Life and the music trade in Edinburgh c1780-c1830,* John Leonard Cranmer, Edinburgh University 1991

Music and Society in Lowland Scotland in the Eighteenth Century, David Johnson, Mercat Press 2003; *Register of Edinburgh Apprentices 1756–1800,* ed Marguerite Wood, Scottish Record Society 1963; *Reports from the Committee of the House of Commons,* Vol X Miscellaneous Subjects 1783–1801 Appendices pg 417 1803; *Poor Law Enquiry Commission for Scotland,* Murray and Gibb for Her Majesty's Stationery Office 1844; *Holiday House,* Catherine Sinclair, William Whyte and Co MDCCCXXXIX; *A Cup of Kindness A History of the Scottish Corporation, a London charity 1603–2003,* Justine Taylor, Tuckwell Press 2003; *Seekers of Truth – The Scottish Founders of Modern Public Accountancy,* TA Lee, Elsevier 2006; *The Rise and Fall of the City of Money,* Ray Perman, Birlinn 2019; *The Edinburgh of John*

Select Bibliography

Kay, Eric Melvin 2017; *Lost Edinburgh*, Hamish Coghill, Birlinn 2008; *Lady Glenorchy and her Churches*, Rev DP Thomson, The Research Unit 1967; *Elegance & Entertainment in the New Town of Edinburgh The Harden Drawings*, Iain Gordon Brown, Rutland Press 1995; *Edinburgh: A History of the City*, Michael Fry, MacMillan 2009; *Time Lord. Sir Sandford Fleming and the Creation of Standard Time*, Clark Blaise, Weidenfeld & Nicolson 2000; *Directory to Gentlemen's Seats &c in Scotland*, James Findlay, WP Kennedy

The Diary and Letters of Edward Irving, ed Barbara Waddington, Pickwick Publications – an imprint of Wipf and Stock 2013; *The Collected Letters of Thomas and Jane Carlyle*, Duke University Press – available free online

The life and times of Leith, JS Marshall, John Donald Edinburgh 1986; *The Place Names of Edinburgh*, Stuart Harris, Gordon Wright Publishing 1996; *Diary of George Sandy Apprentice W.S, 1788*, edited with introduction by C.A. Malcolm, T and A Constable Limited 1943; *The Edinburgh History of the book in Scotland Vol 2 Enlightenment and Expansion 1707–1800*, Ed Stephen W Brown and Warren McDougall, EUP 2012; *Edinburgh History of the book in Scotland Vol 3 Ambition and Industry 1800–1880*, Ed Bill Bell, EUP 2007; *The Enlightenment and the Book*, Richard B Sher, University of Chicago Press 2006; *Edinburgh*, Robert Louis Stevenson, Seeley and Company 1908; *Report on the Sanitary Condition of the City of Edinburgh*, Henry D Littlejohn, Colston and Son 1865; *Insanitary City*, Paul Laxton and Richard Rodger, Carnegie Publishing 2013 *Fugitive Pieces by the Late William Creech Esq, FRS*, George Ramsay and Company 1815; *Calton Hill and the Plans for Edinburgh's Third New Town*, Kirsten Carter McKee, John Donald an imprint of Birlinn 2018; *The Story of Calton Jail: Edinburgh's Victorian Prison*, Malcolm Fife, The History Press 2016; *Quilled on the Cann – Alexander Hart, Scottish Cabinet Maker, Radical and Convert*, Hawkins, Regional Furniture 2002; *Edinburgh in the Golden Age*, Mary Cosh, John Donald 2003; *The Social Life of Scotland in the Eighteenth Century*, Henry Grey Graham, A&C Black 1937; *Edinburgh Revisited*, James Bone, Sidgwick & Jackson 1911; *Edinburgh in the Nineteenth Century*, WM Gilbert 1901; *Memorable*

Edinburgh Houses, Wilmot Harrison, Oliphant Anderson and Ferrier 1898; *The making of Classical Edinburgh 1750–1849*, AJ Youngson, EUP 1966

Annals of the Disruption, Thomas Brown, MacNiven and Wallace 1892; *Alexander Duff*, Thomas Smith, Hodder and Stoughton 1843; *Work of grace at Calcutta, a narrative of the circumstances attending the recent conversions there*, A Duff & T Smith, 1845; *The Indian Rebellion; its causes and results. In a series of letters from the Rev. Alexander Duff, D.D. LLD, Calcutta*, James Nisbet and Co 1858; *Day by Day at Lucknow A Journal of the Siege of Lucknow*, Adelaide Case, Richard Bentley 1858; *The Free Church of Scotland and American Slavery*, Scottish anti-Slavery Society, J and W McDonald 1846; *The Scottish Radicals*, M and A Macfarlane, Spa Books 1981; *Scotland and the Abolition of Black Slavery 1756–1838*, Iain Whyte, EUP 2006; *A Unique and Glorious Mission*, Lesley Orr Macdonald, John Donald 1998

History of British Guiana, Henry Gibbs Dalton, Longman Brown Green and Longmans 1855; *Forgotten Women*, Hannah Young in *Britain's History and Memory of Transatlantic Slavery* ed Katie Donington et al, Liverpool University Press 2017; *Women and Highland Scots in Guyana before emancipation. A forgotten Diaspora*, David Alston, eupublishing 2015; *Crowns of Glory, Tears of Blood: The Demerara Slave Rebellion of 1823*, Emilia Viotti da Costa, OUP 1994; *An Account of an Insurrection of the Negro Slaves in the Colony of Demerara which Broke Out on the 18th of August 1824*, Joshua Bryant, A Stevenson at the Guiana Chronicle Office Georgetown 1824; *Women against Slavery*, Clare Midgley, Routledge 1992; *Captives*, Linda Colley, Jonathan Cape 2002; *Memoirs of a Banking House*, Sir W. Forbes, London and Edinburgh 1869

More monumental inscriptions on Nevis Tombstones of the British West Indies, Lena Boyd Brown Vere, Langford Oliver 2007; *An Account Descriptive of the Island of Nevis, West Indies*, John Alexander, Burke Iles 1871; *Reading the rebels: currents of slave resistance in the eighteenth-century British West Indies*, Natalie Zacek, School of History and Classics, University of Manchester 2007; *The Price of Emancipation:*

Select Bibliography

Slave-Ownership, Compensation and British Society at the End of Slavery, Nicholas Draper, Cambridge University Press 2010; *The Journal of a Voyage from Charleston S.C, to London undertaken during the American Revolution by a Daughter of an Eminent American Loyalist in the year 1778*, Louisa Susannah Wells, New York Historical Society 1906; *Sword Ships and Sugar*, Vincent K Hubbard, Premier Editions International 1998; *Caribbean-Scottish relations: colonial and contemporary inscriptions in history, language and literature*, Giovanna Covi et al, Mango Publishing 2007; *From Harvey River: a Memoir of my Mother and her People*, Lorna Goodison, Emblem Editions 2009; *Coolie Woman: The Odyssey of Indenture*, Gaiutra Bahadur, Hurst & Co 2016; *A Journey to the Tea Countrie*, Robert Fortune, John Murray 1852

The Fifty Second (Lowland) Division 1914–1918, R R Thompson, Maclehose, Jackson & Co 1923; *A Dirty Swindle*, Walter Stephen, Luath 2015; *Jane Austen The Secret Radical*, Helena Kelly, Icon Books 2015

And many trade and Post Office directories and many, many newspapers and periodicals, from the *Caledonian Mercury* to the *The India Mail*

RESOURCES

National Records of Scotland, https://www.nrscotland.gov.uk
Scotland's People, https://www.scotlandspeople.gov.uk
National Record of the Historic Environment, https://www.canmore.org.uk; part of Historic Environment Scotland, https://www.historicenvironment.scot
City of Edinburgh Archives, https://www.edinburgh.gov.uk/managing-information/edinburgh-city-archives
National Galleries of Scotland, https://www.nationalgalleries.org
University of Edinburgh Special Collections, https://www.ed.ac.uk/information-services/library-museum-gallery/discovery/special-collections-museums
Glasgow University Archives, https://www.gla.ac.uk/myglasgow/archivespecialcollections
The National Library of Scotland, https://www.nls.uk
Edinburgh Central Library, https://www.edinburgh.gov.uk/directory-record/1229174/central-library
The Scottish Genealogy Society Library, https://www.scotsgenealogy.com
The Signet Library, https://www.thesignetlibrary.co.uk
The Royal College of Surgeons of Edinburgh Library and Archive, https://library.rcsed.ac.uk
Women's History Scotland, http://womenshistoryscotland.org
Edinburgh Academy Archives, https://www.edinburghacademy.org.uk/859/ea-archives
The Book of the Old Edinburgh Club, https://oldedinburghclub.org.uk/boec
History Links Museum, Dornoch, https://www.historylinks.org.uk
Scottish Indexes, https://www.scottishindexes.com
Old Scottish Genealogy and Family History, https://www.oldscottish.com
Families in British India, https://www.fibis.org
Books and Borrowing, 1780–1830 https://borrowing.stir.ac.uk
The British Library, https://www.bl.uk ; https://blogs.bl.uk/untoldlives

The Georgian Papers Programme, https://georgianpapers.com
Internet Archive – free and borrowable books, https://archive.org
Mitchell Library, Glasgow, https://www.glasgowlife.org.uk/libraries/venues/the-mitchell-library
Mitchell Sydney, NSW, Australia, https://www.sl.nsw.gov.au
The National Archives, Kew, https://www.nationalarchives.gov.uk
Orkney Archives, https://orkneylibrary.org.uk
Imperial War Museums, https://www.iwm.org.uk
University College London Library, https://www.cityoflondon.gov.uk/things-to-do/history-and-heritage/london-metropolitan-archives
Writing about Slavery, https://naacpculpeper.org/resources/writing-about-slavery-this-might-help
The Prize Papers Project, https://www.prizepapers.de
Centre for the Study of the Legacies of British Slavery, https://www.ucl.ac.uk/lbs
The-East-India-Company-at-Home.pdf Free dowload of book on the Munro family, including following prosperity through women, https://discovery.ucl.ac.uk/id/eprint/10043118/1/
Bank of England Staff Working Paper No 1006 Nov 2022, https://www.bankofengland.co.uk/research
Database of British Guiana Colonists 18th, 19th century, https://www.vc.id.au/tb/bgcolonists
Biodiversity Heritage Library, https://www.biodiversitylibrary.org
Ancestry, https://www.ancestry.co.uk
Fold3, https://www.fold3.com
Commonwealth War Graves Commission, http://www.cwgc.org
MyAncestors Australia, https://myancestors.com.au
Library and Archives, Canada, https://library-archives.canada.ca/eng
National Maritime Museum, https://www.rmg.co.uk/national-maritime-museum
British History Online, https://www.british-history.ac.uk
Slavery and British Industry, www.cepr.org/voxeu/columns/slavery-and-british-industrial-revolution